The Bartlett Book of Garden Elements

The Bartlett Book of Garden Elements

A PRACTICAL COMPENDIUM *of* INSPIRED DESIGNS

Michael Valentine Bartlett &
Rose Love Bartlett

DAVID R. GODINE, PUBLISHER

BOSTON

FOR MA AND PA WHO PAVED OUR PATH

First published in 2014 by David R. Godine, Publisher
Post Office Box 450
Jaffrey, New Hampshire 03452
www.godine.com
Text copyright ©2014 by Rose L. Bartlett and Michael V. Bartlett
Photographs copyright ©by Rose L. Bartlett and Michael V. Bartlett
Book and Jacket Design by Sara Eisenman

Cover photo – caption
Library of Congress Cataloging-in-Publication Data
Bartlett, Michael Valentine.
The Barlett book of garden elements : a practical compendium of inspired designs for the working gardener / by
Michael Valentine Bartlett and Rose Love Bartlett. – First edition.
pages cm
Includes bibliographical references.
ISBN 978-1-56792-426-8 (alk. paper)
1. Gardens–Design. I. Bartlett, Rose Love. II. Title.
SB473.B37 2014
635–dc23
2013051178
First Edition
Printed in China

CONTENTS

INTRODUCTION

Michael V. Bartlett, my co-author and husband, did not live to see the publication of this book, which he devoted many years of his life to completing. But his spirit is alive on every page of it.

Michael began designing gardens when he was a teenager and was among the fifth generation of avid gardeners in his family. Both his great-grandfather, Charles Austin Buck, and grandfather, Leonard J. Buck, created gardens that are now open to the public and you will find photographs of their gardens in the pages that follow. Grandfather Leonard encouraged Michael to join him on walks through his garden and rewarded him with a nickel for each plant he could identify—only Latin names allowed!

Michael grew up in a garden of great beauty in Washington, DC. His parents, Charles and Martha Bartlett, built a house that overlooks a lovely woodland park, an oasis of country in the city. They created a green garden planted with hollies and boxwoods, lovely in all seasons. When Michael was naughty, he was sent to the garden to dig a hole for the next plant to arrive. As a young designer, he redesigned and enhanced several areas of the garden. Understated garden ornaments abound, no detail is overlooked and the meticulous attention to maintenance is obvious.

I, on the other hand, grew up in downtown Philadelphia and had sprouted only a few seeds as a child—it wasn't until my twenties that the garden bug bit. Michael and I met as students at the University of Pennsylvania in the early 1970s and became close friends. In 1975, he offered to roto-till my backyard so I could plant a garden, which flourished beyond my wildest imagination. I fell head-over-heels in love with gardening and Michael at the same time.

We married in 1980, united by our shared passion for gardens. The garden design business Michael had begun in 1975 prospered and by the early '80s we were extremely complementary business partners as well. On each project, Michael would lay out the "bones" and focal points of the garden, design the terraces and swimming pools, sometimes even site a new house, while I added the "icing on the cake" for those who wanted flower, herb, vegetable or container gardens.

Over the years, we searched in vain for a book that offered a diverse selection of photographs and drawings we could use for research and inspiration while developing garden design plans. A combination of photos of real places and more abstract drawings, we felt, would help us—and our clients—envision the plans as they took shape. Alas, we could find nothing of the kind—and the idea of creating an archive of our own took root.

From that point on, our extensive travels focused on gardens, gardens and more gardens. Many days, we never got around to eating lunch! The discovery of a beautiful bench tucked into the far reaches of a garden or a handsome gate that led to a secret garden room surrounded by the green walls of an architectural hedge was an absolute thrill. Once we'd captured them in photographs, we would study these pieces of the garden puzzle endlessly. Our collection of photos grew into our own library of garden design details.

With this archive as our source of images, we began giving a series of illustrated garden talks covering the history, design and function of the elements that have played important roles in garden design over the centuries. I wrote the talks and we presented them together, with much extemporaneous embellishment contributed by Michael. Inevitably, members of the audience would ask, "Where can we buy the book?" We soon realized it was time to organize our treasure trove of photographs, our love of the history of gardens and our practical knowledge into a format that could be widely disseminated, read and revisited by gardening enthusiasts everywhere.

Up until his death of cancer in 2008, Michael devoted himself wholeheartedly to the project, working on his laptop even while in the Intensive Care Unit. He took the lead in outlining the text for many of the chapters. He combed through the thousands of photographs we had taken since the 1970s in many of the finest gardens of the world. Since his death, I have further developed his outlines, written additional chapters, taken new photos and selected others from our archives. *The Bartlett Book of Garden Elements* is the culmination of our work together and individually. It has been a true labor of love.

All but three of the photographs in the book (in the chapter on lighting) were taken by the two of us over a 30-year period, in our travels to more than a thousand gardens in twenty-one countries around the world. The photos were taken with a number of different cameras and techniques, eventually including digital technology. This accounts for the inevitable variations in color saturation and light quality.

It is our belief that inspiration can be derived from any garden that is well designed, so the locations depicted here range from ancient ruins and grand, historically significant villas to simple yet elegant cottages and urban retreats. It is the well-thought-out and skillfully crafted details in a garden that distinguish a mundane design from one that sparks the imagination and pleases the senses. Although it may be impossible to replicate the most extravagant elements of centuries-old gardens, by examining what makes them special, it is possible to reinvent them. Quality materials and craftsmanship will always form the foundation of beautiful gardens even though materials and fabrication techniques vary from generation to generation.

In each chapter, we've included some historical background of the garden element, in the belief that insight into its uses—both practical and decorative—over the millennia might be relevant to today's purposes. In our experience, historical perspective can inspire creative contemporary interpretations. And of course there are some garden ornaments that have always been appreciated simply for their decorative qualities. Nineteenth-century Pennsylvania Dutch folk carvers referred to these creations as "just for nice" or "simply for pleasure."

Photographs and history can provide inspiration but establishing a garden requires skill, passion and practice beyond what we can provide here. This is not meant to be a comprehensive "how-to" book. Indeed, many of these chapters could be expanded into books of their own. Our aim is to offer enough detailed practical information in the "Design," "Weathering" and "Installation and Maintenance" sections to help gardeners narrow down their options and make pleasing and practical choices right from the start.

Garden ornaments have been a valued addition to garden design for centuries. In 1657, the English writer and gardener John Evelyn wrote to Sir Thomas Browne:

We will endeavor to shew how the aire and genius of Gardens operated upon humane spirit towards virtue and sanctitie, I meane in a remote, preparatory and instrumental working. How caves, Grotts, Mounts and irregular ornaments of gardens do contribute to contemplative and philosophical Enthusiasms.

And in his book *Elysium Brittanicum*, Evelyn describes embellishments he believed might elevate the garden to an art form:

To render [the garden] the utmost accomplishment it might have likewise the addition of walls, architecture, porticoes, terraces, statues, obelisks, pots, cascades, fountains, basins, pavilions, aviaries, vineyards, walks and other artful decorations.

The special features of a garden can guide us through it, help our plants grow, give us a place to rest, keep us cool, offer privacy, invite the birds, reflect the sky, add a note of whimsy and so much more. They reveal the character of the garden, express the taste of its maker and add interest for the observer.

It is with great pleasure that we share our knowledge, experience and photographs with fellow designers, students and all who love gardens.

The Bartlett Book of Garden Elements

ALLÉES

These trees are magnificent, but even more magnificent is the sublime and moving space between them, as though with their growth it too increased.

RAINER MARIA RILKE

1. Orange trees create an allée that is fragrant when blooming and colorful when fruiting. The trees link sculptural accents at either end of the path.

2. This allée named Cypress Lane provides a sense of rhythm for visitors strolling along the terrace at Greystone Park in Los Angeles. Designed by landscape architect Paul Thiene in 1927, the allée consists of upright cypresses spaced to allow views, while defining the path through the garden.

3. This nineteenth-century interpretation of a tunnello guides visitors through the gardens of King Ludwig II at Linderhof Park in southern Germany.

Drawing its name from the French verb *aller* ("to go"), an allée is a lush and inviting walkway lined with trees. Beautifully framing what's ahead while providing a protective bower along the way, an allée can serve as a gracious and dramatic route to and from a house or other destination.

Trees arranged symmetrically in lines have been incorporated into gardens throughout the ages as a way to connect and feature outbuildings, create focal points, frame garden vistas, and provide shade and shelter. In the United States, they are sometimes called alleys, while those of a larger and grander scale might be referred to as avenues.

The early Persians planted allées of mulberry, orange, lemon, cherry, and apricot to provide nourishment as well as a shaded passage through a sun-drenched garden.

The Italian tunnello, most often comprising strong lines of tall, swaying cypresses or pines, unified the garden, linked various estate buildings, provided shade and created pleasing perspectives. By extending the allée beyond the boundary of the garden itself, designers drew the visitor's gaze out to the surrounding countryside, thus creating a sense of limitless space.

Proficient in horticulture and design, French Renaissance gardeners created robust and beautiful allées, selecting tree species that were highly adaptable to training and pruning. These dense, green passages provided welcome shelter while guiding visitors through the garden.

André Le Nôtre (1613–1700), the master gardener employed by "Sun King" Louis XIV, was an expert in both horticulture and architecture. He included allées in most of his garden designs as a way to structure the vast open spaces and provide direction, definition, and welcome shade. Trees of a selected species were planted close together on grids to encourage rapid upward growth.

In the gardens of Versailles and Vaux-le-Vicomte, Le Nôtre worked with a clean slate of enormous proportions. Allées and avenues as wide as forty-eight feet and over half a mile long served to connect the various parts of these grand gardens. Paths dotted with pergolas ran in close proximity to the château, while allées led out to clearings in the forest and hunting grounds. These passageways dappled with light and shade contributed a sense of endlessness—and endless perfection—to the royal gardens.

As was often the case in aspects of garden design, France was in the vanguard in its use of allées. The fashion soon spread to the British Isles, the Netherlands, Germany, and Russia. In these environments, they tended to be designed on an even grander scale yet, and flourished for several generations. In late-eighteenth-century England, however, a number of grand allées were pulled down, fatalities of the landscape movement, which aspired to a more naturalistic style.

Formal allées came back into fashion during the Victorian era, only to be reinvented during the early twentieth century as extended glades featuring various species of trees, rather than just one.

In the New World, President George Washington hired Pierre Charles L'Enfant (1754–1825) to prepare site plans for the proposed capital of the Union in WASHINGTON, D.C. As a youth, L'Enfant had trained at Versailles and knew well the gardens of Le Nôtre. He borrowed heavily from the French landscape architect to create a plan for the city that featured long, diagonal allées connecting a series of circles and squares within an overall square grid. Although his allées no longer exist in their original form, L'Enfant's spirit lives on in Washington DC's design and flow. Even with traffic teeming over its busy roadways, it is easy to imagine what the city was like in its infancy, with trees arching over its main arteries.

On a personal scale, as Americans acquired wealth, they built grand estates approached by allées of trees. Many fine examples still exist and some of the most dramatic are the great avenues of live oaks clothed in Spanish moss that are found in the Deep South. Beautiful and functional, these

4. André Le Nôtre used successive lines of trees to create strong direction and perspective in the Tuileries in Paris.

5. This allée at Vaux-le-Vicomte is unusual in its asymmetry; densely planted on one side, open on the other. It frames the château without limiting views of the gardens.

6. The Prunus Walk at Dumbarton Oaks in Washington, DC., connects Cherry Hill, an informal area of the garden devoted to a collection of spring-blooming Japanese cherry trees, and the Herbaceous Border, composed of two long-blooming planting beds.

7. This allée frames focal points of sculpture and architecture and makes a vast park feel more intimate.

8. This aerial hedge and its twin are part of a strong central-axis allée in a diverse horticultural palette, in the eighteenth-century gardens of Schwetzingen, Germany.

9. Trees trained as an allée of arches provide green architecture at Schwetzingen and preclude the need for paved paths through the extensive gardens.

10. An entrance drive planted in 1843 features an allée of live oaks about 3/4 mile long, offering a cool and inviting entry to Boone Hall in South Carolina.
11. At its maturity, this young allée of disease-resistant elms at the Chicago Botanic Garden will provide a comfortable, sheltered stroll. Its twin stands guard on the other side of the lawn.
12. The slender trunks of this crepe myrtle allée are under-planted with a hedge to reinforce its linear direction. Gravel is a good paving choice as this is a well-used pedestrian path in the town of Beaufort, South Carolina.

13. The precise pruning of the Linden Allée at the Chicago Botanic Garden creates a heightened sense of perspective, while allowing a view of the sky.
14. An allée of birch trees frames the "Blue Steps" at Naumkeag in Stockbridge, Massachusetts. Built into a hillside, this is unusual topography for an allée, resulting in a striking combination of architecture and horticulture.
15. Closely planted trees in an allée will eventually become solid walls and roofs of green.

allées provide welcome relief from the intensity of the thick summer heat.

Allées are not trained to a structural support but are usually pruned into shape at least twice a year to maintain their architectural integrity. With careful planning and species selection, these dramatic landscape features survive and improve over the centuries. Linden, horse chestnut, elm, beech, hornbeam, honey locust, and oak are often chosen for their rapid growth and malleability. Crabapple, cherry, and hawthorn are appreciated for their beautiful displays of seasonal flowers and the fact that they will never grow taller than one story.

Obviously, a full-scale allée is not something that can be added to just any garden; it is a dramatic, defining feature best suited to large-scale landscapes that will benefit from the perspective and gentle sanctuary they provide.

DESIGN The design of an allée should defer to the forces of nature, maintenance, and time. In selecting the plants to be used, it is crucial to take into consideration their growth habits and resistance to pests and diseases. The clever gardener will avoid trees and shrubs that attract bees, have messy fruiting or brittle wood, are short lived, or cannot tolerate heavy pruning.

Almost all allées are placed on a level grade that affords sharp drainage, good ventilation, and full exposure to the sun.

A gradual diminution of the space between the trees at the far end, and/or the use of shorter trees there, can create the illusion of a longer allée.

Turf tends not to thrive under allées, as turf needs ample sunlight and well-drained soil and doesn't stand up well to excessive foot traffic. Sand or gravel are better choices for functional allées. Provided the allée isn't too well trod, fragrant herbs, such as chamomile or thyme, can be planted beneath it, enhancing the general atmosphere of the bower with their subtle and lovely aroma.

One final benefit of this high-impact garden feature: although the effect of an allée is architectural, it is not classified as a permanent structure and is therefore not subject to local building codes.

CLIMATE AND WEATHERING Because allées provide shelter against the sun, frequently they are placed on the south side of a house, where they can best ameliorate the effect of its rays. When placed on the north side, an allée is likely to reduce the amount of light coming in through the windows of an already dim area, so it is often not the best choice for such a location. In colder climates, however, an allée thus situated might serve as a buffer against northerly winds and a way to retain warmth within the house.

Allées should never be positioned so that they funnel the prevailing winter winds; rather, they should favor the prevailing summer winds.

INSTALLATION AND MAINTENANCE As in all garden planning, foresight must be used in designing an allée, the trees selected based on their ultimate dimensions as well as their susceptibility to training and pruning. It is important to avoid trees with aggressive surface root systems, and a good idea to stick with strong species tolerant of climate change and resistant to pests and diseases.

Once you have selected the trees you intend to use, it is wise to have the soil analyzed professionally to be sure it provides the optimal pH and nutrient composition for the species. To ensure consistency in size and growth rate throughout the allée, trees should be drawn from the same pool of nursery stock. The planting areas should be open to allow for ample sunlight and ventilation and the soil must be well drained. Avoid using fertilizer high in nitrogen as this will encourage fast, leggy growth.

Finally, it is important to prune with care. Flowering trees should be pruned immediately after flowering. Deciduous and evergreen trees should be pruned before the flush of new growth. Trees that are deciduous but retain their tawny leaves throughout the winter (such as hawthorn, beech, sawtooth, and pin oak) should be pruned heavily one month before the first frost.

16. These small-scale trees are trained to a compact barrel shape that allows enough sun through to grow grass along the allée.
17. The cypress allée in the distance beckons the visitor to investigate the garden.
18. Live oaks planted in staggered rows create multiple allées with varying views out to the landscape.
19. The stark trunks of palm trees clearly define the path through this garden but provide little shelter or shade.
20. This very narrow path focuses the eye on the architectural qualities of the upright tree trunks and the contrast of their bark with the gravel terrace.
21. Here, the Prunus Walk at Dumbarton Oaks is beginning to show its fall colors. Allées of trees with brilliant autum foliage add seasonal interest, in addition to providing structure to the garden's design.
22. In early spring, pollarded linden trees reveal the structure of this allée in a public square in Bruges, Belgium.

ARBORS

Gardens are the boon of summer. The long, hot, cloudless months make the shelter of a vine-grown arbor a welcome refuge.

ELLEN CHURCHILL SEMPLE

1. The Rose Arbor at Cawdor Castle in Scotland is carpeted with an airy mix of herbaceous perennials that thrive in its filtered light.

2. Intertwining two rosebushes into an arch adds vertical interest to the pathway through the long, herbaceous borders at this garden in Ireland.

An arbor can be defined as either a leafy, shady niche formed by tree branches or shrubs, or a latticework bower intertwined with climbing vines and flowers. Whether fully natural or incorporating a man-made structure, arbors add a lovely area of shelter and repose to any garden large enough to include one.

The construction and use of elements to support climbing plants first emerged in the cultivated vineyards of the Tigris-Euphrates Basin, and as the practice spread throughout ancient Egypt, Greece, and Rome, its purpose was more practical than aesthetic: grape vines were trained to climb upward and off the ground so as to prevent rot. Images of grapes trained onto round arbors can be found in Egyptian tomb paintings circa 1500 BC. The grape arbors of ancient Rome are well documented and the frescoes of Pompeii show outdoor "dining rooms" created by vine-covered arbors.

Arbors of a sort have been a part of Jewish tradition since biblical times. They are integral to the celebration of the fall harvest holiday known as Succot, a weeklong festival during which observant families eat dinner each night under a specially constructed succah consisting of freestanding poles supporting a vine-covered lattice. According to tradition, the vines should provide a covering of some density, while allowing spaces to view the sky and stars above.

Arbors, most likely incorporating fruit trees or vines, were often found in medieval courtyard gardens, providing a pleasant spot in which to enjoy leisure activities. They and their grander kin, pergolas, were commonplace in gardens of the Renaissance as well, as their designers set about re-creating the glories of ancient Roman gardens as they envisioned them. The words arbor and pergola are often used interchangeably— and, in fact, these structures are similar in many ways. They tend to serve the same function and much of their history goes hand in hand. But arbors are smaller and simpler in design, and therefore more versatile. (To read about their more elaborate sisters in detail, see Pergolas.)

Arbors may be primarily functional or first-and-foremost decorative. They can be used to provide shade for plants (and humans) that require it; provide support for plants and vines that need it for health and hardiness; or simply as an aesthetically pleasing, purely ornamental feature that defines the flow of the garden. From ancient times to the present, gardeners have created a kind of practical majesty within their garden spaces by incorporating the height and lushness of an arbor into the overall architecture.

DESIGN Arbors, which may be freestanding or situated against a hedge or building, often shelter seats and even tables. They may be designed simply, so that the structure disappears amid the plants as they grow to maturity, or they may be more ornate and call attention to themselves, featuring arched or peaked tops and sides made of intricate latticework. The range of design choices is wide, but it is worthwhile to remember that, if your plants are well selected and properly cultivated, much of your arbor's architectural detail will ultimately be hidden by the lush growth.

Consider your arbor's main function when choosing its location. Is it meant to screen an objectionable view or direct your visitors' attention to a desirable one? Is it a focal point of your garden or a hidden retreat meant to delight those who discover it? An arbor can even create a "room" within your garden, in which case you might want to include a gate. Finally, an arbor might serve as a pleasing frame for another ornamental feature—a sculpture, urn, bench, or even fountain.

Nowadays, arbors are made of wood, metal, or vinyl, though wood—the earliest material used—is still the most

3. A superbly crafted arbor provides a shaded transition between garden spaces at Sanssouci in Germany.
4. This tall arbor at the Chicago Botanic Garden lifts the eye, frames the view, and provides excellent exposure for the apple trees trained to it.

5. New Dawn roses trained on hoops attached to columns create separate "rooms" in this private garden in Washington, D.C., designed by Michael Bartlett.
6. Trellis panels attached to a fence create an arbor to support grape vines and shelter a bench.

7. At Kiftsgate in England, this very simple arbor set within a hedge defines the garden space and echoes the curve of the sculpture it frames.

popular. It is readily available, inexpensive, and easy to set up, and tends to blend most harmoniously with the plantings that surround it. If wood is your material of choice, it is best to avoid using the pressure-treated variety for an arbor intended to support edibles (grapes or other fruits or vegetables) because of its chemical content. Untreated Douglas fir, spruce, or cedar, are good choices.

As for design and construction, a broad selection of kits and do-it-yourself plans are available. Trellis- and latticework are sold in many garden centers, but if a truly natural effect is

what you are going for—and you have the time and patience of a collector—a rustic arbor can be fashioned from well-chosen fallen branches or driftwood.

There is an extensive array of ready-made metal and vinyl arbors on the market, and many of them are aesthetically pleasing and well constructed. Metal arbors are sturdy and their effect is often airier and more open than that of a wood or vinyl structure.

Your choice of plants or vines must be taken into consideration when choosing both the material and design of the arbor. Woody, heavy, or dense vines, such as wisteria or roses, require a much sturdier arbor than do clematis, sweet peas, or most annual vines. To insure the long-term success of this dramatic garden feature, be sure to think about the underlying structure and the overtaking greenery at the same time, working out the best combination of substance, style, and embellishment. In the end it is the verdant growth that will draw visitors to its sanctuary.

CLIMATE AND WEATHERING Arbors should be sited in a sunny location so they do not become too cool and damp. In rainy climates with high humidity, heavy vines should be pruned regularly to permit light and breezes to penetrate. This will also prevent the development of mildew within the arbor.

Alternatively, select vines with a naturally light and open growth habit, such as clematis, noninvasive forms of honeysuckle, or annual vines that naturally die back.

In winter, heavy loads of snow and ice may accumulate on top of dense vines, so it is best to keep them pruned to be as open on top as possible, allowing snow to fall through to the ground. Removing snow and ice can be difficult and might prove dangerous for both the remover and the arbor.

In windy areas, arbors should be sited to provide shelter from the prevailing winds, and must be securely anchored to the ground. In colder areas, the protection provided by a well-sited arbor can extend the precious time during which you can enjoy your garden.

INSTALLATION AND MAINTENANCE The level of invasiveness of a particular variety of vine may vary from region to region. For that reason, it is important to check with a reliable local source, when choosing vines for your arbor. If you select a perennial or woody vine, it should be cut back to about half

8. Rustic supports mingle with tree trunks to provide a sheltered place to rest on the benches so invitingly placed within.
9. In the potager garden at Villandry in France, a latticework arbor made of oak provides good air circulation for the roses it supports and a private nook for a bench.
10. The curved path here adds an element of mystery rather than framing or focusing on an object or view, as most arbors do.

of its height before planting. Sacrificing some of the first year's growth is worthwhile in that you are directing the vine's energy to its roots and encouraging the long-term strength of the plant.

Many vines will not automatically cling to a structure; initially, they might need some additional support, such as wire, string, or pieces of lattice attached to the arbor's supports.

Arbors vary tremendously in size and substance. If you are planning a full-scale structure that is visible to others, it is important to find out whether you need to have your plans okayed by your county or neighborhood association before beginning construction. (Even if this isn't the case, sharing plans with your neighbors before undertaking an outdoor construction project can go a long way toward keeping the peace!)

Arbor kits are designed for easy and efficient installation. Whether or not you use a kit, you must make certain that the posts you are using are strong enough to support the vines you've selected—and they must be securely anchored with concrete or spikes. In any kind of garden structure, from a fence to an arbor to a shed, the wood must never come into direct contact with the moist earth, lest it rot in a few short seasons.

Rather than painting your arbor, which can create an on-going maintenance problem, try letting it weather naturally. Stain or a sealant can be used if you feel it necessary, and metal structures should be powder coated. Aluminum and vinyl require little maintenance, although vinyl tends to fade and yellow with UV exposure.

11

13

12

11. A garden path full of color is punctuated by a green arbor that adds scale and intimacy.
12. This urban park in Prague welcomes visitors with a series of benches nestled into arbors covered with roses.
13. A natural wood arbor covered in grapevines works as a shade house for plants, whether newly repotted or being transitioned to a sunny spot. A raised shelf built on the outside of the arbor can serve as a potting bench or a place for plants requiring more sun.

14. Choosing arbor plants for fall color adds late-season interest to a garden, as seen at this one in Williamsburg, Virginia.
15. This kitchen garden in Christchurch, New Zealand, features a succession of arbors with a pear tree in fruit trained to the one in the foreground.
16. At Heale House in England, apple trees are trained to the arbor vertically, their strong lateral branches connecting the trees.

14

15

16

17. A topiary Buddha at Ladew Gardens in Maryland is approached through a tunnel of trees and framed by an arbor.

18. At Giverny in France, tall arbors of roses rise out of the flowerbeds and frame the house from different vantage points.

19. The walled garden at Kellie Castle is an oasis of flowering plants, and the rose arbor adds to the feeling of walking through flowers.

20. The arched woodwork design of this arbor is revealed in the winter but concealed by the end of spring.

21. This arbor at Bodnant in Wales is painstakingly pruned to create a dense and formal shaded spot with a large seating area.

22. This passageway between two buildings in Antwerp, Belgium, has been turned into a garden area with seating by the addition of an arbor.

23. A bed of frittilaria and tulips in the foreground of an arbor of trees lures the visitor to the fountain beyond.

BIRDHOUSES & BEEHIVES

*"For so work the honey-bees,
creatures that by a rule in nature teach
the act of order to a peopled kingdom."*

WILLIAM SHAKESPEARE

Not every living thing in a garden is rooted to the ground or clinging to a wall. As much as any flower or vine, the winged creatures that buzz, chirp, and linger over our carefully cultivated blooms are functional as well as beautiful aspects of the landscape. So it stands to reason that many gardens include structures designed to be inviting to our airborne friends.

For their crucial role in the process of pollination, bees have long been referred to as "angels of agriculture." The early Egyptians housed bee colonies on barges in the Nile, near the fertile soil where their crops relied upon the insects to flourish. The Greeks refined the cultivation of bees by creating artful and functional straw hives in which they might thrive and multiply.

In Europe and the United Kingdom, beekeepers wove conical baskets from coils of grass or straw (bee skeps) and inverted them to house bee colonies. Alternatively, they relied on hollow logs they called gums. To harvest the honey from these types of hives, the keepers had to drive the bees out, usually by the use of smoke. Many bees died in the process and sometimes the entire colony perished.

Honeybees are not indigenous to the United States. They were introduced by British colonists in the 1620s and were valued for their honey, wax, and, of course, their role in pollination. Locally cultivated honey was less expensive than imported sugar, and the wax was fashioned into candles and used as a waterproof coating for fabric. Many colonial gardens included an area specifically set aside for keeping bees.

In 1851, Rev. L. L. Langstroth (1810–1895), a native of Philadelphia, developed a new kind of beehive. Now known as the Langstroth hive, it remains the standard in many parts of the world. Boxlike in shape and fitted with easily removable frames, it encourages the bees to construct their honeycombs in such a way that they can be removed, inspected, and harvested without destroying the hives. The ability to observe the colonies as they work also allows for the early detection of diseases and parasites.

1. Tucked into a corner of the flower gardens at the Villa Ephrussi de Rothschild in southern France, this small stone building welcomes birds and adds rustic charm to the garden.
2. A sculptural ode to beekeeping is carved in limestone in this private garden in Washington, D.C.
3. At Ladew Gardens in Maryland, a birdhouse playfully painted in the colors of a bee stands guard over a collection of bee skeps raised off the ground and protected by a shake roof.
4. Lively colors make these modern, functional beehives in Asheville, North Carolina, a bit more decorative.

Straw hives are still used to catch swarms of bees that can be moved subsequently to permanent wooden hives. The bees are attracted to the scent left in the straw by previous swarms, signaling that they have found a good home. In modern gardens, straw hives or bee skeps are more often purely ornamental, their function as a source of honey and wax having been replaced by utilitarian wooden hives based on the Langstroth design.

The orchard mason bee is a gentle, nonaggressive variety native to North America whose pollination rate greatly exceeds that of the honeybee. Because these bees are native, they are resistant to many of the parasites and diseases that can harm the honeybee—making them an ideal choice for amateur beekeeping, should you decide to undertake it. They do not live in hives; rather, they create nests in whatever wood cavities they can find, within living trees or even stray pieces of lumber. To help attract orchard mason bees to your garden, a variety of ready-made nesting blocks and kits are available—or, if you are more inclined to start from scratch, instructions for easy do-it-yourself versions abound.

The benefit of inviting bees into your garden goes beyond the reward of harvesting their honey. Just as they did for the ancients, bees continue to function as "angels of agriculture," pollinating your flowers, vegetables, and other plants.

Just as it would be rare, if not impossible, to find a garden neglected by bees, it is difficult to imagine one without visits from the local bird species. In fact, many gardeners enjoy the parallel pleasure of bird-watching within the environment they have so lovingly created. To encourage the presence of feathered visitors, some add birdhouses and feeders designed with their local avian population in mind.

Birdhouses are a relatively recent innovation in Europe and Britain. Prior to the nineteenth century, those who yearned to fill their gardens with birdsong caught and caged wild birds, sometimes even blinding them to dampen their instinct to fly. Eventually, various means of attracting wild birds replaced their capture and containment. Food, water, and shelter were provided in the hope that the loveliest and most tuneful species would come, nest, and thrive.

Bird feeders, birdhouses, and birdbaths began to appear in gardens as both functional and ornamental pieces. In America, Choctaw Indians observed the nesting habits of their local population and used hollowed-out gourds to attract the birds they knew would devour bothersome insects. Henry David Thoreau described the rewards of feeding birds at Walden Pond in 1845 and writer Abram L. Urban remarked in his book *The Voice of the Garden* of 1912, "Poor indeed is the garden in which birds find no homes."

Forebears of the birds we know today as pigeons (Columbidae) were raised in ancient Egypt, China, and Persia for their eggs and fertile manure, and as a source of protein. In Rome, pigeon farming was considered a privilege. The Romans designed round stone towers called columbaria that could house thousands of pigeons, and the structures were prevalent for centuries—until the birds became less important as a source of food and fertilizer. Smaller structures called dovecotes, either freestanding or built into turrets on top of a building, replaced the massive early columbaria.

Attracting birds to your garden can benefit both you and the garden. Many birds consume unwanted insects; some aid in pollination; and others eat weeds or seeds, thus helping to curb unwanted plants. Their effect on the hard-working gardener is self-evident: they make beautiful and captivating companions and their song can be a soothing reward at the end of an afternoon's labor.

5. Birdbaths attract birds in search of drinking water or a splash.

6. This superbly crafted birdhouse from the 1860s, featuring finely detailed woodworking and paint, is more sculptural than functional.

7. Reminiscent of a hollowed-out gourd, this clay birdhouse is positioned high off the ground, on the wall of a house in Williamsburg, Virginia.

8. The decoy may not attract birds to this birdbath, but its fresh, clean water does. Birds of many species have been enjoying this birdbath since the 1880s.

9. A pigeonnière in Williamsburg, Virginia, and its content occupants.

10. A dovecote built into the roof of a brick outbuilding in Williamsburg.

11. Straw bee skeps are used solely for ornament in this herb garden.
12. This rustic gazebo is topped with a birdhouse of contrasting architectural detail.
13. A bluebird house is protected from climbing predators by a metal baffle.

14. This birdhouse at Ladew Gardens in Maryland features a graceful roofline that is enhanced by its patina.
15. This ornate birdhouse has been carefully modeled on the house itself.
16. Multi-tiered birdhouses should provide adequate "standing room" on each level.

DESIGN OF BEEHIVES The modern, movable-frame beehive is utilitarian rather than aesthetic, so, unless it is your intention to take up beekeeping in earnest, it might not be an appropriate element for your garden. Straw bee skeps, on the other hand, are often used as decorative elements in historical period gardens or to suggest beekeeping in a more artistic way. A variety of ready-made ones are available and should be selected to fit in harmoniously with the size and style of your garden.

DESIGN OF BIRDHOUSES A garden birdhouse or dovecote—particularly in a small garden—should be designed to blend harmoniously with the architecture and feeling of the house. In a larger garden, where the structure might be farther from the house, they can be more adventuresome in style, detail, and materials, or can be designed to complement another garden structure, such as a gazebo or pavilion.

Birdhouses and dovecotes can be circular, square, hexagonal, or octagonal, their dimensions dependent upon the species you wish to attract. Wood is an excellent choice of material because it insulates and breathes. Roofs can be made of wood, cedar shingles, vinyl, thatch, metal, or slate. A shiny metal roof isn't a good idea, though, because it makes the structure more visible to predators.

When designing and positioning your birdhouse, ventilation, drainage, and access for cleaning must be considered. To keep climbing rodents and reptiles at bay, your birdhouse should be mounted on a sturdy pole several feet above ground level. You might even want to outfit it with baffles to further discourage squirrels and other clever interlopers.

Most birdhouses are built on a single level but you can find a variety of examples of multistoried towers. These "high-rises" can be sullied as the droppings from one level land on a lower one, so careful design is in order.

Some birds, such as the mourning dove and eastern phoebe, will not use enclosed birdhouses, while others are particular about the specifics of size, number of openings, and so forth. If you are intent on attracting a particular type of bird, it is wise to research the preferences of that species.

Many commercially available dovecotes and birdhouses are beautifully crafted and less expensive than those made from scratch. These structures are often easier to install as well. If it suits your taste, dig around for an antique or vintage birdhouse; it can add a unique and whimsical touch. Just be sure that the interior is properly sanitized before installation. Small birdhouses are usually not regarded as permanent structures and do not require permits, but, as always, make sure you aren't running afoul of any local

17   18   19   20   21

17. Even a minimal feeding platform will attract birds, but be ready to feed the squirrels (and bears), too.
18. The roof pitch of this birdhouse is well suited for shedding the snow endemic to its location in Hyannisport, Massachusetts.

19. Birdhouses like this one are readily available from any number of shops or on the Internet.
20. An antique feeding platform made of finely detailed, unstained wood.

21. This wood birdhouse with pottery details is surrounded by a landing platform and offers multiple entrances for the birds.
22. An electric fence is essential to protecting any beehive located in bear territory.

regulations before you add a new structure to your garden.

CLIMATE AND WEATHERING OF BEEHIVES Durable and healthy bee habitats must remain dry inside; dampness speeds the deterioration of the beehive's structure and weakens the colony's resistance to the many parasites and diseases that threaten it.

Hives should be made of hardy wood with low porosity. Joints should be inspected often and any gaps that occur over time should be sealed immediately. The roof of the hive (these are often made of galvanized metal) should also be monitored regularly for signs of weather damage and corrosion.

CLIMATE AND WEATHERING OF BIRDHOUSES In cold climates, birdhouses are often built against or near a wall so as to block the harsh northerly winds. Facing the structure toward the south or west facilitates the retention of solar heat.

If you experience heavy snowfall in your area, it is wise to reinforce the roof of your birdhouse (just as you would that of your own house) so that it can withstand the extra weight. The roofline should be strongly pitched to help shed snow and ice. In temperate climates, roofing materials that heat up and cool down rapidly should be avoided. In windy and hurricane-prone areas, it is important that the structure be well anchored to the ground. Multilevel designs on tall poles are most susceptible to wind damage.

INSTALLATION AND MAINTENANCE OF BEEHIVES If you are serious about keeping bees, and not interested merely in the decorative value of the hive, you should know that the use of straw bee skeps is prohibited in most places because they do not allow for proper monitoring of the colony's health and may contribute to the spread of disease and parasites. Plus, as noted earlier, they tend to require the sacrifice of the colony

so as to harvest the honey.

Modern movable-frame wooden beehives are available from suppliers of beekeeping equipment. If you live near a forested area that might be home to bears—and you don't want to share your honey—fence your hives! An electrical fence is usually necessary.

The simplest nests for orchard mason bees can be made by drilling holes about 5/16 inch in diameter and 3 to 5 inches deep in a piece of untreated wood. As noted earlier, many detailed plans for the construction of nests can be found online, as can a plethora of ready-made nests and bee houses.

INSTALLATION AND MAINTENANCE OF BIRDHOUSES Most birdhouses are made of cedar, spruce, bald cypress, pressure-treated pine, or redwood. When selecting a birdhouse, pay attention to this factor, as some wood types, including redwood, attract carpenter bees. Use pressure-treated wood only if it is clad in another wood because it is infused with potentially toxic chemicals. The densest grade of decay-resistant wood will last the longest. All wood should be stained or

22

sealed with water-based latex on the exterior—but don't use it inside the structure, as many birds are extremely sensitive to the fumes. Birdhouses and dovecotes should be set on footings or posts that extend below the frost line. To avoid rot, wood posts should never come in contact with moist earth; they should be set within cement. For sturdiness, it's best to make sure that all wooden parts are notched together and any fasteners are galvanized or, better yet, made of stainless steel.

Once it is installed and inhabited, check your birdhouse or dovecote regularly for signs of parasites. It should be cleaned at least once a year, after the breeding season, which will vary by species. For easy cleaning, birdhouses and dovecotes should be floored with wood or metal screening that can be removed.

Proper ventilation and drainage are essential to moderate temperature and to guard against disease and parasites.

Making your garden attractive and inviting to the local winged population is sure to increase your own enjoyment of your surroundings as well. The riot of color and sound they bring adds new sensual dimensions to any garden.

23. This rustic feeding platform also has a swinging perch.
24. A departure from the typical box used to encourage bluebirds to nest.
25. A man-made island for ducks is landscaped with trees and includes a roofed shelter for their comfort in inclement weather.

BOLLARDS

Americans will put up with anything provided it doesn't block traffic.
DAN RATHER

Sturdy garden barriers known as bollards tend to be more functional than beautiful—but when carefully chosen and artfully placed, they can add form and visual interest to your grounds, as well as protect delicate flora and direct the flow of garden traffic.

The term bollard comes from the Middle English word bole—tree trunk—but the first bollards cropped up far away from gardens: they were heavy wood, metal, or stone posts, wider at the top than bottom, used on docks as mooring structures for ships. Gradually, they migrated landward, where they continue to be used today to guide the flow of pedestrian and vehicular traffic.

In ancient Rome, stone mile markers, horse troughs, and tethering posts found along busy roads also served as bollards, discouraging travelers, horses, and chariots from straying off the beaten path.

Bollards started appearing in England in the early nineteenth century, typically made from French cannons removed from battleships during the Napoleonic Wars. The French cannons were larger than English ones so they couldn't be used on English warships. Instead, the English decided to recycle them as street bollards. Some were buried muzzle down and others muzzle up with a cannonball fixed on top. These historic bollards continue to inspire modern reproductions.

In today's urban green spaces, bollards perform the essential function of separating fast-moving traffic from meandering cyclists and pedestrians. More gracefully shaped than their stolid forebears—and sometimes even topped with a planting of grasses or colorful annuals—they can add a sculptural element to the pocket oases that dot busy cityscapes, while performing the essential function of directing the flow of traffic. In private gardens, an attempt is usually made to install bollards that are ornamental as well as functional. While their main purpose may be to remind visitors not to park on the lawn, tread on delicate ground cover, or stray too near a water feature, there is no reason why they can't be aesthetically pleasing while doing so.

1. Sandstone rocks nestled against a hedge protect its roots from foot traffic in the gardens at the Taj Mahal. Although they serve as bollards, their natural form masks their function.
2. Stone bollards with metal caps are reminiscent of those made from repurposed cannons in England. Here, they steer cars away from a steep drop-off next to an entrance driveway in the south of France.
3. A canal in Courance, France, is cordoned off by bollards connected by chains. Note the attractive grass growing around the bollards, connecting them to the brimming water.

DESIGN In selecting bollards for a home garden, look for a style that blends appropriately with the surrounding architecture. They should be visually pleasing while optimally functional for the task at hand.

Bollards can be made of metal, concrete, stone, or wood. They may be fixed, removable, telescoping, collapsible, or concealable, and all of these possibilities should be weighed in selecting the type that will best fulfill your needs. In some situations, even sturdy living plants can serve as bollards.

Metal bollards come in a wide variety of styles and are far less expensive than those made of stone, while being more durable than wood or concrete. They may be painted dark green or black so as to keep them from standing out too starkly against the landscape. If necessary, they can be made sturdier by filling their interiors with concrete and reinforcing bars. Many metal-forging companies produce replicas of historic period designs that might complement the existing architecture.

4. Rising out of the flowerbeds, these bollards are meant to remind guests to remain on the path, while allowing adjacent plants to ramble onto it.
5. Originally, this would have been a continuous circle of delicate metal bollards connected by chains. A number of them have been removed, probably due to damage.
6. These stone bollards connected by chains are strong enough and placed closely enough together to stop a car from veering into the canal in Eyrignac, France.
7. The relatively delicate chains connecting the wood bollards at Mount Vernon in Virginia are weighted with decorative pears that add to their visual impact.
8. These bronze bollards in Cap Ferrat, France, have weathered to a lovely patina of green.
9. A single bollard of sculptural form, such as this one found at Williamsburg, is friendlier than a keep-off-the-grass sign.
10. An elegant 1880s cast-iron hitching post in the shape of a swan's neck serves as both bollard and sculpture.

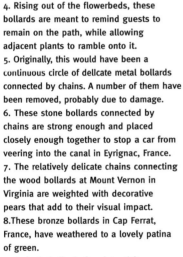

11. **This log warns of a steep drop into a ravine and also provides a welcome spot to rest during an uphill hike.**
12. **Bollards connected by rails create a mini-fence.**
13. **Planters functioning as bollards mark an entrance in the town of Antigua, Guatemala.**

14. **Bollards with lights are most often found in commercial settings, but some people find them useful in defining driveways or entrances.**
15. **A stack of heavy spheres marks the corner of a planting bed close to a driveway and echoes the shape of the nearby shrubs.**

If placed fairly close together, bollards may serve as a fence. The initial cost of such an installation is comparable to that of a fence, but bollards require less maintenance and allow for a more transparent view. Replacing one bollard is usually easier than replacing a section of fence.

All bollards on a single site should be of the same material, color, and design detail. At a comfortable height of 18 to 24 inches, they might also function as seating. On the grounds of the White House, for example, where hundreds of visitors daily must be guided gracefully through areas accessible to them, granite benches of the same color as the paving under foot function as bollards along the promenade.

Sadly, many urban centers feature poorly designed bollards in the form of concrete planters. Too often, these unnaturally dyed, faded, or chipped structures clash with the historic facades of the architecture they are meant to frame and protect. The plants within these bollards often fail to thrive due to extreme temperature change, lack of maintenance, and inadequate irrigation. On the other hand, a phalanx of well designed and properly tended planter bollards can enhance the surrounding landscape while doing their job.

A current trend in bollards involves the incorporation of solar collectors that power nighttime lighting. In the most attractive of these, the solar panels are located away from the bollards themselves. These "green" glowing bollards should be placed carefully; too many of them in a straight row may give off more light than necessary, producing an undesirable "landing strip" effect.

If your tastes run to natural rather than man-made elements, small to medium shrubs or trees planted close together can serve the function of a row of bollards. If security is a concern, iron tree guards placed around the trunks will increase the strength and functional protection provided by the plantings.

CLIMATE AND WEATHERING The design and material of a bollard affect its ability to withstand the elements. Look for a shape that will readily shed water and airborne debris, rather than allowing these things to stand or settle into crevices.

Just as you consider the effects of your local weather when choosing materials for building exteriors, you must think about this factor when shopping for bollards. Wood may decay or crack. Iron will rust. Concrete will chip. Fiberglass and plastic will yellow. A certain amount of weathering is a fact of life for outdoor elements, but careful selection can keep it to a minimum.

Bollards that include solar lighting must be placed in sunny locations, away from overhanging trees or structures that might cast shadows over them and affect their performance.

In areas of heavy snow, bollards may become hidden and therefore hazardous to pedestrians and vehicles. Snow should be removed as necessary, while taking care not to damage the bollards in the process.

INSTALLATION AND MAINTENANCE Bollards should not be sited close to steps or within the swing radius of the doors of parked cars. They should never be placed so as to obstruct an active entrance door or gate.

Fixed bollards should be set in concrete footings with a faceplate or dowel. In temperate climates, the footings must be deeper than the frost line.

Some removable bollards fit into sockets cemented into the ground. These should be equipped with covers that slide into place over the sockets when the bollards are removed, so as to avoid creating tripping hazards.

Powder coating is recommended for metal bollards. From an aesthetic perspective, all natural metal finishes should be satin in order to blend best with the surrounding landscape. Copper-clad bollards should be avoided as the copper will leach and stain the surrounding paving, and may stunt the growth of adjacent plants.

The sides and corners of rectangular stone bollards should be beveled and rounded off to eliminate sharp, potentially dangerous edges.

Bollards placed on manicured lawns are certain to be chipped and gouged by lawn mowers and weed trimmers, so it is a good idea to install a mowing edge around these bollards.

16. These stone bollards have been stained by the leaching of their copper collars and chains connecting them.

17. In Udaipur, India, subtle waterworks are separated from the entrance path by cast-iron bollards painted white and joined by a double line of rope.

18. The spare number of bollards here suggests a barrier without really creating one.

16

17

18

BOOT SCRAPERS

The world is mud-luscious and puddle-wonderful.
E. E. CUMMINGS

Until recently, most roads and streets were unpaved and very little was done to maintain them. Consequently, they were often muddy, unclean, littered with animal dung, and foul smelling. The boot scraper (sometimes called a foot scraper or boot cleaner), on guard adjacent to busy doorways of homes and businesses, emerged as an effective solution for keeping the detritus of streets and grounds outside buildings.

These handy devices rose to popularity in industrial England, where the pervasive grime was anathema to those fashionable types captivated by a widening array of posh footwear. Stylishly crafted boots were coveted and expensive, and well-heeled ladies and gentlemen could not be expected to leave them outside the door when they came to call. The boot scraper became a necessary accoutrement for fastidious hosts and guests alike.

There seemed no reason that this humble, utilitarian item had to be unattractive: graceful examples were produced from wrought iron right from the start, and impressive antique versions can still be found today among the many reproductions and more contemporary designs.

In the United States, manufacturers of fine ornamental ironwork sprang up in many major cities, including Savannah, Georgia, and New York City. In addition to producing freestanding versions of the device, these companies incorporated them into the railings they designed for the entrance staircases of elegant townhouses.

1. An iron boot scraper, featuring an ornate motif of flowers and vines, is recessed into the wall of a limestone building in Bad Ragaz, Switzerland.
2. In many urban areas in the United States, England, and Europe, boot scrapers were incorporated into the design of the stair rail.
3. This three-dimensional boot scraper is set into the corner of the first step of a front stoop and attached to the stair rail.

4. An elegant wrought-iron boot scraper mounted just outside a doorway in Williamsburg, Virginia.

5. Four boots scrapers are incorporated into the design of these double wrought-iron stair rails, which are set into granite front steps in Boston, Massachusetts.

6. Here, a boot scraper is integrated into a section of railing. Note the pleasingly simple stair treads made from single, well-proportioned flagstones.

7. The shape of this boot scraper mimics the stone gothic arch above.

8. Cast-iron boot scrapers are sometimes designed in animal shapes; the dachshund is a natural.

9. This boot scraper set into a freestanding stone could easily be relocated.

Few examples of boot scrapers can be found in India or Asia, and it's no wonder. In India, it is common practice to leave one's shoes outside of a home or temple; elsewhere in Asia, street shoes are exchanged for house or garden sandals upon entry. But in virtually any country where guests were expected to cross thresholds shod, boot scrapers became a popular option.

As paved roads became the norm everywhere, boot scrapers fell out of fashion in urban settings. But country dwellers—and gardeners in particular—can attest to their continuing usefulness, as well as the nice old-world touch they lend to any doorway.

DESIGN As noted, boot scrapers are usually made of cast or wrought iron, which offers the necessary heft and sturdiness while allowing for an airy look. Early examples were designed with an eye toward the man in the field rather than the lady in town, featuring bold symmetrical patterns and an absence of fine filigree or detail. More elaborate boot scrapers, sometimes designed by architects to conform with their buildings, were mounted directly to the stairs or facade. Occasionally, the devices were even provided with their own recessed niche.

Boot scrapers for use on wooden porches or steps are most effective when mounted on their own supporting bases. In any case, they should always be installed solidly, so that they remain steady against the most strenuous scraping.

With the rise of mass production, boot scrapers were cranked out in cast iron, sometimes in the form of silhouetted animals that could be anchored to the stoop. These were usually painted dark, flat black, though it is possible to come across one that is highly decorated and painted. Later examples incorporated bristle brushes for more effective cleaning, but the bristles had to be replaced often; generic brushes had not yet become common. Some designs incorporated a built-in cast-iron tray, making them portable (if not quite as sturdy).

These humble devices are first and foremost utilitarian; though they can be attractive—even whimsical—the most effective ones feature a clean, narrow scraping surface that is as broad as practicable. The detail should never get in the way of the scraper and decorative embellishments should be reserved for the flanges.

Both antique and contemporary boot scrapers are readily available, and many foundries will replicate a favorite design on demand.

CLIMATE AND WEATHERING Because most boot scrapers are made of iron, they are prone to rust with exposure to rain and snow, so care must be taken to prime and coat them appropriately. Those that include bristle brushes are also subject to mildew and rot. The only antidote for this, alas, is replacement of the brush itself.

In snowy regions, expect your boot scraper to spend a certain amount of time buried. To keep it from becoming a tripping hazard or getting in the way of the shovel, remove snow from around it frequently.

INSTALLATION AND MAINTENANCE Boot scrapers should be located near the primary entrance to your house and—even more important—as close as possible to the garden door. If possible, place them in an open space, in direct sunlight, so they will dry quickly after a rain or snow and can easily be swept clean.

Before you install new scrapers, it's best to have them powder coated. Every two to three years, sand down and paint your well-worn scrapers with a metal primer followed by a final coat. This should ensure that they will stand sentry at your doors for years to come.

10. Set into the corner of a step, this boot scraper gets extra strength from an amusing vertical support.

11. A graceful wrought-iron boot scraper set into a stone mounted on brick paving.

12. This boot scraper should be restored to preserve the beautifully crafted wrought iron. The horizontal top member is made of one piece of metal worked into double spirals with arrowheads at each end.

13. The functional lower part of this boot scraper contrasts with the ornamental scrolls above.

14. A cast-iron boot scraper with handles in the shape of sea serpents found in Ghent, Belgium.

15. A wrought-iron boot scraper with double scrolls is mounted on the wood porch outside a front door. Note that the unprotected hardware has started to rust.

10

11

12

13

14

15

BRIDGES

"We build too many walls and not enough bridges."
SIR ISAAC NEWTON

1. Built in the 1840s, the Long Bridge at Magnolia Gardens in South Carolina is one of seven bridges in the oldest picturesque-style garden in the United States.

The first bridge was undoubtedly formed accidentally, when a tree fell over a stream—but it probably didn't take long before prehistoric man figured out how to expand upon the concept for his own convenience. Early straight-beam bridges, consisting of several trees lashed together and topped by planking, washed away with the spring rains and had to be rebuilt annually, using the next two closest trees. It wasn't the most efficient system, but these rudimentary bridges were the earliest ancestors of today's elaborate spans.

Legendary for their engineering skills, the Romans built masterfully precise roads and bridges throughout their vast empire, including the Ponte Rotto (Rotto Bridge), spanning the Tiber River, in 142 BC. Constructed of skillfully interlocked stones solid enough to resist the powerful force of moving water, Roman bridges featured tall piers and arches designed to allow floodwaters to flow easily beneath. Roads over them were often as wide as 15 feet and always slightly crowned in the center, again to facilitate runoff during flood season. Ponte di Augusto, which spans Rome's Rimini River, was completed in AD 20 and is still traversed today.

Bridges in the Far East were usually made of wood and arched steeply over the water to allow pleasure boats to pass underneath. Built for foot traffic rather than vehicles, many had steps instead of ramps. Some were designed in a zigzag formation, with planks set close to the water on submerged piers. This configuration owed more to cultural belief than function: it was meant to keep evil spirits, believed to be able to travel only in straight lines, from crossing. Early garden ponds of the region often included bridges made of stepping stones with flat tops partially submerged in the water. Over narrow streams, massive rectangular slabs of stone provided sure-footed passage from one bank to the other. Longer slab bridges were supported by an upright submerged stone pier in the middle.

The Incas of Peru developed swing bridges made of wood planking suspended by intertwined ropes strung from stone anchors. As precarious as they may have seemed, especially in strong winds, these could span great distances and could be built using a minimum of material and labor. When the Spanish invaded, they were amazed to find suspension bridges that could support as many as eight horses and riders at a time.

2

3

2. An ancient bridge built in the Roman style, in the Pyrenees of northern Spain. The force of the water that flows through it is a testament to its strength.

3. An example of a zigzag bridge that forces evil spirits, and all who cross, to deviate from a straight passage across a small stream.

4. This bridge in a Japanese stroll garden is elevated to provide the best possible view from its crest as well as allowing boats to pass under it.

5. A modern interpretation of a swing bridge in Frederick, Maryland.

6. Circular stepping stones across a pond slow the pace and encourage contemplation of the water's surface.

7. The absence of a bridge in the Lemon Garden of Villa Marlia in Italy forces visitors to walk around the water tank to reach the other side.

4

5

6

During medieval times, bridge building was the province of the Christian Church, which was eager to improve the ease and speed with which it could spread the gospel. The Brotherhood of Bridge Builders, formed by a group of French and Italian monks, designed and built bridges throughout the twelfth century. Castles of the era included their own bridges of a sort: drawbridges that provided passage over moats during the day and could be drawn up for security at night.

The Ponte Vecchio, built over the Arno River in Florence in 1340, was one of the first designed with segmental rather than round arches. (A segmental arch is shallow, comprising less than a half-circle.) The use of these broader and shallower arches reduced the number of piers required, while allowing water to flow beneath them at a greater volume during flood periods without risking damage to the structure. Today, the Ponte Vecchio is one of Italy's most beloved and busy structures, lined with shops just as it was in medieval times.

Although water features are integral to many Italian and French gardens, they are rarely spanned by bridges of any kind. At Versailles, visitors must walk the entire length of the canal to reach the other side; the same is true of the water tank in the Lemon Garden at the Villa Marlia in Lucca, Italy. Perhaps the necessity to stroll the full length of these bodies is meant to encourage guests to view and appreciate more of the gracious gardens.

7

The English landscape tradition, which unified gardens around lakes, ponds, streams, and waterfalls, ushered in the return of bridges. In redesigning the gardens at Blenheim Palace, prominent landscape architect Capability Brown (1716-83) believed that the massive Palladian bridge that contained more than forty rooms was too overpowering for its site, dwarfing the lake it was intended to enhance. He raised the dam and water levels to flood half the rooms within the bridge, thus enlarging the lake and reducing the visible portion of the bridge.

Today, bridges are a popular enhancement to sizable gardens on all continents. Ready-made versions in a variety of styles and materials are available, and it pays to choose carefully, keeping in mind that this dramatic as well as functional element will attract attention from wherever it is visible. Do-it-yourself plans for the construction of smaller-scale pond bridges can also be found if your carpentry skills are sufficiently advanced.

DESIGN A wide range of materials can be used to construct a bridge, including stone, brick, concrete, metal, fiberglass, vinyl, and wood. Stone is the most expensive and requires the highest level of skill to set properly, but it is durable and time tested. Arch-style stone bridges can bear a tremendous amount of weight.

In areas where stone is scarce, bridges are often built of brick, then set on stone or concrete piers. As the bricks themselves are small, many concrete bonding joints are required, and these tend to deteriorate long before the brick does. They must be inspected and repointed on a regular basis.

Reinforced concrete bridges, often employed in highway construction, are usually veneered with stone, brick, stucco, or tile to give them a more pleasing appearance.

Metal offers the greatest structural strength with the least amount of mass: these bridges can look graceful while ferrying multiple lanes of traffic. If routinely painted and well maintained, metal bridges will last for centuries—and the material is less expensive than veneered concrete.

Fiberglass bridges are best for long spans in hard-to-access areas. The substance is lightweight, virtually maintenance free, designed to carry heavy loads, and will not rot or corrode. Fiberglass bridges are also relatively easy to install.

8. An arched stone bridge built in 1762 in the English landscape gardens of Stourhead was designed by its owner, Henry Hoare II.

9. Stone facing protects the brick structure of this small bridge at Dunloe Castle in Ireland.

10. The Iron Bridge in Worlitz Park, Germany, was built in 1791. It is a one-quarter scale replica of the cast iron bridge built over the River Severn at Coalbrookdale, in England, in 1777.

11. An elegant arched bridge of finely worked natural wood in Kyoto, Japan.

12. A moon bridge made of reinforced concrete in a garden called Les Quatre Vents, in Quebec, Canada.

Vinyl bridges are the most lightweight of all, and fabricators claim they are completely maintenance free. They do, however, attract algae bloom, can crack and scratch, and always feel and look like vinyl.

Most garden bridges are made of wood because it is the least expensive material to use and also the most natural looking. Wooden bridges do require the most maintenance, though, and are subject to rot and insect damage.

A wood substance called glulam, made by gluing together layers of laminated wood, is available in much longer lengths than is conventional wood—upward of 100 feet—and it is structurally stronger. Believe it or not, pound for pound, glulam is stronger than steel.

Garden bridges come in three basic styles: straight-beam or truss, arched, and suspension. Straight-beam or truss bridges are supported by piers at each end and are the least demanding to construct. They should be positioned above the flood level and, if necessary, high enough for boats to clear.

An arched bridge allows a higher volume of floodwater to pass, provides more headroom for boats, is structurally stronger, and can span greater distances than a straight-beam bridge. On a smaller scale, these are prevalent in the Asian garden tradition, where they are known as moon bridges because the half-circles they describe, paired with their own reflections, complete the revered circle of the full moon.

A suspension bridge supports its deck with cables attached

13. A colorful, modern wood bridge based on an Asian design, located outside of Dunedin, New Zealand.

14. A stairway passes through manicured hedges leading to a narrow suspension bridge that floats over the stream in Ohinetahi, New Zealand.

15. This bridge in Kyoto's Imperial Gardens was built during the Edo period (in the mid-19th century), before modern building codes; thus, the absence of handrails.

16. The stone bridge at Chiswick, in England, was built in 1774 to replace the original wood bridge designed by William Kent between 1724 and 1733.

17. The wood deck of this bridge is enclosed by cast-iron railings punctuated by sculptural panels.

18. Although the white railing distracts from the view beyond the bridge, its reflection is quite lovely.

19. The pattern of this railing at Worlitz is uncommonly open for one made of wood.

to overhead towers and can be designed to have the greatest distance between piers of any bridge type. The swinging bridges of the Incas, made of braided grass ropes with flooring of interwoven branches, were their forebears and could extend to great lengths. The Golden Gate Bridge in San Francisco, one of America's great suspension bridges, carries six lanes of traffic as well as pedestrians and bicycles over a span of 1½ miles!

Whatever the length of your bridge, rails or restraining edges will probably be required by local building codes. Typical codes mandate that the top of the rail be 34 to 36 inches from the deck of the bridge and designed with a maximum gap of 4 inches between the vertical elements connecting the rails. Railings can be made of stone, brick, concrete, metal, vinyl, or wood, but of course you will want them to blend harmoniously with the bridge itself as well as the surrounding landscape.

Stone cheek walls provide the most durable restraining edges and can provide seating, while offering a sense of security to all who cross. The downside here is that they are the most expensive to build and their solidity limits the view. Freestanding stone piers connected by metal or wood elements offer a more affordable alternative and allow for virtually uninterrupted views. Well-designed, patterned metal rails make the perfect foreground for distant vistas.

Vinyl railings are popular but more expensive than those made of wood and are often designed to mimic the wood variety. They don't require painting (or repainting) and are not subject to rot or insect damage. They may, however, crack or scratch over time.

A wood railing—the most common kind, though they are not as unobtrusive as their metal counterparts—should be made of the densest, most durable wood possible, put together using mortise and tenon joinery, and stained or painted every three years.

Bridge decks can be paved with stone, brick, concrete, metal, wood, or turf. If you choose stone paving, take care to select a finish that will not be slippery. Bricks should be selected to absorb as little water as possible, for the same reason. Moss thrives on brick in shady locations and can be treacherous underfoot.

If concrete must be used, the surface should be broom finished perpendicular to the slope. Presuming it is properly installed, concrete with crushed aggregate is the best choice.

Heavy-gauge metal mesh can be used for bridge paving and is lighter-weight than concrete. A lighter gauge of metal mesh is often nailed to the planks of wooden bridges, offering traction on what can be a slippery surface.

Wood paving for bridges should be dense and of high quality. Good choices include ipe (sometimes called Brazilian walnut), mahogany, teak, redwood, cedar, and pressure-treated pine. The boards should be at least 6 inches wide and set perpendicular to the supporting beams or arches. Try to avoid installing a wooden deck if your bridge is located in a shady area, as the inevitable moisture will create a breeding ground for moss. Abrasive paint helps somewhat; heel ridges installed at regular intervals or light-gauge mesh are even better.

Turf paving is an elegant alternative as it blends seamlessly with the surrounding lawns. Be aware, though, that turf-covered bridges must be located in full sun and require soils that are lightweight and quick-draining.

Garden bridges are conventionally placed where the water is narrowest between the two banks, but this can be modified somewhat for aesthetic purposes. The design of your bridge should reflect the surrounding architecture as well as the style and proportions of your garden. Depending on the design

20. A footbridge of Georgia gray marble crosses the koi-filled moat that surrounds the Bok Tower Carillon, built in 1929 in Lake Wales, Florida.
21. Two slabs of stone overlap to form a dogleg path over a small stream.
22. Because of its muted color and simple design, this bridge blends harmoniously into the garden.

23. Well-worn metal mesh has prevented many an accident on this shaded, rail-less and often slippery footbridge in New Zealand.
24. A wood bridge with sturdy planks crosses a canal in the garden at Schwetzingen. Notice how the span rests on stone shoulders built into the path.
25. The garden flows seamlessly from one side of this stone bridge to the other, thanks to the turf lining its deck.
26. The gravel surface of this bridge is elegantly edged with moss.

27. This white Chippendale bridge at Paca House in Annapolis, Maryland, blends elegantly with the architecture of a nearby outbuilding. The structures on the property are re-creations of the original eighteenth-century buildings.

28. At the Mount Usher gardens in Ireland, extensive natural plantings designed by William Robinson line the riverbanks of the River Vartry and are linked by charmingly subtle footbridges.

29. Tucked into the greenery, this one-railed bridge seems to disappear.

30. A pavilion built across a stream provides a variety of vantage points from which to enjoy water views.

31. A bench built into a railing provides a pleasant spot to pause and appreciate the scenery.

32. Bridges are often partially or completely roofed in Japan, to provide protection in rainy weather.

33. The chains supporting this small bridge can be disengaged and the two-piece deck raised during high water.

and materials you choose, it can be a prominent and focal feature in the landscape or a more subtle element that blends in with its surroundings.

In addition to providing passage from one bank to the other, bridges offer the best views of the water that passes under them. Many bridges in the Far East have roofed viewing platforms at center span. (In addition to providing a sheltered viewing spot, the cover helps the bridge last longer and keeps it from getting slippery.) The Brooklyn Bridge in New York City has several extended platforms on each side with secure railings and benches, encouraging visitors to stop a moment and take in the beautiful views both up and down the East River.

CLIMATE AND WEATHERING All surfaces of a bridge are exposed to the elements, making them vulnerable to corrosion and subject to rapid expansion, contraction, and—in colder climates—

freezing. If you've ever driven over a bridge in the winter, you know that they tend to be more slippery than the road surface leading up to them. You might want to discourage foot traffic over your garden bridge in winter, to avoid potential mishaps.

In windy and hurricane-prone areas, bridges must be properly anchored and structurally engineered to withstand the lateral and upward forces of high winds. In flood-prone areas, beam bridges can be anchored with cables to two upstream trees, allowing them to rise and fall with the surge of the water and resettle on sound piers.

In areas of deep snow and ice buildup, bridges must be designed to withstand the extra weight. It is best to shovel snow off a bridge rather than using salt or deicing chemicals that can pollute the water below.

INSTALLATION AND MAINTENANCE Most counties consider bridges to be permanent structures that therefore require permits for construction. If your bridge is meant to span a stream or river, your plans will undoubtedly be scrutinized for their impact on surrounding wetlands. Be ready to jump through a number of hoops and fill out masses of paperwork to obtain the necessary permits.

Streams often change course during floods, leaving alluvial soils that are unstable, so it is best to bore test your soil if your piers and abutments will be located next to streams. Setting piers on unstable soil without bedrock is a dangerous practice. The footings for the piers and abutments should always be excavated, poured, and set during the dry season.

Prefabricated fiberglass and wooden bridges are relatively easy to install. The supporting piers are constructed on site and must extend below the frost line to solid soils or bedrock to prevent washout.

Bridges made of stone, metal, or concrete should be designed by structural engineers and made by professional masons and iron fabricators. Your engineers and contractors should be the first to walk or drive across the new bridge they've created!

When planting trees and shrubs near or overhanging a bridge, avoid those that shed an overabundance of messy flowers, fruits, leaves, or bark. Site any trees with vigorous root systems far enough away from piers that they are unlikely to undermine or compromise them. Bridges must be inspected on a regular basis and after every flood to be sure that no structural damage has occurred.

For all of the challenges involved in their construction and maintenance, bridges are functional and beautiful additions to gardens featuring water, and can provide memorable views that can't otherwise be enjoyed. Careful planning, design, and selection of materials—and the help of experienced professionals—will ensure a pleasing outcome and a distinctive element within your landscape.

34. Although visually appealing, plants growing on or near a bridge create additional maintenance.

35. Some bridges span ravines that only occasionally carry water.

36. The reinforcing structure of rustic bridges must be inspected on a regular basis.

37. Wood steps ease the steep ascent from this arched, stone-decked bridge.

DRAINS

No individual raindrop ever considers itself responsible for the flood.
ANONYMOUS

Even the earliest farmers understood that good drainage was necessary to the health of their crops. More than nine thousand years ago, the Mesopotamians devised a drainage system in the form of trenches lined with gravel, stone, or bundles of small trees. The earliest record we have of pipes being used to direct drainage dates back to 3100 BC, in the Indus Valley of present-day Pakistan and northern India. In this elaborate and effective system, covered drains lined the streets and collected rainwater as it fell, thus preventing flooding.

The ancient Persians considered storm water runoff sacred and the pollution of it to be a sin. They protected this valuable natural resource by collecting the water in underground cisterns.

The Romans, early masters of road construction, often finished them off with graded surfaces designed to direct runoff from the streets into drainage channels. The backbone of the Roman water system was the Great Drain, or Cloaca Maxima. When completed, this conduit was strong enough to resist the fiercest storms and large enough for horses and carts to pass through it to perform any necessary maintenance. It continues to function today as part of Rome's main sewer system, helping to prevent backwash from flooding the ancient Forum. Minor drains, connected by tributary pipes to the Cloaca Maxima, appeared on the surface as simple holes in the paving covered with V-shaped arches formed by two terracotta tiles. Some surface drains in the Cloaca Maxima were named and their covers decorated appropriately. For example, a sculpture thought to be a decorative drain cover (or prototypical "manhole cover") is decorated with the face of a pagan god, his mouth agape. It has come to be known as the "Mouth of Truth" and was made famous in the 1953 film *Roman Holiday* as the spot where Gregory Peck and Audrey Hepburn test each other's truthfulness.

In the Middle Ages, much of the infrastructure created by the Romans—including their sophisticated system of drains—fell into ruin, though farmers remained aware of the crucial role proper drainage played in successful agriculture. Their best efforts yielded furrow-type channels carved into the soil with farm implements.

1. A drain cover carved out of local sandstone blends with the paving pattern at Fatehpur Sikri in India, built during the late sixteenth century.
2. The fundamentals of Roman drainage engineering have been adhered to globally for centuries and have been adapted to local conditions and domestic use.
3. In Japan, drainage is incorporated aesthetically into the design of the garden.

4. A channel drain follows the outline of the building and is sited to collect the runoff from the roof.

5. A system of double drains collects rainwater in a channel, while any overflow is slowed and filtered by the adjacent trench.

During the fifteenth century, the Incas—a sophisticated society in its own right—designed an elaborate drainage system at Machu Picchu, Peru, to direct the runoff from heavy rains. The network of conduits covering the overall site was augmented by carved channels running directly to some one hundred and thirty individual houses, helping to protect the area's complex series of earthen terraces from landslides.

Heavy annual rainfall, typhoons, and frequent torrential downpours made adequate drainage a high priority in Japanese garden design. Reluctant to sacrifice their aesthetic ideals, Japanese gardeners devised ingeniously understated drains, highly efficient in dealing with the harsh realities of the environment, yet elegant and inconspicuous within the landscape. In the Netherlands, drainage has been a national concern for centuries due to the country's low-lying geography. Skilled engineers called drainers and dykers emerged and quickly became invaluable for their expertise in preserving land prone to flooding. In the middle of the sixteenth century, many such professionals migrated to England and took their skills and techniques with them.

During the agricultural revolution of the eighteenth and nineteenth centuries, a full-scale effort was launched in Europe and America to come up with new ways to maximize the productivity of farmlands. It was soon determined that a key factor was a thoughtful and more efficient approach to drainage. One innovation, the "French Drain," came from the United States, though it doesn't sound like it. Henry Flagg French (1813–1885) of Concord, Massachusetts, was a lawyer fascinated by the phenomena associated with flooding. He studied the natural flow of water in a variety of situations and wrote numerous articles about drainage as it related to house construction and the landscape. In his 1859 book *Farm Drainage*, French described several designs, including "a rough ditch filled with bark to collect and direct water to an outlet drain." Although he is credited with inventing the drain that bears his name, versions of the French drain have been used since the Roman era and remnants were found during archeological excavations at Monticello, Thomas Jefferson's Virginia home, which was completed in 1772. French was certainly responsible for popularizing the use of French Drains in American landscape design.

As recently as the early 1900s, surface water in America's urban areas was still being diverted to curbs and swales on its way to a geographical low point, usually a river or creek. Inevitably, some water was left standing in the channels, where it became foul smelling, attracted mosquitoes, and polluted waterways. Clearly, a better system was needed—and soon, most cities had broken ground to construct the storm sewers and drain inlets we now take for granted.

6. A simple and functional design is enhanced by the developing patina.

7. Gaps in the mortar of the brickwork banding a gravel path act as a slit drain, allowing water to seep into the ground. In general, the use of pervious surfaces eases drainage.

8. A series of opposing diagonals forms a geometric design for a drain cover in Madrid, Spain.

9. The conservation and management of water has become a pressing concern to people of all ages. At an elementary school in Asheville, North Carolina, the students created this outbuilding for their vegetable garden, complete with a green roof and rain barrels.

Modern cities are built densely, and paved within an inch of their lives, their surfaces almost completely impervious to water. For that reason, drains are more important than ever in preventing flooded roads and sidewalks with every hard rainfall. In highly populated areas as well as more open ones, proper drainage is also essential as a means of safeguarding our waterways from dangerous pollutants.

Landscape architects and skilled gardeners understand that a sound drainage plan is essential to good garden design. If you neglect your garden's "plumbing," you run the risk that beds, terraces, lawns, and driveways will be overrun during downpours, leading to erosion and causing damage to plants and ornamental features. A good system of pipes, installed underground and out of sight, can be designed to work harmoniously with ornamental drain covers, downspouts, landscaped or perviously paved drainage swales, rain barrels, and green roofs to harness rainwater—thus protecting the garden while conserving water. Green roofs (rooftops covered in plants) can reduce water runoff, serve as insulation and minimize reflected heat. Many green roofs use trays as shallow as four inches but provide sufficient growing medium, drainage, and irrigation for succulents and carefully selected low-growing plants. Seventy percent of new, large buildings in Germany have green roofs and they are catching on in contemporary architecture worldwide.

DESIGN Once you've settled on the overall plan for your site, you must develop a drainage pattern and piping scheme of sufficient size and scope to absorb water at a rate equal to the maximum amount of rainfall per hour for your local climate. Some drains and/or their grates will have to be aboveground and visible, so it is important to select designs for these that are as visually pleasing as possible.

Drain grates come in many types, sizes, and finishes. Most are made of cast iron, aluminum, bronze, or stainless steel and are designed to be visually appealing as well as easy to maintain. A channel drain set at the edge of a paved area is less distracting than a drain placed within the paved surface itself. Well-crafted slit drains made of the same material as the paving blend nicely into their surroundings and can even add visual interest.

Drains with catch basins sometimes emit an unpleasant smell as debris decays in the standing water, so they should not be located near benches or seating areas. Similarly, all drains connected to a storm sewer drain should have a trap to prevent a backflow of foul odor. Drains located in loose gravel pavement should have a beveled collar to prevent the gravel from being washed into the drain. When possible, several small drains are preferable to one large drain.

An alternative to a grated drain is a modern version of the French drain described above: a ditch or trench filled to ground level with gravel or rock that directs surface and ground water away from an area you wish to keep dry. The trench may also contain a perforated pipe wrapped in filter fabric or geotextile to prevent clogging and ensure drainage along the entire length of the pipe.

Since the storm sewer systems of urban areas often run at maximum capacity, it is beneficial to consider an alternative on-site option, such as an underground groundwater retention and discharge pit or a rain barrel. Another option is the installation of a rain garden—a shallow, planted depression located strategically to collect and filter the rain that falls on

11. A slit drain cut out of the same stone as the surrounding steps.
12. A mass-produced metal slit drain set in pervious brick paving.
13. A slit drain on the grounds of the Taj Mahal is carved from sandstone.

14. A tile-lined trench filled with river rocks directs rain water and protects the surrounding garden.

11
12
13
14

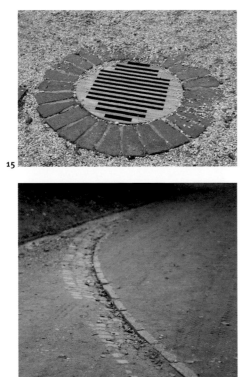

15. Surprisingly, the drain cover for this catch basin is made of wood.

16. The channel created by these granite blocks set into the slope of a driveway directs the water away from its surface.

17. The elevated-dome shape of this drain cover protects it from a buildup of debris.

impervious surfaces, such as roofs, streets, and driveways. All of these alternatives can effectively reduce the damage done by excessive runoff on lakes and streams.

CLIMATE AND WEATHERING In climates subject to heavy rainfall or freezing weather, optimal drainage is a necessity. It is best to locate all drains where people or automobiles will not traverse them, to maintain their structural integrity.

The accumulation of puddles can lead to plant disease and root rot and they also provide a breeding ground for mosquitoes. Proper drainage can eliminate most of this standing water, while alleviating other problems associated with soil or turf that is constantly wet, such as the compacting and marring caused by foot traffic and lawn mowers.

Snow and ice should be removed promptly from over and around drains to prevent the formation of ice dams that can clog the drains and cause flooding in the garden or even the house.

INSTALLATION AND MAINTENANCE For large-scale projects, it's best to consult a drainage expert who can analyze such factors as porosity of the soil, existing low-lying areas, and rain flow from downspouts and gutters. And (as any expert will tell you) it is essential to locate all underground utilities before beginning installation.

All drainage collection systems should be set on a firm base with discharge piping of adequate size and a minimum pitch of $1/8$ inch per foot away from existing structures. Hand dig around trees or use an air spade to minimize damage to the roots.

Certain metal alloys should never come in contact with one another due to the risk of reaction and corrosion. Be sure that the grate metal you choose is compatible with the metal of your drain basin. Regularly inspect and clean out catch basins, downspouts, and drain covers.

And finally, as always, check for any local codes regulating drainage plans—and use common sense (and common courtesy) when it comes to assessing the effect your drainage plan might have on neighboring properties.

18. Gravel and stone paving are graded into a V-shape and then chanelled to direct water toward an iron drain cover.
19. Water outlets artfully carved into this sandstone paving are essential during the monsoon season in India.
20. Curved stairs are shadowed by a stone-lined drain bordered by a low bamboo fence.
21. A channel drain at the base of a dry stack wall in Japan works hard in the hours after a typhoon.

22. Moss grows on this garden wall due to the backsplash from an elevated downspout.

FENCES

He is all pine and I am apple orchard.
My apple trees will never get across
And eat the cones under his pines, I tell him.
He only says, "Good fences make good neighbors."
ROBERT FROST

1

❧ *Fences Made of Metal* ❧

WROUGHT IRON If you think that the wrought iron that has been used in modern times to make beautiful and durable fences, railings, and the like is a recent innovation, you underestimate the ancients. The Hittites, early inhabitants of present-day Turkey, invented a way to smelt iron ore at around 1500 BC, removing its impurities to create a metal strong enough for use in fashioning weapons and tools. This "wrought iron" could be bent and worked into spades, spears, shields, axes, and more. The Hittites were admired for the fine detail and ornamentation of their ironwork and—although they tried to keep details of their smelting process secret as it was key to their military prowess—their advanced metallurgy techniques eventually spread throughout the Middle East and China, then west to Greece, Spain, and Northern Europe.

In ancient Greece and Rome, blacksmiths were thought to be sorcerers who could transform raw earth into useful tools through a kind of alchemy, using fire and water. The Greek god of fire, Hephaestus, was often portrayed wielding the tools of a blacksmith. Vulcan was his Roman counterpart, and his name has become synonymous with strength. A cooperative of blacksmiths existed in Rome between the fourth and first centuries BC and all in the trade were treated as privileged citizens.

During medieval times, wrought-iron screens protected the inner sanctums of great churches and cathedrals. Castles were decorated with wrought-iron ornamentation that was sometimes intricately inlaid with gold and precious stones.

In the 1600s, Spain and Italy became masters of the art, creating geometric grillwork and railings as beautiful as they were strong. By the 1650s, French architects and garden designers set the standard for wrought-iron fences, balconies, and gates. The French ironwork of that period was exceptional in both design and craftsmanship but it was also quite costly. André Le Nôtre, Louis XIV's famed landscape architect, used decorative wrought-iron fences extensively in the gardens he designed, as they provided structure and protection while allowing visitors to look through them at the beauty of the distant scenery.

Jean Tijou, a French Huguenot and master ironworker, emigrated to England in 1689, where he was commissioned to work with Sir Christopher Wren at Hampton Court. Tijou's 1693 design handbook, *A New Book of Drawings Invented and Designed by Jean Tijou*, profoundly influenced English iron craft. He was a master of production, but more important, he was fluent in all the latest French designs and techniques, including repoussé (French for "push back"), which, in metalworking, refers to a technique for creating relief design by pressing or hammering the inside or back side of a metal surface.

By the 1750s, Germany had ushered in the fashion for elaborate wrought iron and Eastern Europe enthusiastically followed. Soon, beautifully designed and crafted fences, gates, and balconies were ubiquitous throughout the continent.

Eighteenth-century Americans took a more utilitarian approach, using wrought iron primarily for tools, hardware,

2

4

5

3

1. A succession of simple circles separates garden spaces without diminishing the view—and echoes the form of the topiary at left. Ladew Gardens, Maryland.
2. This metal grillwork was inspired by seventeenth-century Spanish and Italian motifs but can be found in the south of France, at Cap Ferrat.
3. The metal fence surrounding the Château de Chantilly provides foreground interest without concealing the building in any way.
4. Panels of golden suns are set into an iron fence in the gardens of Schwetzingen Castle, built in the mid eighteenth century. Note the graceful ribbon of ironwork wrapping the top and bottom rails.
5. A fluid design of scrolls, vines, and tendrils ornaments this railing in Dresden, Germany.

6. A simple but beautifully made cast-iron fence at the Owens-Thomas House in Savannah, Georgia, is topped with tridents and set into a stone base. Elaborate cast-iron acanthus leaves supporting the side porch (from which the Marquis de Lafayette once made a speech) provide contrast.

7. This fence made from iron wire that was bent, intertwined and secured with cast iron rosettes was fabricated in Charleston in the mid nineteenth century.

8. A wrought iron rail in an elegant reverse S pattern, erected in Charleston in the late eighteenth century.

9. A cast-iron fence in Boston, dating from the 1830s, features lotus bud posts connected by scrolls of vines and stylized flowers.

and horseshoes. Some ornamental ironwork was made but its high cost limited it to grand homes, churches, parks, and public buildings. Some southern plantation owners enticed European craftsmen to come over and teach their art to slaves, thus beginning a rich tradition of locally produced fine wrought iron in such places as Savannah, Charleston, and New Orleans. Beautifully ornate iron balcony railings and other adornments are a hallmark of southern city architecture. During the second half of the nineteenth century, wrought-iron fences and rails became popular in Boston, New York, Philadelphia, and Washington, d.c., though their styles varied in accordance with the typical local architecture. Sadly, the high cost of wrought iron relative to that of low-carbon steel (which is similarly malleable but corrodes faster) eventually led to a halt in its production. The last wrought iron manufacturing plant in the United States closed in 1969.

Today, the limited supply of true wrought iron, used mainly in historical restorations, tends to be produced by recycling scrap from the past. Much of what is commonly referred to as wrought iron is actually low-carbon or "mild" steel.

CAST IRON Bronze and gold were the first metals to be cast; artifacts fashioned from these substances have been discovered dating back as far as the Shang Dynasty (1600–1046 BC). Although it seems more pedestrian, cast iron—made by pouring melted iron into molds—wasn't fully developed until considerably later. The first-known example of the substance, a lion made in China, dates from AD 502.

The rise of cast iron paved the way for mass production of innumerable objects of various designs and functions, as the process required far less skill and time than did the art of wrought iron. For that reason, although its high carbon content made it more brittle and susceptible to rust than was wrought iron, cast iron quickly became popular for many humble items from cookware to hardware.

The earliest European cast work is thought to have appeared in the fifteenth century, but the technique didn't reach England until the early eighteenth century, when a cast-iron fence was fashioned to surround St. Paul's Cathedral. In the decades that followed, an industry in cast iron established itself in England and came into its own between 1820 and

1860. In his 1839 book *The Builder's Guide*, Asher Benjamin expounded on the merits of cast-iron ornamentation and included patterns for designs.

By 1850, cast iron had all but replaced wrought iron in the United States and employment in the field tripled between 1845 and 1855. Affordable, mass-produced fences, gates, and furniture became the standard for Victorian gardens. Foundries were as numerous as the design choices offered up in shops and catalogs. Designers and fabricators pilfered designs from one another because finished pieces were rarely signed or credited. Throughout the latter half of the nineteenth century, cast iron gradually replaced wood for use in fences, gates, and balustrades, as advertisers promised "Iron Fences Cheaper than Wood." Skilled wrought ironwork was almost completely eclipsed until the art deco period of the 1900s, at which point a number of designers revived the art for its use in architectural embellishment.

More recently, cast aluminum—which may be cast in fine detail while remaining quite rigid—has advanced as an alternative to cast iron. Among its advantages are the facts that it is less prone to corrosion and lighter weight. By 1970, American fence companies were offering the first hollow cast-aluminum rail and picket panel system, considerably less expensive to ship and install than its predecessors. Needless to say, aluminum has become the most popular choice for large-scale fencing projects.

DESIGN As you begin to explore your alternatives, you'll find fences made of wrought iron, cast iron, bronze, stainless steel, and aluminum. Wrought iron is prized for its strength and the fact that it can be formed into intricately detailed and textured designs. Cast iron is more brittle, softer in detail, but far less expensive. Bronze and stainless steel share the best attributes of wrought iron and they don't corrode as fast, nor do they need to be painted. Wire fences, formed from molten iron, were the ornamental precursors of modern-day chain-link fencing. Cast aluminum is characterized by high corrosion resistance, low maintenance, durability, strength, and its ability to be fashioned into detailed designs, yet is light in weight.

10. Cast iron harps connected by chains and "weighted" with tassels adorn this fence at Dumbarton Oaks in Washington, D.C.
11. A transparent aluminum fence in Berlin, Germany. Note how the grass grows beneath it, drawing the eye to the other side.
12. An art deco cast-aluminum rail in Buffalo, New York.

13. In Benitz, Germany, panels of brightly painted wrought iron topped with gold finials are set into stone footings.
14. An elegant alternative to chain link, this aluminum wire fence allows plants to grow through it. Eventually, they will form a green wall.
15. A graceful secondary fence on the grounds of Sanssouci. Thin iron rods are formed into gothic arches and join an upper scalloped rod to top the fence with a sleek diamond shape.

16. This section of rusted fence may soon be on its way to the salvage yard.
17. The Shaker design aesthetic is apparent in this understated iron-wire fence in Pleasant Hill, Kentucky. Overlapping arches are strengthened by top and bottom rails supported by unobtrusive posts. The fence meets the gate at a simple white stone pier. Note how the colors of the fence and house work in harmony.
18. Substantial stone piers punctuate an iron fence set on a low stone wall. The piers are topped with stone finials, each of a different design.

19. These wrought-iron rods are set in a diagonal pattern and secured by cast iron rosettes. The fence is topped by tridents and secured by cast-iron posts.
20. A fence of iron bars set into a stone base, topped by alternating spear designs and supported by fluted columns.
21. Iron rods curved into heart shapes are set in stone and secured to simple upright rails, framing a view over the city of Prague.

All metal comes in standard dimensions in round, square, and polygonal profiles. There are endless choices of preformed scrolls, finials, and point tops for the vertical bars. As you sift through the possibilities, keep in mind that the design of the ironwork should not compete with the architecture or the views beyond, and, most important, it shouldn't impede the surfaces' ability to shed water. If you choose a design with a lot of dimension, be sure that it isn't likely to harbor an unsightly accumulation of windborne particles in its crevices.

When it comes to fences, iron has a number of advantages over wood, including its longevity, strength, and malleability. Unlike most wood, iron can be curved and twisted into complex shapes. Although iron fences are more expensive than those of wood, they can be cheaper in the long run because they last longer and require less maintenance. And they aren't the most expensive choice by any means: stone, brick, and stucco tend to run higher.

It's no surprise that there are more examples of antique ironwork fences than there are wooden ones—but before you go with an antique, there are several factors to consider. Keep in mind the high cost of shipping it as well as the possible need for restoring any damaged or corroded sections. And remember that the quantity available may be limited; you don't want to get caught with half a fence in place!

Metal fences tend to be relatively low—3 to 4 feet high—unless they are intended for security. Low iron fences do not require substantial piers for support because of the inherent strength and rigidity of the material. Tall fences do need the support of brick, stone, or stucco piers placed at intervals of not more than 12 feet. Wooden piers, though rarely used, provide a less expensive alternative and can be decorated with molding, painted, or coated with a stucco finish.

Most iron fences have top and bottom rails. A more expensive and elegant design involves eliminating the bottom rail and extending each picket into the underlying wall or pavement.

When used around balconies or verandas, metal railings create "outdoor rooms" just as fences do, but are often more detailed or elaborate. You can see some samples of this technique in the "Porches, Decks, and Terraces" chapter.

22   23   24

22. Wrought and cast iron blend harmoniously, forming the shape of a crown. Soft blue paint provides a gentle contrast with the facade of the Schloss at Ludwigsburg in Germany.
23. At Sanssouci, a wrought-iron fence of simple rods is painted blue but punctuated by elaborate stone piers, each topped with the carved bust of a different historic figure.
24. A delicate fence of iron wire is buttressed on the water side by elegant iron scrolls, framing a beautiful view of Lake Konstanz from Mainau Island in Germany.
25. This undulating fence is being overtaken by the hedge behind it, making maintenance increasingly difficult.

25

In the northern latitudes, where winters are long and dark, iron fences are often gilded or painted bright colors so that they can be seen at great distances.

CLIMATE AND WEATHERING Metal fences do not block sun, wind, sound, or views, but unlike wooden fences, they can get extremely cold or hot to the touch. Under a scorching sun, they can even heat up enough to burn tender vines. On the other hand, they are less likely to sag, twist, or swell in response to fluctuating weather conditions.

As noted earlier, corrosion is an issue with iron, and road salt and fertilizers exacerbate this problem. Be sure to paint your iron fence regularly if it is likely to be exposed to these substances. Fence joints should be properly welded rather than filled with such compounds as Bondo or silicone. If the joints separate, water can enter the gaps and cause rust and corrosion. Keep in mind that horizontal sections and intersecting components that are not designed to shed water quickly will eventually corrode as well.

A final warning: Metal fences conduct electricity, so care must be taken to ground all adjacent electrical fixtures.

INSTALLATION AND MAINTENANCE In most counties, fences require permits. To obtain them, you will probably have to have your property lines, setback limits, and easements surveyed and staked. Once you have your permits, you might want to share and discuss your plans with your bordering neighbors. Unlike some garden elements, fences affect their view as much as yours.

The art of forming and welding metal takes at least three years to learn, so, needless to say, metal fences should be fabricated and installed by experienced professionals. It is important to specify that you require the best-quality hardware and to question the use of filler compounds to mask imperfect welding.

Discrepancies between field measurements and fabrication can be a real problem, as metal fencing is not easily reconfigured on the spot. Accurate measurements are essential!

At least once a season, clean your fence with a mild soap solution. If you discover any chips or scratches in the process, be sure to touch them up quickly to prevent rust from developing.

Every three to five years, iron fences should be scraped of all rust, hot-dip galvanized, and painted with acrylic enamel paint. An alternative is powder coating, which involves electrostatically applying a dry powder containing a uv inhibitor, followed by baking or air-drying at high temperatures. A powder-coat finish is two to four times thicker than a paint finish and will not fade. Many aluminum fence fabricators offer a lifetime guarantee that their powder coat will not peel or fade. To protect your fence, install a mowing strip of stone, brick, or concrete where it borders the lawn. Surrounding trees should be pruned of dead and decaying wood regularly to minimize the chance of damage or destruction from limbs' falling on a fence.

1. An elegant Chippendale fence encloses the Lightfoot House in Williamsburg, Virginia.

2. A pale fence at Monticello has been restored in accordance with Thomas Jefferson's design of 1808, specifying 10-foot pales made of two pieces of 12-foot heartwood pine or poplar and 12-foot locust posts sunk 2 1/2 feet into the ground.

3. A Japanese bamboo fence in a diagonal pattern is secured to the rails with black palm fiber.

4. The top rail of this bamboo fence has been eliminated at the prime viewing point to enhance the vista.

5. A wattle fence is used to separate garden areas in this contemporary garden. Naturally short-lived, this kind of fence will last somewhat longer if set on a wall.

❁ Fences Made of Wood ❁

When creating barriers meant to intimidate and repel intruders, early settlers turned to the strongest and most abundant material at hand—trees. Most settlements were surrounded by ditches and enclosed with palisades: closely placed pales (tall logs or stakes) with pointed tops standing on end in the soil. The Egyptians, Greeks, and Romans enclosed their cultivated fields with simple wooden barriers as well.

The earliest gardens in Asia were enclosed with bamboo-and-wood fencing. As populations grew more dense over the centuries, the art of fencing evolved in design, diversity, and craftsmanship. The wood-and-bamboo fences continued to address the issue of privacy but, in accordance with the Japanese gardening principle of shakkei, they were constructed so that visitors could enjoy selected views beyond the enclosed area.

In the Middle Ages, most gardens were enclosed to keep out livestock and provide support for plants. Willow, hornbeam, oak, hazel, and chestnut branches were cultivated to produce wattle and open sapling fences.

During the Renaissance, the art of wrought ironwork rose to extraordinary levels of design and craftsmanship, while wooden fencing was relegated to agricultural use and to the gardens of the lower classes. Fences of iron continued to be preferred in Baroque gardens.

The earliest Americans popularized the wooden "rail fence": there is evidence that these were used in Jamestown, Virginia, as early as 1632. Also known as worm, snake, or zigzag fences, they were found throughout the South, favored for their cost efficiency. Made from abundant local lumber, they didn't require costly nails or hardware (both handmade at the time). They were also fairly easy to construct because they required no post holes or footings.

In Europe, fashions in art exerted an influence on fashions in indoor and outdoor design. Chinese and Japanese prints depicting Asian-style fences and gates had eighteenth-century patrons yearning for chinoiserie—and landscape architects and designers obliged by creating garden elements in the requisite style. Soon, the fascination with chinoiserie spread to the United States. When property enclosures were mandated by law in 1705 in Williamsburg, Virginia, many of the gates and fences were built in the chinoiserie style referred to as Chippendale. Thomas Jefferson admired the Chippendale style and ingeniously incorporated its motifs into his railings at Monticello.

The wood fences of the old American whaling towns were paragons of restrained elegance and craftsmanship. Thanks to the skills of resident shipbuilders, New England's coastal towns and islands, such as Nantucket, Massachusetts, abound in examples of finely detailed wood fences. In Salem, Massachusetts, Samuel McIntire (1757–1811) a master carpenter, wood carver, architect, and artist, created ornate fences with carved finials inspired by the Georgian architecture of England.

During the nineteenth century, the Victorians rejected wooden fences in favor of those made from mass-produced cast iron. The exuberant and varied cast-iron designs were more in keeping with the Victorian aesthetic, and the metal fences were less expensive than wooden ones, too.

By the end of the twentieth century, close-board privacy fencing at a typical height of 6 feet had become the most popular kind erected in the States. Lumberyards and hardware chains now produce premade panels of various heights, designs, and woods, holding their own against custom-made fences that cost more and require skilled carpenters.

6. A worm fence requires more wood than a straight fence, but no posts or hardware.

7. Thomas Jefferson's design for a Chippendale railing at Monticello.

8. A simple picket fence with posts that shed water easily.

9. This closed-board fence of bamboo is topped with bougainvillea.

10. Decorative panels above the closed boards add visual interest to the fence.

11. Cut-outs in this closed-board fence allow light and air circulation, while enlivening its appearance.

12

13

14

12. Its shiny surface betrays the vinyl material of this fence, while sloppy craftsmanship is apparent in the installation of the hardware.
13. Signs of mildew and algae bloom are apparent on this vinyl fence, in spite of its sunny location.
14. Close boards with tops cut on a diagonal provide some additional security.

PVC companies entered the market in the 1980s, offering maintenance-free, high-tensile PVC horse fencing that never rots. The advantage of this material—for both horses and their owners—is that PVC is strong, can't be chewed, and will splinter rather than crack or break off leaving sharp points. The earliest versions had an unnatural shine to them that would eventually become chalky and yellow, but improvements to the finish have been made over time. In the last ten years, PVC fencing has become the fastest-growing segment of the industry and comes in many styles, dimensions, textures, and colors.

Several companies manufacture UV-resistant vinyl and offer guarantees of up to fifty years. But if it sounds like a wonder material, keep in mind that the production of vinyl has a negative impact on the environment—and no matter how sophisticated its fabrication, it will always feel . . . unnatural.

Plastic lumber, made from recycled plastic, is more akin to real wood in texture (and better for the environment than vinyl). On the plus side, it can be milled and joined with wood fasteners and will not rot or crack. The downside is that it is softer than wood, expands and contracts more and tends to fade. The bottom line? For garden use, real wood is best.

Vast areas of land throughout Central and South America that were once cultivated have been reforested with the best varieties of tropical hardwoods. Within the last decade, South American Pau Lope (also known as ipe) has become the premier choice of wood for outdoor use. It is bug-and-rot-resistant, extremely dense, and ages to a soft gray.

DESIGN There are four basic types of wood fencing: close-board, open-board, louvered, and combinations of these.

Close-board fences offer a high degree of privacy and sound protection, so they are usually located on the property line. Although their height must be in accordance with local regulations, they can be used to screen out an unwanted view while containing pets and children. Close-board fences can be double faced, paneled, tongue-and-groove, or made with narrow gaps between the boards. (The wider the boards, the fewer gaps the fence will have). They can be coated with sound-absorbing plaster, but if sound is a serious issue, you can create an even more effective sound barrier with a coated, double-sided fence fitted with a core of sound-absorbing membrane.

Open-board fences effectively enclose an area without blocking the views beyond. Popular styles include chinoiserie, picket, spindle, trellis, post-and-rail, inter lap, and rustic—and of course there are countless variations on each style. Design, construction details, and maintenance bear serious consideration because the wood is usually exposed on all four sides. Most open-board fences are painted or stained, and it's best (and easiest) to paint or stain the components before assembly so that even the unexposed parts are protected. Many fences are made up of a combination of close-board and open-board design, the close-board panels below and open boards above. A louvered fence—whereby the boards are installed at an angle to allow for wind circulation—is more private than an open-board fence, while affording a sense of openness. It's an option to consider in warm climates, where air circulation can be a benefit for much of the year.

Before designing a custom-built fence, research the high-quality, well-designed styles of preassembled panels that are available. If you can find something you like, you'll reduce your costs of both materials and installation and get the job done much more quickly.

Wooden fences require permits, just as metal ones do—and one of the requirements may be that you must face the finished side toward the neighboring property. Making your fence double-sided costs approximately 25 percent more, but you can avoid this expense by going with a design that is intrinsically two-sided: a basket weave, for example, or sturdy lattice.

Lattice fencing should be constructed with premium-grade wood that is at least ½ inch thick, notched together, and painted or stained. Manufactured lattice panels are available, but few are of optimal thickness or notched together.

For privacy, a close-board fence with tongue-and-groove joints is the best choice. Boards that are merely nailed "butt to butt" will develop gaps as nails inevitably loosen.

15. Pickets of graduated height create an arch, adding a graceful rhythm to the fence.
16. A substantial bottom rail set on gravel helps preserve this refined Chippendale fence.
17. A beautifully crafted fence with "through" spindles and alternating post-and-finial designs surrounds The Lindens in Washington, DC. The house was built in 1754 in Danvers, Massachusetts, and dismantled and moved to Washington in 1934.
18. The louvers in this fence are set in alternating directions, limiting the view and varying the light passing through.
19. An open fence with minor differences from pier to pier.
20. Rustic fences tend to be double sided.
21. A fence with diagonal lattice panels has two "good" sides.
22. Lattice constructed on a tight grid provides privacy without impeding air circulation. The lattice panels here are set in solid posts and stained to extend the life of the fence.

23. Here, white pickets are set between brick piers above a low brick wall. The ferns that have sprouted on the piers are charming, but will cause water damage eventually.

24. The color of the weathered wood blends nicely with that of the stone wall below.

25. An open-and-closed-board fence with elevated posts is topped by urn-shaped finials.

CLIMATE AND WEATHERING All wood that comes in contact with moist soil and available oxygen will eventually rot. Posts are most susceptible, because they are exposed to a full 12 inches of soil. In optimum conditions, where the soil is dry and well drained, Osage orange posts can last up to seventy-five years; black locust or "stone wood," forty years or more; pressure-treated pine, twenty years; ipe, twenty-five; cedar, redwood, and white oak, fifteen.

Try to avoid setting wood posts directly into the ground. Consider such alternatives as galvanized pipes clad in wood or concrete piers with galvanized metal cleats. Other options for prolonging the life span of your posts include setting them on a low, masonry wall or treating them with additional waterproofing protection. A larger post, 6 inches square, will last longer than the more commonly used 4-inch variety, as will a post of top-quality, premium heartwood.

Cedar posts should be of heartwood, treated with a preservative and set in gravel, not concrete. These will not shrink, crack, split, or twist, whereas pressure-treated pine is prone to do so. If pressure-treated pine is used it should be hand selected, premium grade, and painted or stained. An additional word of warning: although it is subject to regulations, pressure-treated wood still contains toxins and should be used and handled with caution.

Close-board fences provide protection from the wind and, when sited facing south to block winter winds, they are adequate shelter for marginally hardy plants. In areas of strong winds, the posts of a closed fence must be set more deeply than normal or buttressed for added stability. A well-placed wooden fence can also prevent snowdrifts. However, if it is placed at the bottom of a hill, it will restrict the flow of colder air and create cold pockets, possibly affecting the growth of marginally hardy plants.

Whatever your climate, consider the benefits of fencing that will allow prevailing summer winds to pass through. You may be giving up a bit of privacy with an open-board or louvered fence—but the cooling benefits will allow you to enjoy the summer landscape on even the sultriest nights of the year.

INSTALLATION AND MAINTENANCE Wood suitable for exterior use is available in lengths of 6, 8, 10, 12, 14, or 16 feet. It may be smooth-cut or rough saw-cut.

As noted, fences should only be constructed of the densest and most durable woods. Ipe is 370 percent denser than teak, which is 280 percent denser than red cedar. All three are resistant to cracking, as the wood naturally expands and contracts.

In Europe, the woods most often used for fences are western red cedar and oak. In the United States, redwood, pressure-treated pine, and red or white cedar are favored. The average life span of fences made of western red cedar and redwood is twenty to twenty-five years; pressure-treated pine, twenty to thirty years; pressure-treated hemlock and spruce, ten to twelve years.

Wood is available in a variety of grades and it is not surprising that the best is the most expensive. Starting with the best, the grades are as follows. Clear: no knots; Premium: same appearance on both sides, small tight knots; Select #1: same as premium but one face with more knots; and Standard: more knots and defects, possible knotholes that jeopardize durability.

Posts are usually the first element of a fence to fail, so be sure to select the best wood and footings for your soil conditions. Never set posts more than 8 feet apart. Their tops should be cut to a profile that sheds water or capped with wood, copper, or lead.

Rails (the horizontal boards connecting the posts) are usually the second element to fail, so design your fence and choose your materials to mitigate against sagging. Specify a strong joint (top joint, mortised joint, butt joint, grooved joint, slotted joint) or, if they won't be visible, use double-dipped galvanized hangers. The tops of all horizontal pieces should be tapered to shed water. The lowest rail should be set at least 2 inches above ground level.

Open fences over 4 feet tall should have three rails. If they are constructed of panels or tongue-and-groove boards, they can be as tall as 6 feet without a middle rail. Fasteners and screws are more secure than nails and should be of the highest quality. They should be chosen with regard to the type of wood used, as some metals react and cause corrosion or staining. Likewise, hardware that might stain or corrode should be coated in epoxy, painted with a polyester finish, or powder coated.

Consider finishing with latex paint or semitransparent or transparent stain to protect the wood. If you are fond of the natural, weathered gray finish of wood, hose down your fence frequently when the sun is out and it will turn gray faster.

26   27   29

28

26. A wood cap angled to shed water protects this delicate open fence.

27. These spear-topped pickets are attached to three rails for strength—but because they are in direct contact with the soil, they will deteriorate quickly.

28. Triangular pickets with rounded tops are painted to contrast with the rails. This adds visual interest while protecting the wood.

29. This well-made but weathered fence, featuring through pickets of alternating heights, is in desperate need of maintenance.

30. A fence along a gorge in Bad Ragaz, Switzerland, is simply constructed but requires careful attention
to the fit of the timbers within the notches of the metal piers.

31. A teak fence in an understated open pattern delineates the Japanese garden at Tatton Park in England.

32. Modest but elegant wood piers support a picket fence at Mount Vernon in Virginia.

33. A very open fence signals that a pond is off limits without interfering with the view.

FOUNTAINS

Happy in all that ragged, loose
Collapse of water its effortless descent
And flatteries of spray . . .

RICHARD WILBUR,
from "A Baroque Wall-Fountain in the Villa Sciarra"

Great civilizations have always developed around water. From the Nile Valley to the banks of the powerful Yangtze, fertile land rising up from the world's great rivers, lakes, and springs has provided sustenance both physical and spiritual to mankind since the dawn of time. As the Greek philosopher Thales of Miletus wrote, "Water sustains all."

Today, water features most often serve a decorative purpose, while early fountains were first and foremost functional, providing fresh water for drinking, bathing, and irrigation, as well as serving as a communal gathering place. Yet, even in ancient times, the intrinsic beauty of water did not go unappreciated. Egyptian tomb paintings dating from as early as 3000 BC depict walled courtyards and gardens of fruit trees designed around gravity-fed, rectangular pools populated by schools of fish.

British archaeologist Austen Henry Layard (1817–1894) discovered a fountain in the Gomal River gorge of ancient Assyria (modern-day Iraq) that he described as "a series of basins cut in solid rock, with water led by conduits basin to basin—the lowest ornamented with lions in relief." During the first millennium BC, the Persians constructed systems of channels and aqueducts called qanats. These underground tunnels used gravity to feed water to settlements in areas remote from large rivers, where aquifers were too deep to be accessed by wells. Sometimes a qanat would surface in a garden or courtyard as a fountain.

1. Neptune's Fountain sits at the bottom of a cascade cut into the mountainside at Linderhof Park in Germany. The fountain is connected by two tunnellos to the Music Pavilion that sits atop the cascade.
2. A channel rill of the same sandstone as the paving connects two ablution pools.
3. The ruins of a folly at Veitshöchheim pay homage to the spirit and influence of ancient cultures.
4. The centuries-old site of a town fountain in Bad Ragaz, Switzerland.
5. In this Japanese fountain, water flows through a bamboo spout into a granite basin carved into the shape of a boat.

6

7

8

6. At the Alhambra in Spain, water serves a multitude of purposes. Here it brings light into the recesses of the courtyard.

7. The Generalife, an oasis of gardens and waterworks, was the summer palace set across a ravine from the Alhambra. Now referred to as the Water Parterre, the fountain there has jets that can be adjusted to spray the hot summer paving with cooling water.

8. In the Court of the Water Channel, an arching succession of thin water jets creates the illusion of abundant water.

The Greeks were blessed with an abundance of freshwater springs, inspiring their skilled engineers to build fountains dedicated to nymphs and heroes. Usually located near temples, they varied in design but always featured a basin to contain the water and often a roof of some kind to protect its purity. Decorative masks provided a playful outlet for the flow, and some were adorned with sculptures and included places to sit.

We have the Romans to thank for the word fountain itself, which is derived from the Latin word fons, "spring." The first so-called fountains, dating from just before the Common Era, could be found in the courtyards of Roman baths and houses and in the streets for public use. They were gravity-fed via eleven aqueducts constructed to carry fresh water to the city from as far as 60 miles away. In nearby Pompeii, many were elaborately decorated with mosaics and natural seashells.

In the Far East, fountains developed in their own way. The earliest examples found in Japan were called chozubachi or tsukubai. Simple bowls fed by a bamboo spout, they were placed near shrines and used for ritual cleansing. The Japanese poet Sen no Rikyu captured their spiritual dimension:

"When you hear the splash of the water drops that fall into the stone bowl, you will feel that all the dust of your mind is washed away."

The Moors, accomplished hydraulic engineers in their own right, introduced water into the gardens of sun-baked southern Spain for its natural cooling quality as well as its appeal to the other senses. Water from the melting snows of the Sierra Nevada Mountains flowed to these gardens through a network of qanats. The Moors were masters at making the most of the limited water available in the region, and many of their fountains featured multiple small jets rather than one large one, creating the illusion of a bountiful supply of water. Two of the most famous Moorish gardens, at the Alhambra and the Generalife, can still be visited; their fountains, pools, and rills flow much as they did in the thirteenth century.

In the medieval period in Europe, many fountains fell into disrepair as aqueducts were neglected or destroyed. Those that survived could be found in monasteries or the gardens of the nobility. Intricately carved with scenes from history, the Bible, or allegorical tales, these fountains came to represent purity and innocence.

9. A raised basin in the courtyard of a Spanish Colonial monastery in Antigua, Guatemala.
10. At the Fountain of the River Gods at Villa Lante, the oversized hands of the gods signify the abundance of water they supply. Below, a narrative frieze embellishes the basin.
11. The catena d'acqua ("chain of water") at Villa Lante is decorated with carved shrimp in recognition of the family crest of its owner, Cardinal Gambara.
12. The famous Trevi Fountain in Rome.
13. Neptune's Fountain at Villa d'Este uses water to create light at dusk.
14. La Rometta, the "Little Rome" fountain, features sculptural representations of iconic sites in Rome. Over its history, the low, multi-tiered wall was sometimes used for seating, complete with giochi d'acqua ("water jokes"): When a guest sat down, a spray of water would be released, dousing him!
15. The garden at Herrenhausen, begun in the seventeenth century, is packed with fountains, many forming the focal point of a parterre de broderie such as this.

As the Renaissance dawned, Italian scholars became fascinated with the civilization of ancient Rome and set about translating the writings of Vitruvius, Pliny the Younger, and Pliny the Elder. The remains of Hadrian's Villa and other structures were excavated and soon, gardens and fountains in the early Roman style came back into fashion. In 1453, Pope Nicholas V began the reconstruction of the Roman aqueduct, Aqua Virgo (renamed Aqua Vergine), in an effort to bring more fresh water to Rome. He crowned it with a Roman mostra, "grand fountain," at the place where the water surfaced in the city. Today, the Trevi Fountain is the most famous in Rome and many consider it to be the most beautiful.

Throughout the Renaissance, the Italians took advantage of the bountiful supply of water and their topography of steep slopes to create gardens with gravity-fed fountains extraordinary in scale and craftsmanship. Villa Lante and Villa d'Este are just two examples of gardens united by water, the flow creating separate "rooms" for various fountains that display many forms of moving water.

Today's Rome remains touched by the magic of baroque master sculptor Gian Lorenzo Bernini (1598–1680), who was commissioned by no fewer than eight popes to restore and create fountains in squares throughout the city. His Fountain of Rivers, Triton Fountain, and Trevi Fountain (finished by Nicola Salvi) have been admired for centuries and continue to serve as lush oases and gathering spots within the bustling modern capital.

While the French long admired the gardens and waterworks of Italy, they faced the challenge of making water flow gracefully over flat terrain. In the seventeenth century, André Le Nôtre, the master garden architect of Vaux-le-Vicomte and Versailles, used an abundance of jets and fountains to create large expanses of water. The aqueducts and cisterns of Versailles were sufficient to store and supply the water required by his designs, but there was no way to generate enough pressure to run all 1,400 fountains at the same time. A solution to this problem was found: As Louis XIV and his entourage passed through the gardens, fountains were turned off and on successively along their route, so that they might enjoy a continuous display of waterworks.

German landscaping of the baroque era included flamboyant water features. Elaborate parterre gardens were designed around sculpted fountains whose powerful jets shot water to magnificent heights; the cascades of rushing water followed the contours of the land.

Like their French neighbors, the English admired Italian water gardens, and they were fortunate to share Italy's rolling terrain and abundance of water. Formal gardens in the Italian style sprang up through the seventeenth century, featuring waterworks and fountains. During the English Landscape

16. At the Château de Courances, La Bagneuse ("The Bather") overlooks one of fourteen fountains called Les Gueulards ("The Loudmouths").

17. Nymphs frolic in the three-basin Naiad Fountain at Linderhof.

18. The Apollo Temple overlooks a cascade surrounded by rusticated stonework in the gardens of Schwetzingen Castle.

19. The Stag Fountain is one of a pair in the central axis of Schwetzingen Castle sculpted by P. A. von Verschaffelt in 1767.

20. Naturalistic ponds framed by well-placed trees and shrubs replaced formal fountains in England as the aesthetic philosophies of the landscape movement took hold. This view at Sheffield Park deftly highlights the manor.

21. A cast-iron and glass basin, circa 1870, sometimes referred to as an aquarium fountain, might be a temporary home for goldfish at Ladew Gardens in Maryland.

22. In another part of Ladew Gardens, a cast-iron fence welcomes visitors into a garden room with a three-tiered cast-iron fountain at its center.

25. A Provençal fountain added in 1927 provides the central focus for the Ellipse Garden at Dumbarton Oaks, considered by many to be among the finest of Gilded Age gardens.
26. An interpretation of a moon gate frames this fountain built in the 1920s at Pinewood Estate, Florida. In Chinese lore, a moon gate prevents the entry of evil spirits.
27. At La Fronteira in Portugal, a tiered fountain marks the central axis of a parterre garden.
28. A tiered fountain of imported tile on the terrace of the garden at Pinewood.
29. A fountain of many asymmetrical tiers in Frankfurt, Germany.
30. The side garden of a house in Charleston with a tiered fountain as its centerpiece.

23. A fern motif embellishes the tree trunk pedestal of this cast-iron fountain in Savannah, Georgia.
24. The Frog Fountain at Vizcaya, a Gilded Age garden in Florida, is named for the zinc frogs that cling to the edge of its rectangular marble sarcophagus.

Movement of the eighteenth century, however, formal gardens and ornate fountains fell into disfavor. Inspired by Dutch landscape paintings, designers moved toward naturalistic landscapes on a grand scale, dotted with lakes, ponds, waterfalls and rills.

In 1772, clockmaker and scientist John Whitehurst invented the manually operated hydraulic ram pump that made many of the elaborate water displays possible. A quarter-century later, the French inventor Joseph Michel Montgolfier (an innovator of the hot-air balloon, among other things), perfected the first self-acting ram pump. Able to run continuously without human or animal power, it could raise water to a height of three hundred feet, allowing for ever more exuberant displays.

Fountains made of cast iron came into fashion in the Victorian era. Foundries responded to the demand with a wide array of affordably priced designs suitable for gardens of all sizes.

By the beginning of the twentieth century, America's moneyed aristocrats were constructing lavish estates. Borrowing extensively from European architecture and garden design, their massive houses were surrounded by gardens with lakes, waterfalls, and fountains.

Today's technology has put fountains within reach of virtually anyone who enjoys the sight and sound of rushing water. Those who relish the hunt through antique and salvage shops or estate sales might be rewarded by a gem from an earlier era

31. Fountains with rising water jets mark the cross axes of the expansive garden at Herrenhausen.
32. Even when the fountains at Herrenhausen rest, there is beauty in the sculpture of the nozzle.
33. The Great Fountain at Herrenhausen includes a central jet that can reach 250 feet.

34. The Fountain of the Muses, designed by Carl Milles and located at Brookgreen Gardens, South Carolina, is made up of fifteen discrete parts and was inspired by Greek mythology. The four figures on the right signify the fine arts of poetry, architecture, music, and painting, while the figure on the left represents sculpture.

35. A rill built into the side of the stairs at the Alhambra.
36. The Patio de los Naranjos at the Cathedral of Seville surrounds a stone fountain, possibly Roman. Rills provide irrigation to the orange trees.
37. An ornamental rill at Schwetzingen is tucked between hedges.

that can easily be retrofitted. For do-it-yourselfers, a wide variety of new components can be configured into something unique. And, of course, ready-to-install, prefabricated fountains may be purchased in just about any material or design one can imagine.

DESIGN Fountains fall into four classic types: the tiered basin; the basin with a water jet; the rill and its more boisterous incarnation, the cascade; and the wall fountain.

The tiered fountain, the most elaborate and expensive type, is made of raised basins or garden sculptures that spout and cascade water into lower basins. They are designed to distribute water evenly over the sculpted surfaces while maintaining a handsome appearance when dry. Many antique tiered fountains can be found, as well as a wide range of reproductions.

The basin with the water jet has evolved considerably from the original single-spout version. Hundreds of nozzles are now available that produce a wide variety of spray profiles described as cascades, geysers, bubblers, fan, dome, rotating, and so on. When the pump is switched off and the jets are still, there is often a less-than-pleasing view of the plumbing and nozzles — but it is possible to find beautifully crafted nozzles that serve as sculptures in themselves. Aquatic plants can be added to soften the view as well, but they must be kept out of the spray area, as moving water will inhibit their growth. (They also fail to thrive in chlorinated water.) Basins with water fonts tend to be less expensive than tiered fountains.

The rill is a narrow, shallow canal that channels the flow of water down a slope or series of steps. In ancient civilizations, public and private fountains were gravity-fed, the excess water diverted via rills that were frequently used to irrigate fruit and vegetable gardens. Many rills are designed to flow down the center or along the sides of a set of stairs.

Obviously, the best location for a rill is on an inclined slope. Designs may be architectural and formal or naturalistic and informal. Most rills are designed to be attractive even when dry. Rills must be created on site: manufactured rills cannot be found outside of miniaturized desktop fountains.

A large version of the rill that can accommodate a greater volume of water is called a cascade and is meant to conjure up a fast-moving stream or waterfall.

The wall fountain shoots water from a wall into a basin. This is the most economical of water features in terms of its spatial requirements, and is usually one-sided. A wall fountain

may be as simple as a single unadorned spout dispensing water into a plain basin or as elaborate as a carved mask projecting water so that it cascades into a series of multilevel, tiered basins.

Fountains are usually placed on axis with the primary view of the landscape. In the great gardens of the past, they were located so as to draw visitors into and through the garden. Even in the most formal and symmetrical gardens, fountains tend to vary one from another rather than being restricted to a repetitive design throughout the garden.

Although they might be constructed of metal, concrete, terra-cotta, fiberglass, vinyl or rubber, stone is the preferred material for fountains, as it is the most durable and can be carved into virtually any design. Metal fountains are usually made from bronze, lead, or cast iron. They are sturdy and can be mass produced. Precast concrete fountains are also mass produced and durable, but their dyes tend to fade unless sealed. Terra-cotta fountains, though attractive, should not be considered for use in temperate climates unless they are glazed because of likely damage from the freeze-thaw cycle.

46

47

48

38. A water channel at Humayun's Tomb in India feeds a basin, which in turn releases water into the rills that circulate throughout the garden.

39. In Japan, rills are informal and lined with natural stone.

40. A cascade tumbles down a hillside but there are many opportunities to cross it.

41. Thirty marble steps propel water down the cascade at Linderhof Castle.

42. A series of sculptural ledges create a cascade when water flow is increased.

43. Water spills from a simple terra cotta spout set in a wall in Antigua, Guatemala.

44. A sculptural wall mask spurts water into a swimming pool below, in this private garden in Washington, DC.

45. Multitiered wall fountains at the Zwinger Museum in Dresden, Germany. Note the unusual placement of the top tier in front of a window.

46. A flat rectangle of copper spills water from one band of metal to the next and finally onto a bed of river rocks. Staining from the copper is beginning to appear on the wall at the bottom left of the fountain.

47. Recessed pools are surrounded by gravel paths set into the lawn.

48. A single jet rises from a pool with a slightly raised edge surrounded by stone paving at the Villa Marlia in Italy. The fountain sits at the intersection of two paths and marks the entrance to the garden room beyond.

49. This recessed pool is covered with a decorative grill to insure safety, in this Washington, DC, garden designed by Michael Bartlett.

49

Fiberglass, vinyl and rubber fountains are the least expensive but can be punctured easily and will degrade over time from exposure to UV rays.

Fountains may be raised, level or recessed into the ground but should never be less than 18 inches deep so as to obscure any view of the mechanical parts at the bottom. They should always be filled to the brim; dark-colored interiors can create the illusion of greater depth.

Fountains that are flush with the ground are less expensive to construct, but without barriers they pose a potential hazard to onlookers who could step or slip into the water. And of course fountains with raised perimeters offer a welcome spot to sit and enjoy the display.

Designing a fountain so that it spills into a swimming pool is an elegant way to enliven the scene with the sound of splashing water. These fountains should be plumbed separately, though, so that they may be turned on and off without affecting the filtration system of the pool.

For those with an eye on energy efficiency, solar-powered water pumps are available—but be aware that they require full sunlight and do not propel water to great heights. They are best used in places where electricity is not readily available.

CLIMATE AND WEATHERING In temperate climates, fountains should be drained during the winter months. If possible, the pump should be removed and protected from freezing. Only basins that have been designed and reinforced to withstand the pressure of expanding ice can remain filled when temperatures drop below freezing. (There are some lovely fountains that have been specially designed to freeze over and create icicles.)

Never use antifreeze in a fountain, as it is toxic to children, animals, and birds. In a fountain stocked with fish, they will need pockets 30 inches deep to survive.

In hot, arid climates, fountains and mist systems are appreciated for their cooling benefits. In windy, exposed areas, a great deal of water will be lost through evaporation, creating a risk that the pump will run dry and fail. The best solution is to install a wind vane controller selected to accommodate the height of the jets, as well as an electronic water-level sensor that will trigger a refill of the basin as needed.

INSTALLATION AND MAINTENANCE Fountains must be set on precisely level footings that are deeper than the frost line. During construction, special attention must be paid to the areas most vulnerable to leakage, including spots where wires and plumbing enter and exit the basin.

50

50. Water seeps from a wall through inconspicuous pipes and spills onto ledges of stone, before finally reaching the swimming pool of a private garden in McLean, Virginia.
51. This cast-iron, tiered fountain has been winterized quite imaginatively.

51

Lighting tiered basins and sculptural fountains can be tricky. Placing a light fixture too close to the feature being lit creates a "hot spot" and contrasting dark shadows. If done correctly, however, lighting a fountain not only enhances its beauty but transforms it into a dramatic addition to the nighttime vista.

It's very important to maintain the quality of water in a fountain, and this takes constant monitoring and care. Algae growth is the most common problem and can be controlled by chemicals as well as by shading the water with aquatic plants and/or darkening its color with a nontoxic black dye. In ponds and lakes, floating jets can be used to aerate the water and reduce algae growth.

To remove salt and mineral deposits, the basin must be emptied and scrubbed. Water should also be filtered to prevent nozzles from clogging. Plants that shed an abundance of flowers, fruit, leaves, or bark should not be planted near a fountain. Surface water should drain away from the basin or be directed to a trench drain encircling it.

52. An exuberant figure of cast iron shoots a jet toward the sky, while water flows over the scalloped edges of its pedestal to the basin below.
53. A profusion of jets surrounds a carved elephant as he sprays water into the surrounding pool.
54. Beautifully carved ornamentation decorates a font of still water at Brookgreen Gardens in South Carolina.
55. An ancient well head that originally served as a water source for the cloister now forms the ornamental focus of this herb garden.

52

53

54

55

FURNITURE

To sit in the shade on a fine day and look upon verdure is the most perfect refreshment.

JANE AUSTEN

1. The embracing curve of this bench echoes the shape of a pond, at Blithewold Gardens in Rhode Island. The subtle color gives it presence without overpowering its informal surroundings.

2. Inspired by Greek exedrae, this curved stone bench sits on its own terrace with added seclusion provided by the surrounding hedge. Mythological sentries stand guard.

3. A Chippendale bench in a quiet corner of the gardens at Tintinhull sits near its own small reflective fountain.

4. Vita Sackville-West made this turf seat planted with chamomile for her herb garden at Sissinghurst.

When Socrates engaged his star pupil, Plato, in philosophic dialogue, the two were probably sitting under the Grecian sun on a permanent outdoor bench called an exedra. These stone seats, usually set into semicircular porticoes, were commonly used as gathering places for scholars, politicians, and others. Occasionally they took the form of freestanding "chairs" with semicircular seats and high backs. The ancient Greeks must have understood what we know today: being outdoors can free the mind and spirit.

Pliny the Younger (AD 61–121), a lawyer, author, and magistrate of ancient Rome, wrote many letters detailing the layouts of his villas. Describing his home in Tuscany, he commented,

"In different quarters are disposed several marble seats which serve as so many reliefs after one is wearied with walking. Next to each seat is a little fountain."

In medieval gardens, turf seats were a common feature. Usually rectangular in shape, their living "upholstery" sometimes included herbs, such as chamomile, which released a pleasing fragrance when sat upon. These gracious resting spots could most often be found near a fountain or tree or against a wall so as to offer back support.

Garden furniture was rare in historic Japanese gardens, many of which were designed to be viewed from a teahouse, monastery, temple, residence, or viewing platform. These structures had sliding doors and screens, sometimes translucent, which framed views of the garden and served as graceful portals to sheltered spots designed for contemplation. To sit comfortably, one was expected to bring a mat. Some Japanese gardens weren't designed for sitting at all: "stroll gardens" were meant to be walked through or, in some cases, viewed from a boat on a pond.

Renaissance and baroque gardens took many design cues from the ancient Greeks and Romans. Ornate, hand-carved marble benches based on the exedra abounded, often located near fountains, strategically placed at optimal viewing spots or nestled in cool, shady areas.

With the rise of England's picturesque garden movement in the eighteenth century, garden ornamentation and furniture took on a more natural look. Designers created "forest" furniture and "rural" chairs fashioned from indigenous branches, while tree stumps and logs often formed the basis of seats and benches.

In the colonial United States, the earliest seats specifically designed for garden use were made of wood and very simple in design, sometimes incorporating a Chippendale-style back. The

Almodington bench, made in 1780, is considered to be the oldest extant example of wooden garden furniture in the United States. It is made of pine, with a simple Chippendale back consisting of four panels of diagonal slats. Originally found on the Almodington plantation in Somerset County, Maryland, the bench is now on display at the Museum of Early Southern Decorative Arts in Winston-Salem, North Carolina.

Quite often, garden seating was created simply by taking indoor furniture outside. The Windsor chair was often used in this way. As they were frequently composed of more than one type of wood and then painted, Windsor chairs were affordable and extremely durable (presuming that the woods were joined soundly). Airy and elegant, the style was harmonious with an outdoor setting without sacrificing comfort. George Washington used groupings of Windsor chairs on his porch at Mount Vernon.

In the nineteenth century, iron furniture became popular for outdoor use, valued for its longevity and the fact that it could be forged into sophisticated curvilinear forms by skilled ironworkers. Eventually, wrought-iron furniture gave way to the cast-iron variety, which could be mass produced by

5. Based on the shape of an exedra, this carved stone bench with a wrought-iron back becomes a balcony overhanging the rugged landscape of Extremadura, Spain.

6. The river gods preside over the outdoor dining room at Villa Lante in Italy. The central table has a trough that can be filled with water to float serving dishes shaped like boats.

7. A carved stone seat of Renaissance design at Cà d'Zan in Florida.

8. A hollowed-out log used as a bench in a private garden in Tryon, South Carolina.

9. The red Chippendale pattern of the back of this bench stands out against a tall hedge at Ladew Gardens in Maryland.

10. Landscape architect Beatrix Farrand took special interest in the garden furniture used at Dumbarton Oaks, either designing or hand selecting it. These sturdy chairs, designed to resemble interior side chairs, have seats cleverly patterned for quick drainage.

11. A somewhat busy example of a cast-iron bench with differing patterns on the back, seat, arms, and legs. Referred to as the "Gothic settee," it was produced by a number of iron foundries in the United States between 1890 and 1940.

12. This cast-iron bench with a fern motif on its back was popular in the late nineteenth century.

13. Muted gray-green paint makes this cast-iron bench in Williamsburg, Virginia, recede into its surroundings.

14. Flat ribbons of metal are twisted and overlapped, then set on a seat of diagonals that rests on cast legs.

15. Chairs inspired by the traditional Adirondack model at Chanticleer in Pennsylvania.

16. Custom made to fit the trunk of the tree, this bench has panels of varying designs for its back and is set on gravel to preserve its legs.

pouring molten iron into molds. Elaborate patterns—ranging from geometric shapes and Gothic motifs to intricate depictions of plants, musical instruments, and mythical creatures—were readily available, affordable, and appealing to Victorian tastes. Sometimes, wooden seats were added to make the unyielding metal chairs and benches more comfortable.

Evocative of lazy afternoons at a lakeside cabin, the Adirondack chair remains one of the most recognizable and popular styles of outdoor furniture in the United States today. Its life began in 1903, when one Thomas Lee determined to make a comfortable and easily constructed outdoor chair for his vacation home in Westport, New York, on the banks of Lake Champlain. His large family critiqued a number of designs and declared the "Westport Plank Chair" their favorite. The definitive version was made of eleven pieces of knot-free hemlock or hickory, all cut from the same board. Lee showed his chair to a local carpenter named Harry Bunnell, hoping that Bunnell might make some for him during the winter months. Without informing Lee, Bunnell patented the design under his own name and made and sold Adirondack chairs for the next twenty years, never sharing his profits with Lee.

Known for its low seat, slanted back, and arms wide enough to balance a drink or plate, the chair is widely available in a variety of materials, as are many companion pieces, such as rocking chairs, loveseats, tables, porch swings, and the like.

Today, garden furniture can be found in a wide range of materials, styles, and price ranges, from precious twig-style antiques to simple reproductions of classic wrought-iron designs. There are plenty of contemporary choices, too. In choosing furniture for your garden, it is important to consider function, durability, location, aesthetics, and budget—and don't forget to sit on it before you make your final choice! You will want to enjoy it in comfort for years to come.

DESIGN The addition of furniture to a garden can instantly create an inviting outdoor room, guide visitors' focus to a striking view or provide a resting spot—all while acting as an ornamental feature in its own right. Chairs, benches, rockers,

17. A brick wall becomes a bench with the addition of a wrought-iron back.
18. In the 1950s, Russell Woodard designed outdoor furniture called "Sculptura," made of woven wire with wrought iron. This example is in a private garden in Washington, D.C.

19. In Washington, D.C, blocky stone chairs of severe design.
20. This bench at Dumbarton Oaks, designed by Beatrix Farrand in the early 1930s, is made of teak and iron wire.
21. In Williamsburg, Virginia, a slat-back wood bench with an undulating skirt beneath the seat features arms of two different designs.

swings, chaises longues, tables and ottomans suitable for outdoor use are available in wood, stone, metal, and a variety of synthetic materials. Designs that coordinate with just about any architectural style and appeal to a broad range of individual tastes can be found at garden centers, through designers, online, and even at the hardware store or supermarket. They range from permanent, custom-designed pieces built directly into the landscape and one-of-a-kind antiques to simple pieces that fold or stack for easy removal and storage.

The most durable wooden furniture is made from woods that are warp, rot, and insect resistant. For decades, hardwoods, such as teak and mahogany, were the material of choice—but overharvesting have made them hard to come by and quite expensive. Fast-growing and sustainable alternatives have emerged, including shorea, eucalyptus, acacia, ipe, balau, iroko, jarrah, and kempas. These woods are tight grained, durable, and laden with natural oils that resist damage from insects and moisture.

Of the softwoods, cedar is the best choice for use in outdoor furniture, as it is naturally resistant to insects and moisture

damage and rarely splinters. Pine is commonly used, although it is susceptible to rot and should be treated with a wood preservative. (Pressure-treated pine should be avoided for this purpose, as it is impregnated with toxic chemicals.) Willow, cypress, and alder are most often used for twig or rustic furniture because of their malleability. Bamboo—which is eco friendly, fast growing, strong, and lightweight—is emerging as a popular material for outdoor furniture. Keep in mind, however, that it is susceptible to wood-boring insects.

Outdoor furniture made of woven natural materials, such as wicker, rattan, or water hyacinth, can be lovely although not particularly durable. It's best to confine its use to porches, gazebos, pavilions, or other sheltered areas. For use in unprotected spots, you might want to consider woven furniture made from stronger synthetic fibers or treated with a protective sealant. Some of these pieces replicate the look of natural fibers well but are considerably longer lasting.

Stone outdoor furniture—though not the most comfortable—is certainly the most durable, as it is impervious to rust, rot, and damage done by insects. Marble, granite, limestone,

22. This bench with a rustic back and a seat of bent wood can be found outside the Phipps Conservatory in Pittsburgh.
23. Blocks of stone arranged to look like upholstered furniture at Chanticleer in Pennsylvania.
24. Hard surfaces are made more comfortable with the addition of cushions, at the Lake Palace in Udaipur, India.

25. The remaining arm of this carved stone chair is shaped like a swan's neck.
26. A stone dining set with detailed patterns of tree trunks behind, flowers on the backs, and cushions on the seats—complete with fringe and tassels.
27. Stone furniture at Naumkeag, conceivably the furniture Mabel Choate described to Fletcher Steele as "uncomfortable".

sandstone, and jade have been used for centuries. In addition to the fact that stone furniture can feel cold and hard, particularly in cool or damp weather, its weight makes it difficult to move—so site it carefully and think of it as a relatively permanent addition to the landscape. Mabel Choate, the original owner of an estate, known as Naumkeag, perched above the town of Stockbridge, Massachusetts, once remarked to her garden designer, Fletcher Steele, that the stone seats he'd added to the garden were uncomfortable. He replied, "You're not supposed to sit in them. You are supposed to look at them."

Cast stone is a form of architectural concrete processed to simulate natural stone. By adding a fine grade of aggregate to a mixture of cement and sand, fabricators of this material have eliminated the "pebble and voids" look of concrete and created a denser substance that is less affected by freezing and thawing. Because it is lighter and warmer than natural stone, it can be an excellent choice if you like the monumental look of stone furniture. And, of course, it is less expensive than quarried and carved stone because, once a mold is created, any number of copies of a particular design can be made.

(In this way, it resembles cast iron.) There is often a selection of finishes, too.

These days, metal furniture is usually made of cast iron, steel, or aluminum, though wrought-iron pieces can be found in antique shops and at estate sales. It is prized for its strength and the fact that it can be intricately detailed and textured. Cast iron is more brittle and softer in detail, and can be a bit cold and bumpy for sitting—but it is far less expensive and easier to come by. Steel can be fabricated to look very much like wrought iron and it has the added benefit of not corroding as fast.

Aluminum furniture comes in three types: tubular, wrought, and cast. Tubular aluminum furniture is made from hollow tubing cut and bent into shape and then welded together. Its joints are relatively large because of the diameter of the tubing, so clean welding is imperative. Wrought-aluminum furniture is similar to the tubular variety but stronger, with smaller joints and less welding. Cast aluminum is made by pouring molten aluminum into molds to create solid furniture that can be detailed easily.

28. A bench formed from a large sheet of metal.

29. An unusual circular seat made of lattice-patterned metal with a central cone forming the back.

30. A modern bench of smooth, seamless aluminum.

31. A bright blue wood bench draws the eye into an alcove.

32. A weathered bench of salvaged wood with moss and lichen growing on it becomes an organic part of the garden.

33. A high-backed bench in a modern interpretation of Chippendale design tames the scale of the tall stone wall and makes the space more intimate.

34. A bench designed by William Kent is protected inside the loggia known as the Praeneste at Rousham House in Oxfordshire, England.

35. The flamboyant back of this wood bench is attached in only three unsubstantial places, meaning that it is probably intended more for ornament than comfort and durability.

36. Rust from the wrought back of this bench has stained the stone seat.

And then there's plastic. For decades, the plastic furniture market has been dominated by cheap, disposable products fabricated at a high cost to the environment. The good news is that since the 1990s, some manufacturers have developed ways to recycle plastic bottle waste (milk jugs, water bottles, etc.) to create thermoplastic: a high-density, solid-colored material with the heft of wood that is resistant to UV damage.

Although you would never mistake it for wood, furniture made from thermoplastic has a variety of merits, including its eco-friendliness. It is worth considering for some types of gardens.

After you've decided on a particular material for your outdoor furniture, and a style that is in keeping with the architecture and garden, you must decide on a color scheme. Neutral, dark, or natural colors blend in more readily with the

37. Even strong native stone such as that of the Mermaid bench at Bomarzo will deteriorate over the course of four centuries.

38. Though the design has been copied ad infinitum, a well-made Lutyens bench, such as this one at Sissinghurst, maintains its integrity. Fine carpentry and stone paving beneath increase its longevity.

39. A curved seat with a two-panel back in a trellis pattern is charming tucked into a corner. Unfortunately, it is in direct contact with the earth and mud is splashing onto the legs and bottom rail. This will lead to rapid deterioration of the wood.

40. At the Chicago Botanic Garden, this elegant bench of natural wood features a back crafted to embrace the circular view through the wall. Protected by a roof and set on a stone terrace, it will remain well preserved.

41. Benches in this common contemporary design can be found in numerous gardens in Germany, almost always placed on a paved surface.

42. This chair made of teak and iron at Dumbarton Oaks is properly sited on a gravel terrace.

43. This cast aluminum rendition of a traditional design is lightweight and long lasting.

44. Even when placed on a paved surface, paint-on-metal benches will chip and should be touched up regularly to curtail rust.

45. A trio of benches with attached tables, set on a paved area, creates a spot to congregate at Nymans Gardens in England.

landscape, whereas white or bright colors draw the eye to the furniture itself and away from its surroundings.

CLIMATE AND WEATHERING As noted, furniture made of stone is the least affected by the forces of nature. It will not rot, rust, or be blown about by the wind. Different types of stone vary in their porosity; in cold climates, porous stone (or any stone that has cracks that might collect water) should be protected with waterproof covers, firmly secured so they won't blow away.

All wood furniture is subject to moisture damage so it is important to keep the legs from direct contact with the ground. If they must stand directly on the lawn or soil, they should be soaked in wood preservative.

Painting or staining your wooden pieces will protect them against weathering. Finishes are available with mold inhibitors for added protection and these should be considered if you live in a wet climate. Similarly, a finish that includes UV inhibitors can be a good idea in a particularly sunny area.

Some dense hardwoods, such as ipe and shorea, will not readily absorb paint and should be left bare and allowed to weather to a lovely natural gray. Whatever wood and finish you choose, be sure that all of the joints on your furniture are tight and won't collect rainwater.

Furniture made from rattan, wicker, and other natural fibers is the most vulnerable to the effects of weathering and climate. Sun will bleach it and dry it out; exposure to rain will cause it to rot and mildew. That is why we suggest you confine its use to protected areas.

Iron furniture is highly conductive of heat and cold, which can make it uncomfortable—even downright dangerous—to sit on during some times of the year. A wood seat added to an iron bench or chair can ameliorate this problem. Rust is always a concern with iron, and joints that might harbor water are particularly susceptible. Heavy iron furniture should be set on paving so it will not sink into soft, moist surfaces.

Powder-coated aluminum furniture is extremely resistant to corrosion and weathering. The downside is that individual pieces can be very light, making it a poor choice of material for windy spots unless you intend to take your chairs and tables indoors when the wind kicks up.

Inexpensive plastic furniture—a pox on the environment in any case—fades and becomes chalky when exposed to sun. It is also lightweight and subject to the vagaries of prevailing winds. Thermoplastic pieces are quite weather resistant and similar to wood in weight, so are less likely to end up in the swimming pool during a windstorm.

A final precaution: All lawn furniture should be located with an eye on the possibility of falling tree limbs, fruit, and bird droppings. Shade is lovely, but be careful not to put your family and guests in the line of fire! And—of course—take pains to protect or store all furniture during winter months in a cold climate.

INSTALLATION AND MAINTENANCE Furniture should always be placed on a firm and level surface—preferably a paved area—so as to keep it from direct contact with the moisture-retaining earth.

Apply the appropriate stain or sealer to wood furniture, unless the natural, weathered-gray effect is your preference. (This natural patina is not harmful to the wood; rather, it is a thin, superficial layer that protects what is underneath from UV rays.)

Most outdoor furniture benefits from cleaning with a mild solution of detergent and water at least twice a year. If it is located near a pool or spa, this should be done more regularly so as to reduce the effects of the chlorine. Powder-coated pieces can use an annual waxing.

If your furniture is painted, check it regularly for chips that might open the door to rot or rust. Sand down any chipped areas and touch them up. Joints should be checked regularly for water damage. If a filler compound was used to mask imperfect joinery, make sure that it has not separated and exposed the underlying layer to the elements.

Finally, avoid getting varnish or paint on screws because they are prone to loosening in response to freezing and thawing and may require tightening. Inspect all hardware regularly to ensure that it is tight, intact, and not leaching onto adjoining surfaces.

46

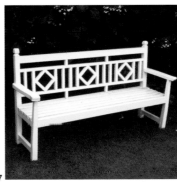

47

46. Benches encircle a sculptural tree trunk and are sheltered by the tree's dense canopy.
47. A bench of a rather simple Chippendale pattern is tucked into a group of hydrangeas. Unfortunately, it is in direct contact with the turfed earth.
48. An elegant wrought-iron bench accented by graceful curves and scrolls.
49. Reeded strap metal is curved to create an elegant bench but marred by the use of inferior fasteners that have oxidized.

48

49

50. **These chairs with wings of Corten steel could be considered sculptures.**

GATES

Still round the corner there may wait,
A new road or a secret gate.
J. R. R. TOLKIEN

1. This mid eighteenth-century gate at Veitshöchheim, in Germany, lifts the eye. Its graceful swaying verticals, alternating with thin rods topped by tassels of wheat sheaves, is strengthened by crossbracing and set into substantial sandstone piers.
2. The geometric design of this circa-fifteenth-century gate in Mallorca, Spain, shows a mix of Spanish and Moorish influences.

In our discussion of fences, we didn't delve into the subject of gates—but of course, the two go hand in hand. Nearly every fence needs some sort of gate, and many of the particulars regarding materials, maintenance, and weathering apply similarly to both. But gates can be used in a wide variety of decorative and ceremonial as well as utilitarian ways—and a number of significant historical examples survive.

❧ *Gates Made of Metal* ❧

The earliest metal gates were functional and used primarily as barriers to control the flow of human and animal traffic, thus providing security as well as protecting crops from roaming livestock. Gates were found in fortress walls surrounding settlements and they formed the entrances to walled cities. Sometimes their effect was purely functional, but often they were ornamented with sculptures, reliefs, or symbols of the resident gentry, such as coats of arms.

In ancient Greece and Rome, gates were rarely used in domestic architecture. They tended to be monumental in scale and reserved for grander uses: entryways to towns or temple complexes, for example. Working in the fifth century BC, the architect Mnesicles designed the Propylaea, the majestic gateway to the Acropolis. This massive structure was made of marble and limestone that was reinforced with iron. The overall edifice included several gates that separated pedestrian, animal, and carriage traffic. Before passing through, all were

expected to be ritually clean. The gates served also to protect the state treasury housed within and to bar those who might unlawfully seek sanctuary. This still impressive remnant of a great civilization has undergone extensive restoration over the years and is open to full view today.

In Spain, the art of creating ornamental ironwork is known as *rejería* and dates back to the ninth century AD. *Rejas*, the iron gates and grilles found in churches and cathedrals, are designed to protect shrines and relics and are sometimes used to separate the choir from the congregation. *Rejas* still abound, particularly in southern Spain, where they often function as gates just inside the entrance doors of private homes. When the exterior doors are opened, the *reja* keeps the interior secure, while affording a view of the courtyard at the center of the house. *Rejas* are also used as balcony railings and window grilles.

During the Renaissance, Italian artisans looked to their Greek and Roman predecessors for inspiration—but when it came to gates, they had few artifacts to study. Being highly skilled goldsmiths and silversmiths, they drew upon these skills and techniques to elevate their ironwork gates from well-made utilitarian objects to elegantly patterned entrances to villas. Gates also became focal points within gardens and provided graceful transitions between garden rooms.

During the baroque and rococo periods (17th–18th centuries), ironwork gates became more flamboyant and intricately patterned, often embellished with gilt. They served the same functions as those found in Renaissance gardens.

By the 1650s, French home and landscape architects had set the standard for wrought iron fences, balconies, and gates. (You can find more about the French influence on ironwork in our chapter on fences.)

Decorative gates fell out of favor in eighteenth-century gardens as the English landscape style—favoring nature over structure—took hold. As the closures were relegated to their earlier, more utilitarian purpose, their designs became simpler.

The use of lavishly ornamented gates reemerged during the nineteenth century in England, Europe, and the United States. Handcrafted wrought-iron gates reappeared, while mass-produced ones made of cast iron became affordable, popular alternatives, available in a vast array of designs.

3. The gardens at the Château de Courances in France have undergone numerous alterations since their creation in the sixteenth century, making it difficult to date this wrought gate. Note the similarity in the shape of the vertical element above the lower rail to the pattern of the gate at Veitshöchheim in the first photo.
4. The ornate double gates to the arboretum on the grounds of Schwetzingen Castle are set into stone piers topped by urns and surrounded by hedges. Blue paint enlivened by gilt flourishes makes a cheery sight on a dreary day.

5. Scroll and heart wrought-iron designs provide a framework for the simple gate at Isola Bella in Italy.
6. A renowned wrought gate on the grounds of St. Michael's Church in Charleston, South Carolina, was signed by its creator, J. A. W. Iusti. Fabricated sometime between 1752 and 1761, it consists of flat pieces of iron formed into scrolls and urn shapes.
7. This Charleston gate was inspired by the historic scroll patterns of the area but made with smaller-gauge metal components.

3

4

5

6

7

8. Red paint gives this unassuming gate more presence, bringing it into harmony with the flanking stone piers.

9. A mix of wrought and cast iron provides contrast between the band of circles at the bottom of the gate and its cast and fluted upright components.

10. Sculptural peacocks anchor the complex pattern of this cast-iron gate. The overhanging stone arch both frames and supports it.

11. Elaborate entrance gates combine scrolls, hearts, leaves and flowers at Cà d'Zan, one of last mansions of the Gilded Age, in Sarasota, Florida.

12. The Trefoil Gate at Dumbarton Oaks in Washington, DC, was faithfully restored in 2010. Designed by Beatrix Farrand for what remains one of the finest examples of a Gilded Age garden, construction began during the 1920s.

13. Gracious curved stairs lead to a gate separating garden rooms in this private Washington, DC, haven built during the Gilded Age.

Mark Twain is credited as the first to describe the era that began in the late 1800s and lasted until the Great Depression as the "Gilded Age." In America, newly rich "robber barons" as well as the established wealthy built sprawling estates modeled on the châteaux, castles, and villas of Europe. When it came to their vast gardens, they spared no expense—so it is no surprise that they included lavishly designed gates throughout the landscape as well as at the formal entryway to the property.

World War II brought rationing and recycling of iron, and its use for decorative purposes began to feel downright unpatriotic. By war's end, iron gates and fences had fallen out of favor both in England and the United States, and American house design began to emphasize a more private backyard. Some subdivisions and communities even outlawed the use of gates and fences in an effort to create a more open neighborhood feeling, a sense that the properties flowed seamlessly from one to the next. But in recent decades, as variety of architectural styles has reemerged as a virtue throughout suburban and rural enclaves—and the issue of security is ever present—gates and fences have once again taken hold as an expression of the overall personality of the property and its owners.

14 15 16

14. A simple gate set into a spare fence on a low wall defines the space without defending it.

15. Diamond and anthemion shapes in this simple fence in Boston find their way into the ornate cast-iron piers. The open gate welcomes visitors.

16. A view through these Savannah gates to the triple porches of the house piques the curiosity of passersby.

17. Although located in Buffalo, New York, this gate sets the tone for a garden featuring Asian influences.

18. A gate made of iron with sharp spear tops and set within a substantial wall provides a high level of security.

19. A gate with an open, trellislike design is surrounded by a stucco wall.

20. A beautifully constructed stone wall encloses the garden, while the open design of the gate visually joins the spaces.

21. There is strong contrast between the relatively small gate set into sizeable sandstone piers and the soaring fence that surrounds it, as designed by Sir Edwin Lutyens in New Delhi, India.

DESIGN In 1887, Thomas Meehan wrote in The Gardener's Monthly, "Tasteful entrance gates are like clothing to a man. The dress of a stranger is our first clue to his character . . . So we get the first impression from the entrance gate and the landscape gardener should give it close study."

Meehan understood that a gate is responsible for our first impression of the garden and should be reflective of its style, scale and proportion. It should be thoughtfully placed to frame the views within and without, and should provide an invitation to enter and circulate—all without drawing focus away from the garden's own intrinsic beauty. Excessively ornate ironwork, no matter how remarkable, can easily overshadow the views a gate is meant to enhance.

Gates can be employed within fences, walls, and hedges—or a combination of these. When used as fence openings, they should, of course, coordinate with the pattern of the fence—but should be distinct from it as well, so that the location of ingress is always obvious. In small gardens, metal gates with a sufficiently open feeling can serve to secure the garden while seeming to extend the space itself.

The six basic forms of metal gates include the single-swing, double-swing, gate within a gate, accordion, sliding, and false.

Single-swing gates are rarely more than 5 feet wide. They should swing in, away from the pedestrian space and any adjoining steps. Double-swing gates are never less than 4 feet wide, total, and, like their single-swing counterparts, should always swing in. Latches are difficult to align in both of these types but especially in double-swing gates, which require the aligning of two sets of latches.

The gate within a gate provides a separate, more easily maneuverable pedestrian entryway within a large gate for vehicles.

Largely an urban invention, the accordion gate is usually

17 18 19 20 21

22. A single gate cleverly crafted from horseshoes.
23. The design of these double gates set into brick piers is in harmony with the medallions of the fence mounted on the surrounding bricks walls.
24. This highly unusual swiveling iron gate must be difficult to swivel after a snowstorm.
25. A false gate, sometimes called a clairvoyee, allows views through a solid wall without permitting passage.

26. These iron double gates are taller than the surrounding brick piers but they are well supported because the piers are so substantial.
27. An optically interesting and very unusual double gate is surrounded by stucco walls capped with tile.
28. Low double gates without piers, set directly into a minimal wall, act as a decorative introduction to the flower garden rather than a physical barrier.

wide enough to accommodate vehicles while folding to the side like an accordion, thus minimizing the swing area needed when opening it.

Sliding gates are most often used in commercial settings and are rarely found in gardens. Requiring no swing area at all, they are useful in tight spaces.

False gates do not function as gates at all, but are decorative and focal, creating the illusion that a garden continues beyond its walls.

Metal gates are often shorter than wooden ones, though entrance gates, particularly those leading to imposing estates, can be conceived on a grand scale with elaborate ornamentation.

The best supports for iron gates are metal posts encased by brick, stone, or stucco — but they can be clad in wood as a less expensive alternative. Wooden piers can easily be made to blend with surrounding architecture by adding appropriate molding and then painting them a harmonious color or finishing them with a coat of stucco.

Metal gates can be self-closing with the addition of springs, counterweights and electric openers — and if you are concerned that the presence of the opener will mar the overall effect, it can be hidden from view by recessing it into the pavement. A solar-powered gate opener can significantly reduce your electricity cost.

Gilded iron gates — bright spots in the landscape — can add a striking note in latitudes where nights are long, or

29.

30

31. 32

33

29. This lightweight, cast-aluminum gate is attached to slender wooden piers and features a simple "snap into place" latch.
30. Magnificent gilded gates brighten the garden space and heighten one's expectations while offering a glimpse of what awaits within.
31. Cheerfully painted wrought iron gates are topped with urns of flowers. Note the stationary iron picket panels that attach the gate to the stone piers.

32. Wrought-iron driveway gates at St. Michael's, based on the J. A. W. Iusti's design, welcome visitors to the gardens at Boone Hall Plantation in Charleston.
33. Driveway gates cut out of sheet metal soar to great heights with scrolls of bent metal in Christchurch, New Zealand.

climates with frequent cloud cover. The French landscape architect André Le Nôtre was fond of them, believing that their elegance captivated observers while offering a suitably grand frame for the wonders within. Bright paint provides a similarly imposing effect if that is what you are interested in—whereas black or dark paint can make your gates seem to disappear.

Driveway gates have come into vogue in areas where capacious new homes are abundant—but they can sometimes seem forbidding or ostentatious. They are also expensive to install and maintain, so think twice before going for the "gated mansion" look. If you do opt for a driveway gate, the addition of an auxiliary entrance for pedestrians will add friendliness (along with some additional expense). In any case, security, rather than grandiosity, should be your guiding principle. As far as style is concerned, the artfully designed double wrought-iron gates flanking the entrance drives to historic southern estates are worthy of emulation.

Pedestrian gates should be at least 3 feet wide; and those meant for vehicles, at least 8 feet wide. The width of the path beyond the gate should relate to the size of the gate.

CLIMATE AND WEATHERING We've covered the effects of climate and weathering on metal in our "Fences" chapter, but gates have additional issues because of their hinges and other hardware. Freezing and thawing may loosen screws and joints; exposure to rain may cause the hardware to rust and weaken.

INSTALLATION AND MAINTENANCE It bears repeating: Always consult with local utility companies before beginning any project that requires digging.

The installation of metal gates in gardens can be complicated; we recommend that you hire experienced professionals with a keen understanding of the potential difficulties. To reduce the need for maintenance as the gates weather, insist that your fabricators and installers use the highest-quality hardware at every stage.

Hinges are the heart of a gate's operation—and are the most vulnerable to damage because of the weight they support and the wear and tear they sustain through constant use. They should be oiled and inspected for rust regularly.

A few final notes: Remember that your gates must have enough clearance below them that they can swing freely; and avoid any filler compounds, as they tend to weather differently from the metal itself, often breaking loose and exposing cracks that might fill with water.

34. A wrought-iron gate opens into a small courtyard between the front entrance and the sidewalk.

35. A small gate in the foreground of this majestic Live Oak allée is much more welcoming than a fence without a gate.

36. The subtle ironwork of the gate and fence creates visual interest as well as separation from the sidewalk, without obstructing the view of this charming house in Wilmington, NC.

37. A wrought-iron gate in a trellis pattern, topped by by a sunrise motif, is securely hung from sturdy brick piers.

38. In this garden in New Zealand, a gate of twisted metal rods attached to assymetrical curves on top and bottom is hung on wooden piers that disappear into a surrounding hedge rather than a fence or wall.

39. A gate fashioned with three-dimensional fruits and flowers in Savannah, Georgia.

40. A tall gate, a bit narrow to open from the middle, aligns with the front door as well as the curbside stoop once used to ease entrance to a carriage.

41. The delicate filigree of this double iron gate is beautifully enhanced by the brick arch that frames it.

⌘ *Gates Made of Wood* ⌘

The earliest wooden gates were fashioned from thorny branches such as acacia, sandwiched by wood frames that had to be slid out of the way manually.

During the tenth century AD in Japan, *torii* gates appeared at the entrances to sacred shrines. Consisting of two vertical pillars, usually painted vermillion, topped by two black lintels held together by a tie bar, these gates had no door and were not surrounded by a fence. Clearly, they were meant

1. A diminutive double wood gate suits the cottage garden that it encloses and is in keeping with the architecture of the house.
2. A gate in India made in much the same way that gates were made centuries ago.
3. A rustic gate fashioned with natural branches with the bark intact, topped by a vine-covered arbor.

4. This gate in Japan provides a harmonious transition between the outside world and an area reserved for peacefulness.

5. The double gates and their surrounding fence blend several Chippendale patterns, providing a cheerful welcome to this house in Williamsburg, Virginia.

6. Broad double gates are well supported by sturdy hardware secured to substantial brick piers.

to be ceremonial rather than utilitarian: a symbolic entrance to the spiritual world. The earliest *torii* gates were usually made of wood, but some stone examples have been noted. Later ones were made of metal, concrete, and other materials.

The elegantly choreographed tea ceremony emerged in fifteenth- and sixteenth-century Japan as a reaction to the flamboyant lifestyle of the samurai. Zen monks designed the gardens surrounding their teahouses with an eye toward making visitors feel as if they'd stepped out of the worldly realm and into an atmosphere of contemplation. Bamboo fences and gates were used to obscure, reveal, and frame views along the path leading to the teahouse, so as to intensify the experience of moving from one frame of mind to another. The gates were usually very simple and open bamboo lattice latched with a strip of bamboo.

Engravings and prints of European medieval gardens depict wattle fencing with narrow openings and no gates at all. Eventually wood gates were added to secure livestock, and they were hinged with vines or leather so that they could swing or pivot.

Renaissance, baroque and Victorian gardeners preferred metal gates of cast or wrought iron for their wide array of intricate design possibilities and their longevity. The more humble wooden gates tended to be relegated to utilitarian, mainly agricultural purposes—that is, until Chippendale gate design emerged in the eighteenth century. (This ornamental style remains popular today, and we discuss it in more detail in our section on wooden fences.)

The Székely region of Romania offers up rich historic examples of carved oak gates from the eighteenth century, and their heritage stretches back much further. It is said that in the sixteenth century, a tax was levied there, based on the size of one's entrance gate, which was considered an indicator of financial status. This prompted many to destroy their elaborate gates and replace them with smaller ones, although the gates of the nobility were preserved because they paid no taxes. Versions of these impressive gates are still made today in the region, out of oak carved with flowers, vines, geometric figures, or celestial shapes.

As iron hardware became available, making wooden gates more durable and functional, they grew larger, more elaborate, and increasingly fanciful. The cottage garden style and the arts and crafts movement of the late nineteenth and early twentieth centuries revived the use of superbly designed and finely crafted wood gates, and they are still the first choice of many who prefer a more natural and earthy aesthetic.

DESIGN Like fences, the six basic types of metal gates described earlier also exist in wood. They may be designed as close-board, open-board, louvered, or any combination of the three.

Close-board gates provide privacy and sound protection, concealing the view beyond and adding an element of surprise. They can be a simple continuation of the double-faced, paneled, tongue-and-groove, or narrow-gapped construction of the surrounding fence—or they can offer a variation for the sake of visual interest. Wider boards will reduce the number

7. An open gate with a lattice bottom and gothic arches above divides the space with an ornamental embellishment without impeding the view of the garden.

8. This handsomely crafted gate features a smoothly rounded top and spindles that pierce the bracing of the bottom rail.

9. Bentwood slats create a graceful curve for a secondary garden gate.

10. This unusual gate in Williamsburg, Virginia, incorporates sturdy hardware and wood piers carved to continue the cadence of the fence and shed rain and snow. Note the counterweight behind the gate.

11. A double gate with through spindles of alternating height. Note that the stone block below the bottom rail provides support and prevents sagging.

12. A gate within a gate simplifies entry for pedestrians, while providing sufficient clearance for vehicles.

13. An accordion fence may not be particularly attractive but it provides a practical solution when faced with limited space.

14. This open-and-closed-board gate features a raised diamond pattern on the recessed panels below and through spindles piercing the curved upper rail. The adjoining wooden piers are cut to the profile of the surrounding brick wall.

of gaps in the gate, and the added strength of tongue-and-groove construction will help prevent the gate from sagging.

When selecting a garden gate, it is important to consider its function. Is it mainly for privacy and security, or is your primary goal to frame what lies beyond? Whatever its function, the gate must always complement the architecture of the house and other structures on the property.

Because gates form the entry and exit point of the garden, they must be placed with traffic flow in mind. Traditionally, they are equal or lower in height to the adjacent piers, walls,

15. An open double gate with through spindles of alternating heights is separated from a second single gate for pedestrian use.

16. A closed gate of heavy teak with a highly textured surface.

17. Found in Kyoto, Japan, these double gates of silver-gray weathered wood are composed of carved panels of various designs. They are set into well-proportioned wooden posts on natural stone, surrounded by bamboo fencing.

18. Double gates with an open design of diagonal slats.

19. Though light and airy in appearance, these open double gates include four rails for extra strength. Through-pointed top pickets pierce the curved upper rail in ascending height.

20. The louvered top of this large gate with recessed panels allows some ventilation.

21. This very wide, trellis-patterned single gate is topped by forbidding spikes. The hardware seems small for the size of the gate but the stone piers, topped with egg-shaped finials, are substantial.

22. A lovely teak and wrought iron gate at Dumbarton Oaks separates garden rooms.

23

24

25

26

27

28

29

30

23. The Asian influence is obvious here, in the design of the gates and the architecture as well as the way the plants have been pruned.

24. A single gate with a trellis pattern below and pickets above is sure to stay closed, thanks to its heavy counterweight.

25. A cannonball counterweight on a Chippendale gate in Virginia.

26. The hardware on this gate at Dumbarton Oaks is appropriate in both weight and design.

27. It's unfortunate that the extraordinary craftsmanship and hardware here will soon be marred by rust, which is already beginning to develop on the lower strap hinge.

28. Fine-quality wood that ages gracefully and precise woodworking with fine joinery are the best ways to counter the effects of weather.

29. A large-scale gate can be a physical barrier but not a visual one, thanks to a highly contrasting color scheme and proportions that are harmonious with the soaring double porch.

30. This colorful gate in rainy Bamberg, Germany, benefits from its sheltered placement.

or fences. Always keep the style and proportions of the garden in mind when choosing a gate design, since it is the introduction to the garden itself.

As you coordinate your fence and gates, remember that many combinations of styles are viable and attractive, depending on your taste—but be aware that open-board gates allow a view of the vista beyond, while maintaining the sense of a closed environment.

It's best to stain or paint your open-board gates prior to assembly, as the wood is exposed on all four sides. To allow for better wind circulation while preserving privacy, consider using a louvered gate.

For centuries, gates have been designed to close automatically behind visitors. In colonial times, cannonballs were used as counterweights; nowadays, springs are universal and remote controls commonplace.

Hardware should be chosen for its visual interest as well as its functionality—and the two are far from mutually exclusive. You should have no trouble finding well-designed hinges and latches that will add character to your gates. Look around for local craftsmen who can produce unique hardware in custom designs with strength and durability.

CLIMATE AND WEATHERING When using wood in your garden, you must take care to avoid rot. Obviously, wet climates pose a bigger challenge than do dry ones. (More specific information about which types of wood will work best in your particular climate may be found in the "Climate and Weathering" section of our "Fences" chapter.)

Certain woods are also more vulnerable to shrinking, cracking, splitting, or twisting. Premium heartwood cedar is least susceptible to morphing, whereas pressure-treated pine is more susceptible to decaying over time. If you do use pine, make sure to hand select a premium grade. Less dense woods should always be painted or stained to minimize the expansion and contraction that causes twisting, cracking, and swelling.

Metal gate hinges and fasteners should be of high quality—ideally hot-dipped, galvanized, stainless steel, or aluminum—and should be inspected for rust regularly. Sealing and painting hardware will prevent their bleeding into surrounding wood.

INSTALLATION AND MAINTENANCE The average life span of a gate depends on the type of wood you choose, ranging from twenty to twenty-five years for western red cedar to ten to twelve years for spruce. Those constructed of more durable woods—ipe, teak, or red cedar, for example—will last up to three times as long as those of lesser grades, because they are less likely to crack under changing weather conditions.

Prefabricated gates are available in many styles, but it pays to think long term and select one made from high-grade wood and constructed with mortise and tenon joinery, in which a hole, slot, or groove (mortise) in one member is fitted to a projection (tenon) in the other. The frame of the gate should be made of metal with a wood facing, and to further strengthen it, a diagonal brace should connect the top (latch) side to the bottom (hinge) side. All gates should be positioned at least 2 inches above ground level to ensure a smooth swinging motion and avoid contact with the moist earth.

Gates over 4 feet tall need three rails and three hinges. Heavy gates should have posts made of metal pipe clad in wood or masonry, set on a deep footing. A less expensive

31. Hardware can provide visual interest as well as structural support.
32. Oversized strap hinges are particularly practical for the gates of animal enclosures.
33. This sizable gate is firmly supported by three well-placed hinges fastened to substantial brick piers.
34. This low horizontal gate is elegantly reinforced by the arched bracing.
35. A gate in Virginia is strengthened by cross bracing and gently elevated to avoid contact with the ground. It is attached to its piers with obelisk-shaped finials.
36. These sculptural piers are more about form than function: they are considerably larger than necessary to support the gate. Note the latch hardware and gate stop.
37. The overhead cross beam supports this gate well enough that the hinges can be inconspicuous.

alternative involves an overhead cross beam or arch.

As we've mentioned, painting or staining wooden gates helps guard against rot—though this is unnecessary if you select a dense wood such as ipe: stain will not penetrate its fibers anyway. Choose the best wood you can find for your posts, and choose your footings based on local soil conditions and climate. Protect your posts with caps of wood or metal or cut a profile designed to shed water. Be sure that all joints are fitted tightly or otherwise protected from standing water.

Loose hinges or joints are likely to cause your gates to sag and wobble. Try tightening or reinforcing them to fix the problem, but if that doesn't do the trick it may be necessary to take your gate apart, replace some parts, and reassemble it.

Finally, it is advisable to install a gate stop—a solid barrier designed to stop the gate as it closes and reduce impact on the

hinges. This, along with the other precautions and choices we advise, will ensure the longevity and ongoing beauty of a key garden element that is both decorative and utilitarian.

39

38

40

41

38. The hardware and hinges here reflect the Spanish style of a garden originally named El Retiro, in Lake Wales, Florida. The top edge of the gate is protected by metal sheeting. (This garden was created by Michael Bartlett's great-grandfather, C. A. Buck, and is now called Pinewood. It is part of the extended grounds of Bok Tower.)

39. This gate, designed by Michael Bartlett, shows the benefits of thoughtful design followed up by regular maintenance. It is elevated above the ground, secured by a gate stop and regularly painted. The open-and-closed design provides privacy from within while allowing peeks of sculptural interest.

40. Attractive gray-blue stain protects the wood of these large-scale gates while providing a welcome splash of color.

41. A gate with cut-out animal shapes, topped by cast iron, becomes a sculpture.

42. This gate is attached to a brick wall by a wooden half-pier.

42

GAZEBOS

The kiss of the sun for pardon,
The song of the birds for mirth,
One is nearer God's heart in a garden
than anywhere else on earth.
DOROTHY FRANCES GURNEY

1. Beautifully located on the shores of Lake Como, this gazebo at Villa Carlotta is sited on a breezy promontory, providing visitors with magnificent lake and alpine views on three sides.

2. A gazebo set on a hillock overlooks a flower garden. Its slight elevation exposes it to cooling winds.

3. A belvedere peeks over a wall at the end of a peninsula above Germany's Lake Konstanz.

4. The Kiosque de l'Impératrice is a belvedere from which to view the rose collection at Le Bagatelle in Paris. Older photographs show the structure painted brown.

5. A grotto with an architectural façade and rustic interior is built into a hillside with a turf terrace on top.

6. A comfortable summerhouse with a fireplace overlooks a hidden swimming pool.

The term *gazebo* first appeared in English in 1752, in *New Designs for Chinese Gardens* by William Halfpenny. Etymologists have been unable to pinpoint the origin of the word but many believe that Halfpenny invented it himself by adding the Latin suffix *-ebo* ("I shall") to the word *gaze*— a satisfying enough explanation for the name of a structure that enhances the experience of any garden.

Gazebos, belvederes, summerhouses, pavilions—the terms are often used interchangeably—are all freestanding, ornamental, roofed structures. When thoughtfully sited, they provide an airy yet sheltered spot to enjoy pleasing views and the company of friends. Gazebos tend to be open or have lattice walls; belvederes are similar but often set upon a wall or elevated to maximize the perspective. Summerhouses and pavilions are larger and more substantial than gazebos and belvederes and may be designed for year-round use. (Yet another kind of outdoor structure—the grotto—is built into rock rather than freestanding. It resembles the others only in that it is covered on top and open on at least one side.)

Murals on Egyptian tombs dating from 1400 BC depict grand rulers in comfortable pavilions, enjoying the lush paradise gardens they had created as oases in an arid landscape. These pavilions were built of brick veneered in marble or stucco, open on all sides for breezes but covered on the top to shield the sun.

The word belvedere derives from the combination of two Italian words, *bel* ("beautiful") and *vedere* ("to see"). In ancient Rome, the landed gentry built belvederes into the walls along the coastline bordering their summer homes so that they might take advantage of pleasing summer breezes and sea views.

The early Persians, like the ancient Egyptians, constructed pavilions within their gardens. Sometimes these were simple tentlike structures that could be easily moved, their floors cushioned with mats. Others were far more elaborate, permanent edifices made of decoratively carved marble, which might be built over a stream or spring to ensure that the interior spaces remained cool.

As the practice of Buddhism flourished in the Far East, a new kind of pavilion—the pagoda—sprang up on the grounds of temple complexes. (The term pagoda can be traced as far back as the first century AD in China.) These intricately carved wooden structures, painted vermilion, gold, and black, provided a bird's-eye view of the temple grounds, as well as a site for meditation and spiritual retreat.

As Buddhism spread to Japan, the tea ceremony became an important aspect of spiritual practice and teahouses functioned as garden pavilions. In contrast to the pagodas of China, these jewel-like outbuildings were utterly simple but elegant, artfully constructed of wood and bamboo. The entrance to the teahouse was usually so low that guests were forced to bow as they entered—a physical reminder that they were entering a world apart from their mundane preoccupations.

The early pavilions that dotted the European countryside were used as hunting shelters or guardposts. Only occasionally were they created specifically for leisure use—as tranquil places in which to commune with the gods and nature. Gazebos discovered in the ruins of Pompeii seem to have been erected above the upper story of a building to provide a view of the garden or an extended view into the countryside. Beyond creating a picturesque standpoint, these were useful for spotting unwanted visitors, human or animal.

During the Renaissance in Europe, gazebos were most often found in monastery gardens as places for prayer and contemplation. Artificial grottoes that mimicked the caves found along the Italian seacoast were popular as well, sometimes carved out of the earth and sometimes more obviously manmade and meant to look like rock formations. Their interiors

7. One of many outbuildings of varying design in the gardens at Schwetzingen Castle, this one is clearly inspired by a Roman temple.

8. This tensile structure transforms Spanish colonial ruins in Antigua, Guatemala, into a large pavilion.

9. Although of shorter height, the Chinese Tower in the Englischer Garten in Munich is modeled on the Great Pagoda at Kew Gardens in England. Originally built in 1789, it was destroyed during World War II and rebuilt following the original design in 1952.

10. The grotto known as the Mouth of Hell, at Bomarzo in Italy, feautres an inscription that translates as "Abandon all thought, ye who enter."

11. A grotto at the Villa Marlia, near Lucca, Italy, was designed to look like a seaside cavern.

12. Originally referred to as the Temple of Hercules because of its interior decor, this pavilion is now known as the Pantheon at Stourhead. Designed by Henry Flitcroft in 1753, it was sited to be visible from all corners of the garden.

13. At Williamsburg, a pavilion with Chippendale rails now includes panes of glass to protect visitors from chilly winds.

14. This pavilion at Monticello is a faithful reconstruction of the one Thomas Jefferson designed for his leisure use.

15. At Mount Stewart, a pavilion in the Spanish Garden features a tile roof. The hedge of clipped arches, terra-cotta pots and pebble paving reinforce the theme.

provided a cool respite from the relentless Italian sun, and often featured statues and fountains set against walls decorated with seashells, stalactites, and gems.

In the Elizabethan period (1553–1603), gazebos were designed to mimic the architecture of the houses they flanked and were large enough to use for outdoor dining and dancing.

In the eighteenth century, proponents of Britain's landscape movement used gazebos, pavilions, and "follies"—garden buildings distinguished by their extravagant, even eccentric design—to direct the gaze of visitors to the best and most naturalistic views. Follies were most often built in the classical Greek or Roman style, but there are many examples of Moorish, Oriental, and Gothic ones as well. Their primary function was ornamental.

In the late 1700s, European gazebos in the chinoiserie style came into fashion. These openwork structures were made of varying lengths of wood set in a geometric pattern within an open framework. Around the same time in the United States, Thomas Jefferson designed a pavilion for his vegetable garden at Monticello. Still standing, it is 13 feet square and built of brick

in the Palladian style. Surprisingly light and airy, it features double-sash windows similar to those of the main house. A chinoiserie railing surrounds the roof. Jefferson used the pavilion as a tranquil haven in which to read and enjoy the view.

During the second half of the nineteenth century, the successes of the Industrial Revolution led to the rise of America's middle class and a burgeoning culture of consumerism. People had leisure time and were looking for ways to spend it comfortably. Gazebos became status symbols as well as appealing places to relax after a hard day's work. In fact, gazebos and pavilions were de rigueur in Gilded Age gardens large and small. To the wealthy, they served as a reference to the great civilizations across the ocean and were often used for music recitals and literary readings.

During the late nineteenth and early twentieth centuries in America, the porch came to substitute for the gazebo—and by the 1950s, patios and terraces had come into favor for outdoor living. (You'll find more on these in our "Porches, Decks, and Terraces" chapter.) But there is an enduring appeal to a shady outbuilding that is inexpensive to build, a deterrent to

16. A spacious gazebo with clerestory windows of leaded glass.

17. An umbrella-shaped tile roof is quite open but strongly supported by stone columns set on a stone wall.

18. An open wrought-iron gazebo without vines is primarily ornamental, offering only minimal protection from the elements, while providing views of the sky.

19. A shingle-style gazebo built on a sturdy stone foundation.

20. A modern Chinese pavilion in the Asian Collection of the National Arboretum in Washington, DC.

21. A rustic gazebo with shingles and vines.

insects, and a shelter from the weather. In the last few decades, gazebos have come back into vogue in a variety of styles, mostly assembled from prefabricated kits. Beyond the simple shelters they were originally designed to be, they may be had with such accoutrements as fans, fireplaces, outdoor kitchens, built-in light, and sound systems and hot tubs.

DESIGN For the sake of simplicity, we will refer to all garden shelters as gazebos from here on.

The architecture, materials, and embellishments of gazebos meant for small gardens should be in harmony with those of the main residence. In larger gardens, where they can be sited further from the house, they can—and we feel they should—be more idiosyncratic in style, details, and materials.

Gazebos of all sizes and types may be purchased and delivered in prefabricated sections. Many of these are beautifully crafted, they tend to be less expensive than custom construction and they require less installation time.

In plan, gazebos are usually circular, square, hexagonal, or octagonal. They may be roofed in waterproof fabric, wood, vinyl, metal, tile, slate, or thatch with floors of wood, tile, brick, stone, or concrete. Columns and crossbeams may be made of wood, vinyl, metal, concrete, brick, or stone.

Gazebos are usually confined to one story, though some are taller. A lovely example of a towering garden structure is the ten-story pagoda in Kew Gardens, New York. Cupolas (domed roofs) may top gazebos for ventilation and are sometimes designed as roosting places for insect-eating birds. Weathervanes make a nice crowning touch.

Gazebos are an enticement to come out into the garden and enjoy its views, while remaining sheltered from sun, wind,

and rain. The Irish literary titan George Bernard Shaw (1856–1950), designed a gazebo to serve as his writing retreat. It easily revolved on castors, thus allowing him to take advantage of the best cooling breezes and warming sunlight throughout the day.

A gazebo should never seem to dominate the garden vista but should be tucked into the landscape and provide a modicum of privacy within. Ideally, its roof should be partially covered in flowering vines to create a sense of embrace by the

22. The Great Pagoda at Kew Gardens was built in 1762 and stands 163 feet tall. At its center is a stairway of 253 brick steps.

23. The Pigeonnière at Les Quatre Vents in Quebec is an impressive pavilion. Featuring a reflecting pool, its first level opens out to the garden, while its upper level is completely enclosed, handsome, and comfortably appointed.

24. A white clapboard pavilion at Ladew Gardens is tucked away and protected but offers views through its windows on all sides.

25. A gazebo of fine iron wire at the end of a well maintained hedge draws guests into a garden room in Oregon.

26. A gazebo with trellis sides and an elegant oval window.

surrounding environment. In small yards, gazebos should be scaled down and placed subtly near the edge of the garden.

Circular or polygonal gazebos less than 5 feet in diameter cannot comfortably be inhabited by more than two people. Except in the smallest gazebos, fixed benches should be avoided as they are rarely comfortable—moveable (and removable) furniture is best and offers the option of adjusting positions to take advantage of light and breezes. Small tables can be fixed in the center without a problem. In temperate climates the furniture should be removed and put in storage seasonally.

Gazebos should be sited on level ground or set onto a raised platform with stairs. Avoid low-lying areas where water tends to puddle.

CLIMATE AND WEATHERING In cold climates, gazebos are often sited to block northerly winds, retain solar heat, and receive

27. One of a succession of gazebos of extraordinary detail, this structure includes ornate stone columns that support a copper roof topped with floral displays. Within, a fixed table is surrounded by stone seats.

28. Strong wood posts set on a low stone wall enclose panels of trellis and support the slate roof of this gazebo, which includes a fixed table within.
29. The Chinese House at Sanssouci is an extravaganza of rococo and Chinese inspiration. Built between 1755 and 1764 for Frederick the Great, as a place for small social gatherings, its footprint is an unusual trefoil shape.

30. This pavilion can be completely closed to the elements while remaining full of light.
31. The vaulted interior of this open pavilion allows hot air to rise and cooling breezes to blow through.
32. This small gazebo is surrounded by simple paving, but the planters of bougainvillea add a colorful accent to the roofline.

33.

34

35

33. A gazebo designed by Frederick Law Olmsted in Central Park features a roofline designed to support and shed snow.
34. An open gazebo is the focal point of this flower garden.
35. A well-made rustic gazebo is just right for this woodland setting.

maximal exposure to sunlight emanating from the south or west. Larger structures sometimes include a fireplace, which extends the season during which they can be used. Sides are often screened, louvered, or paned to provide protection from wind and mosquitoes.

In hot, arid climates, pavilions can be cooled by fans, running water, or mist systems.

In regions that experience heavy snowfall, the structure and roof of the gazebo must be designed to support the additional weight. The roofline should be strongly pitched to shed snow and ice and adjacent plantings should be able to withstand the force of snow's sliding off the roof (or should be protected with snow boxes).

In windy and hurricane-prone areas, it is important that the gazebo be well anchored. Tall structures and those built on elevated platforms that allow wind to pass below are most susceptible to storm damage.

Most gazebos do not have gutters. In rainy climates, the water splashing from the roof to the earth below may stain and rot a wood structure. With this in mind, it's best to surface the area below the gazebo's drip line with paving material or gravel pitched away from the structure.

INSTALLATION AND MAINTENANCE As with all construction, it is essential to locate underground utilities before breaking ground.

Gazebos should be set on footings or posts that extend below the frost line, to provide stability and extend the life of the structure. Wooden members should be notched together and fasteners galvanized or stainless steel. Cedar, pressure-treated pine, and redwood are common choices of material. (As you consider your options, you might want to consult the information in our section on wooden fences: the principles here are the same.) As for the roof, cedar shingles and metal are the most conventional and practical choices.

Vinyl gazebos have become popular in spite of the fact that they can be 30 percent more expensive than the wooden variety, because they are low-maintenance and do not require painting. Because vinyl boards are now produced with surface texture, they no longer yellow or chalk—though they still have a tendency to scratch and crack (and still look like vinyl up close). As vinyl attracts algae bloom, it should be cleaned regularly with a mild soap-and-water solution. Vinyl gazebos are usually roofed in either cedar, asphalt, or rubber-based shingles.

Because a gazebo is classified as a permanent structure, it must adhere to local building codes. If you don't want to worry about this bit of red tape, a tensile tent structure can be an excellent and inexpensive alternative. Tent structures require no permits, can be festive and are easily relocated or put into storage.

Precast concrete columns are a poor choice of support for your outbuilding. Any texture or color that has been added to them for aesthetic purposes will probably fade, leaving you a look you probably didn't bargain for. What's more, if the columns are cast in sections, the pieces must be joined with epoxy—which never quite matches the color of the concrete as it weathers. As the joint lines reveal themselves, the fakery becomes ever more obvious.

Elaborate metal pavilions have endured for centuries and many good reproductions of the classics are available. It is important that the manufacturer guarantee that no filler compound was applied to any of the joints, though, as these will expand and contract at different rates than the metal and will eventually pop out, causing the exposed metal to rust.

Metal gazebo roofs are usually of sheet metal as well. Some feature fanciful designs, such as interlaced scallop-shaped tiles of lead. Iron gazebos should be powder coated

36. These tentlike structures provide shelter and can be collapsed for easy maintenance.

37. The Music Pavilion at Linderhof is an example of extraordinary detail and craftsmanship.

38. In Sanssouci, a beautiful trellised gazebo reflects the garden's rococo influences.

39. An umbrella-like gazebo is tucked into a corner by a small pond. Patina is developing on the roof and hanging bells sound in the breeze.

40. A cast-iron gazebo on a sidewalk in Charleston provides shelter for a passersby. The rust beginning to show on the roof should be taken care of as soon as possible.

or painted with acrylic enamel paint that is coated with a polyurethane finish—or they may be allowed to rust if that is a look you like.

Well-designed brick and stone gazebos are relatively expensive to build and install but once in, they will seem as if they have always been there and will require minimal maintenance. These usually are roofed with slate or tile.

41. A stone gazebo that shelters birds along with humans appears always to have been in place.
42. A stucco pavilion with a tile roof is timeless and could be found in many locations all over the world.
43. This pavilion is elegant and rustic at the same time, with tree trunks of impressive proportions surrounding panels of cut branches that fit together meticulously to create a chevron pattern.
44. A flamboyant gazebo is set atop a man-made hillock to take advantage of views of the surrounding landscape.

41

42

43

44

LIGHTING

"Light can be gentle, dangerous, dreamlike, bare, living, dead, misty, clear, hot, dark, violet, springlike, falling, straight, sensual, limited, poisonous, calm and soft."

SVEN NYKVIST

Prehistoric man would not have survived had he not harnessed fire for heat and light. It is speculated that the first lamp was fashioned from a shell or concave rock filled with moss that had been saturated with animal fat and set ablaze.

Ramses III reigned as Egypt's pharaoh from 1187 to 1155 BC, and the gifts he bestowed upon its temples were generous. According to surviving records, the following declaration accompanied his gift to the sun temple at Heliopolis: "I give thee the lands with olive trees in the city of On. I have furnished them with gardeners and many men to make ready oil of Egypt for kindling the lamps of thy noble temple."

The Greeks of the seventh century BC produced terra-cotta *lampas* with wicks that burned far brighter and longer than earlier ones, which had been smoky and dangerous. Olive oil, beeswax, and nut oils were the most common fuel sources.

As time progressed, the Greeks and later the Romans modified the design of the lampa until they had devised a covered, shallow dish of gold, silver, bronze, stone, or pottery so efficient that miners were able to strap them to their heads much like modern headlamps without fear of spilling any oil.

During the sixth century AD, the stone lantern was introduced to Japan via Korea in conjunction with the spread of Buddhism. The earliest lanterns were devotional votives

1. A stone lantern with four legs, set low to the ground, is sometimes referred to as *yukimidoro*.
2. Elegant urn-shaped light fixtures sit on a garden wall in Prague. Their classic shape belies the forward-thinking energy conservation in practice: note the compact fluorescent bulbs within.

placed outside of shrines or temples. They were fueled by plant oil and meant to symbolize the light of Buddha bringing wisdom and compassion to humankind. Eventually, candles replaced the oil and the light became functional as well as spiritual. By the sixth century, the stone lantern had become an important part of secular garden design in Japan.

Torches were the most common form of lighting in Europe during the Middle Ages. To make them, branches or sticks of green or wet wood were bundled and bound together, then moss, leaves or rags soaked in pitch, tree sap, or animal fat were attached to the end of the bundle. The result was a bright, portable source of light. Plant oil was preferred over animal fat as fuel because its smell was less objectionable. But in high-altitude areas, such as the Himalayas, or Andes, where plant sources were limited, local butter was used.

Lighting throughout the world didn't advance much until the eighteenth century, when a new device called a central burner was invented. In it, the fuel source was separated from the flame by a hollow tube, allowing greater control of the intensity of light by making it possible to regulate the rate at which the fuel burned. This innovation also greatly reduced the risk of fire. In 1783, a Swiss chemist named Ami Argand produced the first lamp with a central-burner system enclosed by a glass cylinder. This further reduced the chance of fire by eliminating the effect that wind or rain might have on the flame. The central-burner lamp became even more efficient with the introduction of new fuels, including whale oil, coal gas, wood-distilled gas, and kerosene—but even with these improvements, the cost of illumination remained high.

In 1816, Baltimore became the first American city to brighten its streets with gaslights, an innovation that soon spread across the country and throughout Europe. Initially,

3. *Tachi-doros*—stone lanterns set on pillars—can be found near shrines in Japan. This example is at the Chicago Botanic Garden.
4. At the Kasuga Shrine in Nara, Japan, three thousand lanterns known as Kasuga tachi-doro are lit during the annual three-day festival of lanterns called Setsuban.
5. A lantern with two legs, one in water, is called a *kotoji-toro* and signifies a bridge.
6. A copper fixture mounted on a house in Savannah, Georgia, is fueled by gas.

9. "Moonlighting" is about the quality of the light created, not the fixture.

10. A fixture suspended from ironwork connecting the piers that anchor a gate creates an arch as well as providing illumination.

11. A wrought- and cast-iron pole light, though not as old as the railing, complements it.

12. A suspended light fixture made mostly of glass.

13. A pair of extended light fixtures adds to the symmetry of this entryway.

14. The vine growing up this gas pole light connects it to the front garden space.

15. Securely mounted to the wall in two places, this fixture houses a bulb that looks like a pillar candle.

16. A simple wrought iron scroll extends the light from the building.

17. Leaded glass topped by a crown makes this light fixture unique and highly ornamental.

18. A suspended glass orb housed in a framework of worked iron.

7. At Williamsburg, an iron fixture with an incandescent bulb hangs from a hook.

8. Graceful wrought-iron scrolls allow this transparent fixture, lit by an incandescent bulb, to float.

only the wealthy could afford gaslight inside their houses, but by the second half of the century, apartment buildings, modest homes, and factories had adopted it.

In 1879, Thomas Edison perfected the incandescent bulb, ushering in an era when affordable, safe illumination would be available to everyone. Since then, lighting innovations have proliferated, including the carbon arc street lamp (1880), mercury vapor lamp (1901), neon lamp (1911), fluorescent lamp (1927), halogen lamp (1959), and multi-vapor metal halide (1963). The most recent development is the LED or light-emitting diode, which offers peak energy efficiency, the widest range of colors, and the longest life—up to 50,000 hours. (The LED is not a lamp in the conventional sense but a semiconductor diode that converts voltage to light.)

In 1952, John Watson of Houston, Texas, founded Watson Lighting, one of the first outdoor lighting companies. Credited with coining the term moonlighting, he introduced outdoor light to the gardens of the wealthy throughout the United States. Since then, outdoor lighting has become a part of mainstream residential landscape design as more and more people use the garden as an extension of the house.

Incandescent lighting has been a mainstay indoors and out since Edison introduced it—but its days may be numbered for environmental reasons. Beginning in 2012, the United States and United Kingdom began to phase out incandescent bulbs in favor of compact fluorescents designed to fit into the same lamp bases. Although somewhat more harsh in effect—their flickering may even cause headaches and nausea—fluorescents last longer and are considerably more energy efficient. At the same time, LED technology is advancing quickly and promises to be an appealing alternative in the future.

As energy consumption skyrockets and communities flout light standards and grow brighter, concern over "light pollution" increases. The glare can even result in temporary night blindness—a clear hazard to highway drivers. And never mind trying to see the stars if you are within ten miles of a city. Legislators are already attempting to crack down on violations of exterior lighting laws, and in many communities, permits must now be obtained for any major outdoor lighting project.

DESIGN Landscape lighting should be designed for optimal safety, security, and nighttime views. For the best results, do not overlight your garden or create sharply contrasting light levels. Fixtures should be placed, directed, and shielded to light only the intended areas and to avoid glare.

Light fixtures can be mounted on buildings, poles, piers, and trees. They may be suspended from the overhanging arch of an entrance gate or from a portico or porch. Sometimes they are built into steps, walls, bollards, fountains, and swimming pools. And finally, there are in-ground and freestanding fixtures, such as spotlights, wash lights, and path lights.

Fixtures mounted on architectural structures should be both ornamental and functional, and can be mounted flush, extended, or suspended. Select your fixtures to blend harmoniously with the architecture and make sure they are in proper proportion with the structures they will illuminate. Entrance

19. This fluorescent bulb sits within a pole fixture that looks like an incandescent bulb—contradiction in terms?

20. A glass sphere held above a cast-iron pole and mounted on a stone pier.

21. The design of this pole light in Dresden is in keeping with the baroque surroundings.

22. A pair of lights mounted on a rustic locust-log pole.

23. The canopy of a tree is artfully illuminated by unobtrusive light fixtures.

24. Garden lighting can be designed to highlight both trees and architecture.

fixtures, whether single or in pairs, tend to be mounted flush and sharply focused to light a limited area. Extended or suspended "pendant" fixtures provide more light to a larger area and throw interesting profiles and shadows onto adjacent walls and paving. Watch out for glaring downlights over entrances, as these tend to highlight the bald spots, eye bags, and wrinkles of arriving guests!

Decorative pole lighting offers the greatest spread of even light with the least number of fixtures, but can produce the most glare. If you opt for poles, be sure to place most of the lamps at low heights.

Down-lighting from trees creates the closest simulation of moonlight, and can illuminate large areas, while creating interesting branch and leaf silhouettes. Of course, installing bulbs high in trees can be an expensive undertaking, so pay careful attention to the proper placement and angles of the

fixtures and choose the most effective light shrouds.

The lifespan of an exterior light varies by type. Mercury vapor lamps (scheduled to be phased out by 2015 for environmental reasons) last for up to 24,000 hours; metal halide lamps, up to 16,000 hours; MR16 halogen lamps, up to 10,000 hours; and LEDs, up to 50,000 hours.

Ground-level lighting can be flattering as well as dramatic but requires the greatest number of fixtures to ensure even light. These fixtures are more intrusive and can be more vulnerable to damage or jostling by landscapers. If possible, avoid using path lights, as these are invariably intrusive to the daytime garden. Long-running pairs of these will give your garden path the look of a landing strip, and when placed within the lawn, they are bound to be damaged by a mower, shovel, or trimmer.

Proper illumination of steps is your most important practical consideration. Ideally, they should be illuminated from above, as lights placed in stair risers offer only limited illumination and too much contrasting intensity and glare. Flush-mounted wall lights with louvers offer uniform illumination, although in particularly steep stairwells even properly shrouded fixtures can produce glare.

Light fixtures set under water produce dazzling reflections, especially when the water is aerated. They should be made of brass with the most durable seals and watertight connections. Fiber-optic and LED lighting are good options for this purpose in that they use relatively little energy, are easily maintained, and enjoy bulb life of up to 50,000 hours.

Too much contrast in the light levels from one area to the next will cause eye fatigue or even momentary night blindness. Strong interior lighting must be blended with a transition zone near the doors to the darker exterior lighting. Paths and walkways should be evenly illuminated, as hot spots and shadows can be disorienting. The terminus of a path should be lit more intensely to draw visitors in, and all focal points should be blended together with softer illumination to avoid a "spotty" effect. But don't be afraid of shadows; these can add mystery and a sense of depth to the nightscape.

The more intense your lighting scheme, the deeper your garden will appear. Levels of intensity should be layered with the brightest in the background, the least in the middle ground, and a transitional level in between.

When lighting small areas, low-voltage (12-volt) fixtures are the most energy efficient and least expensive to purchase, install, and maintain. Low-voltage lights can be adjusted with a dimmer, but be aware that at lower settings, the light may appear yellow. Fluorescent lights and HID fixtures, such as metal halide, are energy efficient and offer the greatest beam spread but are not easily controlled by dimmers. Halogen lamps, such as the MR16, may be adjusted with a dimmer, but this may decrease lamp life. LED light is usually 12 volts but ranges from 9 to 15 and not all fixtures can be dimmed.

Much residential lighting is a combination of low-voltage and incandescent lighting. Fixtures and bulbs marked with the government-approved Energy Star rating are the most energy efficient.

All outdoor lighting should be separated into zones that can be controlled individually with switches, timers, motion detectors, or photocells. Use of a pressure sensor or motion detector for driveway lighting is a nice way to welcome guests (and alert hosts of their arrival). Many in-ground or well-light fixtures are available for this purpose. Most other outdoor lighting is best controlled by automatic timers and remote controls rather than switches.

25. Can you find the bulb in this highly ornamental, gilded, wall-mounted fixture?
26. This gaslight seems to grow out of the pier.

27. The weathered patina of this copper fixture blends nicely with the color of the wall.

28. A simple but sophisticated triangular fixture mounted on a house.

29. A weathered copper frame houses an interior lantern.

30. A chandelier suspended from a tall ceiling completes this stylish entrance porch.

Exterior light fixtures are made of iron, stainless steel, aluminum, copper, brass, bronze, PVC, and composites. They can be finished with powder coat, anodized, clear sealed, or left to weather to a verdigris finish.

CLIMATE AND WEATHERING Stainless steel, copper, brass, ceramic, and bronze fixtures are durable and the least sensitive to corrosion and pitting. Plastic is also resistant to corrosion but not as impact resistant as other materials and cannot be fitted with high-temperature bulbs.

Light fixtures with many open crevices, poorly drained shields, or inferior lightbulb seals will collect water, causing corrosion and eventually a short circuit. Light fixtures in areas near saltwater should be wiped clean of any salt residue at least once a month to stave off salt corrosion.

Well lights, recessed into the ground, should not be considered for places with a high water table—and should only be used in lawn areas. Be sure to provide a good drainage base of gravel for these, and consider mounting your fixtures on stakes in all planting beds.

High-pressure sodium and incandescent lights set at high intensities may alter the respiration of illuminated plants, as well as their growth and dormancy cycles. Common problems are delayed dormancy in autumn and die-back of new growth in spring. Maples, birch, hornbeam, dogwood, beech, sycamore, locust, and elm are the most sensitive to the effects of intense artificial light. Ash, gingko, crab apple, American holly, spruce, pine, and oak are the least sensitive. Fluorescent, mercury vapor, and metal halide lights are low in the red spectrum and thus will have the least impact on plants. The best way to ensure your plants' welfare is to reduce the intensity of your lights as well as the number of hours they are illuminated.

Finally, keep in mind that light fixtures attract insects. Fixtures should be cleaned regularly to remove bugs as well as fallen leaves and other debris.

INSTALLATION AND MAINTENANCE The design of outdoor lighting is an art as well as a science and we recommend hiring a professional to help. Most lighting designers will provide a list of addresses of properties they have worked on that can be viewed live or in photographs (although photos may not convey the ambience effectively).

Garden lighting can be planned and executed in phases. If you choose this route, you might want to plan ahead by setting 1- or 2-inch PVC conduit pipes under your steps, walls and terraces, with later expansion in mind. When phasing a lighting project, it is best to complete one area at a time rather than installing a few lights here and there, which can make for a spotty effect.

Although garden lighting is typically low voltage, line-voltage (120 volts) is also available but must always be installed by a licensed electrician. Be sure to check your local regulations regarding installation codes. Quite often, line-voltage wires must be placed in a conduit at least 18 inches below ground level. Line-voltage wires should never share a conduit with low-voltage, gas, or water lines.

Lighting trenches should never cross a drip line or the roots of trees. When trenching to trees, consider hand trenching or using an air spade to minimize the cutting of roots, with any returning line set in the same trench to minimize trauma to the tree. If roots must be cut, take pains to cut them cleanly. Magnolia and other soft-wood tree roots are susceptible to root rot and should not be cut when dormant.

The safety of both the installer and the tree must be taken into account when lights are mounted in trees. Insist that whoever installs your lighting is gentle with the bark and avoids using spikes for climbing. If straps are used to affix the lights, they should be expandable or loose enough to allow room for growth. All fixtures should be fastened to junction boxes with stainless-steel screws that can be adjusted as the trunk and branches grow as well. Similarly, wiring should be attached to trees with flexible clips and should be strung loosely to allow for growth. Wire and junction box clips should be checked and adjusted every three years.

Outdoor lighting requires regular maintenance, including the replacement of bulbs, lubrication of sockets and seals, cleaning of lenses, and pruning back of any overhanging foliage. Fixtures mounted high in trees are the most expensive to maintain but the least likely to be damaged or dislodged by landscape crews.

For energy efficiency, there is nothing better than solar lamps—and they produce a pleasingly soft glow. But, for obvious reasons, solar lights are only practicable in sunny climates as they require at least six hours of direct sunlight daily.

It is important to be considerate of your neighbors when lighting your own property. Overlighting will only make your neighbor's property appear darker. The glare from neighboring lights can be eliminated or reduced by lighting the foreground and middle ground areas. Proper aiming and the use of shrouds should ameliorate any unpleasant glare.

Down-lighting from trees, architecture, and walls is most akin to natural sun and moonlight. For this effect, fixtures should be placed at least 30 feet above the ground and directed so as to avoid glare and dark spots. Mounting fixtures on limbs rather than the trunk can minimize stark angles and maximize the spread of light.

Up-lighting trees, walls, sculpture, fountains, and architecture adds depth and drama to the nighttime view, but care should always be taken to ensure that the light is focused directly on the intended object. Trees and sculptures should be up-lit from two or three sides. Side-lighting textured walls,

31. A garden light protected by a terra-cotta casing highlights a highly textured wall.

32. This beautifully embellished lattice fence comes to life in the evening garden with subtly placed and directed uplighting.

33. Understated hardware has been used to attach this elegant light to a warm stucco wall.

34. Ornate ironwork supports this fixture but only partially obscures the wiring.

35. A suspended light is almost flush with the wall.

36. Setting this pole light on a sandstone base helps it blend with the much earlier architecture.

sculpture, or trees with interesting bark will highlight the surfaces and create dramatic shadows.

A thoughtfully and professionally planned lighting scheme can make a garden as lovely by moonlight as by daylight and extend the number of hours you and your friends can enjoy the outdoors.

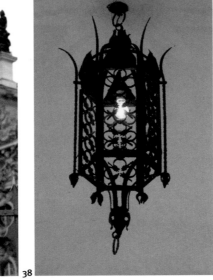

37. Copper patina tops an egg-shaped glass globe set on the stone pillars of a wrought fence. Note that the wiring has been taped to the fence!

38. The ornate ironwork of this fixture helps mute the glare of its bulb.

39. This light extends from an atypical location: the corner of a house.

40. When electrification is difficult, a candle is an easy solution for special occasions.

41. A sculpture tells a story atop a pole light in Ghent, Belgium.

PAVING

When my way is too rough for my feet, or too steep for my strength, I get off it, to some smooth velvet path which fancy has scattered over with rose-buds of delights; and having taken a few turns in it, come back strengthened and refreshed.
LAURENCE STERNE

1. A path through flower borders at Sissinghurst consists of a basket-weave pattern of English bricks set on edge with a central course of running bond bricks designed to draw the eye to the next garden room.
2. Bricks of extended length set on edge in a herringbone pattern at the Alcazar in Spain.

Footpaths and driveways provide essential access to the house and all corners of the garden, and must be designed thoughtfully. Many paving materials are available and should be selected with consideration of climate, cost, and overall aesthetic harmony.

Paving Made of Brick

Fired-clay bricks more than three thousand years old, found in China, were perhaps the earliest form of paving. The ancient Romans used bricks extensively and devised mobile kilns to carry with them into conquered territories so that they could begin rebuilding immediately. With the fall of the Roman Empire, this technology was lost and brick production ceased in European countries other than Italy. Most brick construction elsewhere was made of "mined" and recycled Roman brick.

The fifth chapter of the Book of Exodus is often referred to as "Make Bricks Without Straw," and—whether or not historically accurate—offers insight into the brick-making techniques of ancient times. The exodus of the Israelites from Egypt is thought to have taken place around the fourteenth century BC, after years of slavery and oppression that included the building of many Egyptian monuments. Bricks were considered valuable building blocks but they were difficult to form with only the very fine river clay that was available in the Nile delta. The addition of straw to the clay made for stronger and longer-lasting bricks that dried more quickly. According to Exodus, the captive Israelites were tasked with trampling straw into the clay with their bare feet. When Moses demanded that the pharaoh release his people from bondage, the ruler became enraged, ordering the Israelites to make the same number of bricks without straw—a nearly impossible task that fed their revolutionary spirit.

In the twelfth century, Italian brick was introduced to Germany and formed the basis of the Brick Gothic style of architecture that spread throughout northern Europe. Brick-making was revived in England in the thirteenth century to compensate for the limited availability of stone and timber there. By the time of Henry VIII (1491–1547), handsome brick walks were being laid by skilled masons and many are still in use today.

In the United States, brick-making can be traced back to early-seventeenth-century Virginia as well as New England. Abundant supplies of natural clay in the colonies meant that bricks could be made locally rather than imported from

England. Records have been found describing the construction of a kiln in Salem, Massachusetts, in 1629.

Throughout the eighteenth century, Williamsburg, Virginia, was a center for brick-making and brickwork. Typically, building blocks were fabricated on the construction site by unskilled laborers and then put into place by well-trained and highly skilled bricklayers with a grasp of construction techniques and an eye for design. Eventually brickworks could be found up and down the East Coast in response to an ever increasing demand for building materials.

At the other end of the continent, Mexican and Spanish settlers in what is now California and New Mexico were fabricating adobe bricks throughout the late eighteenth and early nineteenth centuries, Made of mud and straw, these bricks were thinner but larger than today's counterparts. Adobe bricks were eventually superseded by kiln-fired ones,

manufactured at a proliferation of brickyards that sprang up throughout the West to meet growing local demand. As many wooden buildings and settlements succumbed to fire, brick construction was prized as a safer alternative.

During the boom era of the Industrial Revolution in both the United States and the United Kingdom, brick remained popular for both paving and building construction. It was readily available, cost efficient, and relatively easy to use. Although brick did provide a measure of protection from fire, even brick buildings couldn't stand up to the San Francisco earthquake of 1906; their mortar joints crumbled and many toppled to the ground. After that disaster, the use of brick for commercial construction waned, though it remained popular for residences and garden paving.

Today's paving bricks are more durable than ever, thanks to the application of great heat and pressure to the clay. This makes

3. Square bricks in the running bond pattern without mortar joints in Williamsburg, Virginia.

4. Found in Asheville, North Carolina, these glazed bricks with surface texture reduce the risk of slipping.

5. Blue bricks in San Juan, Puerto Rico, echo the color of the nearby sea.

6. A complex pattern of bricks of many sizes and shapes in New Delhi, India.

7. Square bricks alternate with bricks of a different hue set on edge.

them denser, stronger, and more stain resistant than earlier incarnations. More than 1,600 brick types are currently available in the United States, encompassing an extensive range of colors, sizes, patterns, textures, and installation protocols.

DESIGN The size of standard paving bricks varies from country to country. In the United States, bricks meant to be mortared are typically 3⅝ by 7⅝ inches, whereas those intended to be set in sand range from 3¾ by 7½ to 4 by 8 inches. Their thickness ranges from 1 inch for light pedestrian use to 2 inches for heavier use. Paving bricks are solid; building bricks have holes.

A brick's appearance derives from the method of its manufacture. Handmade bricks, prepared individually, show variation from one to another. The irregular edges of machine-molded bricks give them a soft, informal appearance. To create rolled-edge bricks, wheels are literally rolled over their edges to soften them, making them similar in appearance to machine-molded bricks but less expensive. Paper-cut bricks are made by placing paper directly onto the raw material before it is cut, creating a pleasingly irregular surface and soft edges.

Most mass-produced brick is extruded—a process that involves mixing a raw material such as shale or clay with water and forcing the mixture through a die. The extruded column is cut into units of the desired length and then fired. This method produces strong, uniform bricks with crisp edges at a very reasonable price.

Reclaimed bricks instantly provide a weathered look and are eco-friendly, but they may be soft and easily damaged by temperature changes or excessive weight loads.

8

9

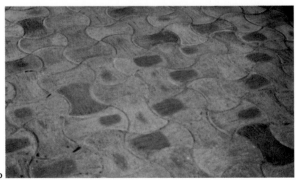

10

8. An ellipse of bricks in the running bond pattern, inlaid with bands of stone slabs.

9. This brick, manufactured in the early twentieth century, is no longer made and is highly sought after for restoration projects.

10. Interlocking brick pavers of abstract shape offer a sense of motion.

11. Rectangular brick pavers with a yellowish hue in Guatemala.
12. Bricks set on a pervious surface in a radial pattern.
13. Oversized brick laid in a herringbone pattern with square bricks forming a restraining edge.
14. Brick set on edge in herringbone panels with a restraining edge of running bond bricks.
15. Interlocking pink-toned brick pavers.
16. The basket-weave pattern.
17. The herringbone pattern.

A brick's natural color is a result of the chemical or mineral content of its raw material. For example, pink hues suggest high iron content and yellow is associated with lime. Firing temperature also affects color; higher temperatures yield darker bricks. Glazed brick, featuring a ceramic coating that glistens, is available in a range of colors—but if its surface is not textured, it will be quite slippery when wet.

Specify a premium-select grade of one or two color ranges of bricks that are proven for your climatic zone, rather than the full range of the manufacturer's varying colors.

Paving bricks are laid in patterns, the most common of which are running bond (sometimes called stretcher bond), herringbone, and basket weave. Herringbone is best for driveways because its interlocking pattern can bear heavy loads without shifting.

All patterns require about the same number of bricks—approximately four and a half to five per square foot. Brick paving should include a border that functions as a restraining edge and visually defines the paved space.

A brick house surrounded by brick walls and paving can be

18. A brick path with square, standard, and cut bricks imaginatively arranged at Lotus Land in California.
19. A brick path in a radial pattern with ribbons of limestone banding.
20. This brick paving is overpowered by its mortar joints.
21. Handmade bricks in a basket-weave pattern at the Taj Mahal.

visually monotonous, but there are ways to ameliorate this. If your house is brick, consider large terra-cotta pavers for the terrace, complemented by small bricks for paths. A good rule of thumb is that horizontal planes should differ in material from vertical planes.

When setting brick on a rigid base, a large number of joints will appear—accounting for as much as 20 percent of the surface area. To avoid a sense that the joints are overpowering the brick, consider tinting the mortar to minimize the contrast between it and the brick itself.

Setting bricks on edge can create a nice effect visually, and the solid feel underfoot is worth the extra material cost.

CLIMATE AND WEATHERING In the era of climate change, storm water management has emerged as an important environmental concern. Surface runoff has been exacerbated by the widespread use of impervious paving materials, sometimes referred to as "habitat for cars." These surfaces shed rainfall, directing it into sewer drains and eventually to streams and rivers—along with surface pollutants it has picked up along the way. Regulatory agencies have proposed a requirement that paved surfaces be water permeable, although this has yet to come into widespread effect yet. Because water can flow through them, these pervious surfaces are also resistant to cracking. It's important to point out, however, that paving materials cannot be porous in freeze-thaw zones. Brick for pedestrian use should have a less than 7 percent absorption rate and a compressive strength of 8,000 pounds per square inch.

In any case, grout joints eventually fail. In the freeze-thaw zone, water saturates the mortar and upon freezing, expands as much as 9 percent. This leads to the fragmentation of the joint. Over time, large areas of paving need to be repointed. Rather than patching as needed, its best to repoint the entire area to maintain a uniform look.

Brick is ideal for southern exposures, as the light-colored varieties don't heat up as much as do many types of stone.

And, because chlorinated water doesn't harm brick, it is an excellent choice for use around swimming pools.

When paving northern exposures, remember that light-colored brick reflects more light and dark-colored brick absorbs it, thus hastening the melting of snow.

In shaded and/or moist areas, moss and algae can flourish, turning your brick surface into a slipping hazard. Brick is best employed in areas that are well drained and receive at least four hours of direct sunlight per day.

Do not use rock salt to remove snow or ice from brick as it can encourage efflorescence. Nonsodium melting agents are best, and are more beneficial to the environment as well. Snowplows should be used with caution and should ideally be equipped with rubber-edged blades.

INSTALLATION AND MAINTENANCE Choose brick that can withstand your particular climatic conditions and is certified for pedestrian and light traffic (ASTM Class SX). To protect it during installation, the exposed face can be lightly waxed and then steam cleaned upon completion.

It is essential to provide good surface and subsurface drainage. The subgrade base must be stripped of all organic matter, compacted and always pitched away from any structures. The base must also be compacted and well drained. Finished terrace and path levels must pitch away from all structures with a gradient of at least ⅛ inch per horizontal foot (¼ inch in the freeze-thaw belt). Make sure that most joints run parallel to the slope of the paved area.

All paving not mortared to a concrete base must have a restraining edge to prevent drifting. Select edging made from the same material as the paving or, alternatively, ¼-inch steel edging that is powder coated to match it.

All rigid-set paving must be pointed with mortar within four hours of setting so that the pointing mortar bonds with the

22. Oversized bricks in the stacked bond pattern (also called jack-on-jack) create a pool terrace in Guatemala.

23. The effect of efflorescence on brick paving.

24. A variation on the basket-weave pattern with a restraining edge of bricks set on edge.

setting bed mortar. Consider adding masonry tint to the pointing mortar to reduce contrast and give the appearance of age.

Bricks should be dampened before setting and pointing so they won't absorb moisture from the mortar and cause it to dry too quickly. Never set or point paving material in extreme temperatures or when expecting rain within 24 hours. When setting rigid paving in full sun, cover completed work with tents, boards, or wet burlap. (Stay away from solid tarps and plastic as they tend to heat up.) Allow the area to cure for 24 hours before admitting pedestrian traffic; a week, for vehicles. As environmentally correct as it is, pervious paving does permit airborne weed seeds to sprout in its joints. Preemergent weed killers, such as glyphosate, will take care of the problem, but it is best to avoid herbicides as much as possible. Instead, try Burnout—an organic weed killer with a vinegar and lemon juice base. Highly acidic vinegar alone will kill some weeds, or you might want to try a landscaping torch or boiling water. As a truly organic resort, seed the gaps with

a desirable species that will overtake the weeds. In the shade, moss can be encouraged to grow between your pavers by increasing the acidity of the soil.

When paving with brick near trees and large shrubs or incorporating new plants into a paving scheme, consider the root system of the species. Those with surface roots will eventually dislodge the paving.

If you are really bothered by the look of joints, which should be a uniform $3/8$ inch wide, it's possible to find brick paving set on a flexible base with no mortar joints at all. In this case, expansion joints should match the brick and be located adjacent to edge restraints.

Most cleaning can be done with water and a stiff brush; avoid harsh cleaning chemicals and acids that can change the color of brick. Unsightly algae buildup can be removed with a dilute solution of bleach and water—but use extreme caution when applying it near plants.

25. A torch can be used to kill weeds growing between pavers—or around any paved surface.

26. This running bond pattern at Dumbarton Oaks is punctuated by ovals.

27. Strips of turf break up a basket-weave brick path and turn it into panels of brick stepping stones in this garden designed by Michael Bartlett.

28. This path of bricks set on edge, found in the town of Verre, Holland, resembles the one at the Alcazar in Spain.

1. A fine gravel path meanders through the herbaceous borders at Castle Drogo in England, designed by Sir Edwin Lutyens. The path's curves oblige visitors to take their time, while its surface blends harmoniously with the overflowing plants.

2. Gravel raked meticulously to represent the water of a flowing stream.

3. A wave pattern has been painstakingly formed and maintained in this *kare sansui* garden. The care required is considered a form of meditation.

Paving Made of Gravel

Gravel has been used for centuries to provide a firm and dry surface for terraces, paths, and roads. The ancient Romans are known for their complex system of roads, many of which were gravel. These were designated *via glareata* "graveled road") or *sternendae*, meaning "to be strewn."

In early Japanese gardens, gravel was spread as a symbol of purity. Later, during the Muromachi period (1333–1568),

gravel stood in for water in Japanese "dry landscape" gardens known as *kare sansui*. Patterns raked into the gravel were meant as abstract representations of waves or flow.

Natural gravel deposits can be found along riverbanks and seashores, in flood plains, and in mountainous regions at the bottom of steep cliffs. In areas lacking natural gravel, limestone, sandstone, or basalt are blasted to create crushed stone

4. Seashells and gravel are bonded to form textured paving in Savannah, Georgia.
5. Gravel intricately raked into a checkerboard pattern.
6. Light gray gravel is the perfect complement to this flower border in Italy.
7. In London, a split aggregate gravel driveway provides a textural setting in the same hue as the house.
8. Finely ground red sandstone provides a vibrant foreground for the Rashtrapati Bhawan (formerly the Viceroy's House) designed by Sir Edwin Lutyens in New Delhi.

or aggregate. Crushed oyster, scallop, and other seashells have long been used in place of pebbles in seaside locations.

An inexpensive paving material to begin with, gravel has become even more cost effective in recent years, with the use of recycled materials. For example, glass gravel in a broad range of colors has been created from tumbled, recycled glass. Other recycled options include crushed hard-nut shells, rubber from shredded tires (but beware of lingering chemicals that should not be in contact with plants), tumbled broken pottery, or terra-cotta and crushed seashells.

Advantages of gravel include the fact that it is porous and costs little to install. Bear in mind, however, that it requires frequent raking and top-dressing to maintain a satisfactory surface. If possible, look into using locally produced gravel rather than importing it from afar.

DESIGN Extremely versatile and available in many sizes and colors, gravel may be found in a diverse range of gardens all over the world. Pea gravel is sandy-colored and round; its white counterpart is made of quartzite. It has a tendency to roll around, but generates little dust. Creek rock is smooth and often gray. Lava rock is ochre in color and very lightweight. Crushed stone varies in color and has a tendency to be dusty. To provide visual interest, gravel is sometimes "seeded" with darker and lighter pebbles to create a "salt-and-pepper" effect.

Gravel pieces are usually less than ¾ inch in diameter, as smaller stones tend to make the space feel more expansive. Angular gravel is best for surface compaction, while round, smooth gravel is apt to scatter. With that in mind, driveways call for gravel of a larger dimension, whereas smaller stones

9. A pea gravel driveway with turf edging at Mount Vernon.

10. Pea gravel with a granite restraining edge at Dumbarton Oaks.

11. A pea gravel driveway with cobblestone banding, designed by Michael Bartlett in McLean, Virginia.

12. A flagstone path gives way to crushed stone of a complementary color.

13. Crushed gray gravel provides a pleasing contrast to the brick of the house and repeats the color of the flagstone cap on the wall. It also speeds snowmelt in this Connecticut garden.

14. Light-colored pea gravel brightens the space between two buildings.

work best for paths and terraces.

For all of its virtues, gravel is not the most user-friendly choice. Walking on it can be perilous, particularly in high-heeled shoes. And it provides a temptation for the young at heart who find throwing stones amusing.

Consider banding all gravel paving with a stone border of the same or complementary material. This will add visual interest and, when properly installed, help contain the gravel.

CLIMATE AND WEATHERING In arid climates, gravel is sometimes used as a substitute for groundcover or lawn, eliminating the need for irrigation, weeding, or other maintenance. In rainy climates, its pervious nature provides excellent drainage.

For northern exposures, select light-colored gravel to increase reflected light or, in colder climates, dark-colored gravel for quicker snowmelt. Southern exposures call for light-colored gravel, which tends to stay cool—although glare can sometimes be a problem.

Gravel roads can be a good option in freeze-thaw climates because they don't crack or develop potholes and are therefore much less expensive to maintain. But snowplows should not be used on gravel as they will scatter it and can damage edging. Instead, environmentally safe melting agents or sand are best.

In dry periods, some gravel roads can be dusty.

INSTALLATION AND MAINTENANCE The key to proper gravel installation is to begin with the correct blend of gravel, sand and silt-clay. Gravel roads should be set below the surrounding grade level so that they blend in and appear more natural. The base for a driveway should be stripped of all organic material, excavated for a 6- to 8-inch base of crushed stone ¼ inch to 3 inches in diameter, compacted and well drained. To keep weeds down, a fabric filter is advisable.

The surface course should consist of a 2- to 4-inch layer of compacted ¼-inch gravel. After the base is compacted, a thin layer of the surface material should be compacted and embedded into the base course, followed by the remainder of the surface gravel.

Because gravel paving is not mortared to a concrete base, it needs a restraining edge to prevent drifting. This should be made of a material that contrasts with or complements the gravel: stone, brick or ¼-inch powder-coated steel. All masonry edgings should have a footing below the frost line.

Periodically, gravel paving must be checked for ruts and then raked and replenished as necessary. To take care of weeds, apply a preemergent weed killer or spot treat as necessary. Alternatives to chemical herbicides include spot-burning weeds with garden torches or spraying them with highly acidic vinegar.

15

16

18

19

17

15. A narrow gravel drive sunk below grade level and lined with stone.

16. Raked sandstone gravel is bordered by flagstone and granite cobbles at Chanticleer in Pennsylvania.

17. A pea gravel terrace with 1/4-inch powder coated steel edging designed in response to the energy of two active spaniels.

18. Metal banding helps contain gravel while adding pattern and visual interest.

19. Squares and rectangles of metal sit on top of gravel, providing contrast in texture and form.

⊗ *Pattern and Mosaic Paving* ⊗

Although the earliest mosaic paving may have been strictly utilitarian—meant only to provide a durable surface and keep dust and mud at bay—it wasn't long before it was elevated to an art form.

The Greeks began to fashion *tesserae*, small, hand-prepared pieces of stone, tile, or glass, and use them to create precise and elaborate designs in a broad range of color. The superb mosaics that can still be found at Pompeii in Italy and elsewhere were very likely the work of Greek mosaic artists. The Romans took up the use of mosaics and the art spread as the Roman Empire expanded, although the designs often lacked the sophistication of those found in Italy.

1. Colorful tiles in a star pattern work as a compass in the gardens at Cà d'Zan in Florida.

2. Stones set on edge create hexagons and diamonds that are filled with river rocks and pieces of terra-cotta to create a complex pattern.

3. Pebbles imported from China are laid on edge at the Dr. Sun Yat Sen Garden in Vancouver.

4. Pebbles of the same color but different shapes form interesting patterns.

5. Mosaics in a courtyard garden at a Roman settlement at Empuries, in Spain.

6. In Udaipur, India, this optically complex pattern employs geometric shapes of varying colors.
7. Diamond shapes made from marble set into sandstone at the Taj Mahal.

8. Pebbles arranged to create a bouquet of flowers in Vence, France.
9. Inlaid stones of different colors creates a beautifully detailed chevron pattern.

10. Interlocking geometric and irregular shapes merge to create new patterns in Jaipur, India.
11. Mosaics designed by Gaudi form fantastic paving, walls, and sculptures throughout the Parque Güell in Barcelona.

Zillij, a highly intricate form of mosaic tilework, featuring interlocking abstract and geometric shapes, developed in Moorish Spain around the eighth century and grew more sophisticated as time passed. Its forms and colors possess iconographic significance in the Islamic tradition and, by religious fiat, never include representational figures. The art of *zillij* is still practiced today and can be found in paving, walls, fountains, tables, and so forth. Motifs similar to the geometric patterns of *zillij* have also found their way into the stone artistry of India and other countries influenced by Islamic culture.

For generations, the art of mosaics was largely abandoned—until the nineteenth century, when the ability to mass-produce tiles coincided with a revival of interest in historic building techniques. The burgeoning upper class took up the fashion of incorporating mosaics into their homes and public buildings.

Adherents of the turn-of-the-century art nouveau movement were particularly passionate about the use of mosaics. The work of Antonio Gaudi (1852–1926) provides a dramatic example, particularly his work with architect and mosaic artist Josep Jujol at Parque Güell in Barcelona. A series of terraces overlooking the city are enlivened by whimsical mosaic forms fashioned out of recycled shards of broken ceramic tiles and pottery.

Gaudi may be the patron saint of excess but he is the exception that proves the rule. Generally, restraint on the part of both designer and mason should be the watchword in the art of mosaics, with contrast among colors and sizes of tiles kept to a minimum.

12. A variety of salvaged materials produces a unique pattern in Barcelona.
13. Cow vertebrae and split-face indigenous stone in Antigua, Guatemala.
14. Granite setts in contrasting colors create a diamond design in Prague.
15. Slabs of marble of different colors laid in a herringbone pattern drift into the sea at Cà d'Zan in Florida.

16. Raised panels of mosaic pebble work flank the main path through this garden room at Lotus Land.
17. Pebbles imported from Mexico and arranged in the design of a wheat sheaf feature the motto of the Bliss family, creators of Dumbarton Oaks: Quod severis metes ("As ye sow, so shall ye reap").

DESIGN Almost any durable material that does not corrode or rust can be set within the paving; stainless-steel washers, glass and porcelain fragments, fossils—even cow vertebrae and other bones—are just a few examples of elements you can introduce into a mosaic. But, before you get carried away, do your research. Look at examples, think about the effect you want and always have a sample made.

Pattern pavings tend to be more formal and symmetrical near the house and less exacting as they move further into the garden. Keep in mind that your design should be "readable" from all directions and views.

When designing mosaic or pattern pavement that will not be walked on frequently, you face fewer constraints. Since you don't have to worry about footing, you can use more exotic materials and create more interesting compositions. Of course, most exterior paving is meant for pedestrians and must therefore be skid resistant.

There are many joints in mosaic and pattern paving, so care must be taken to use a mortar color harmonious with the composition.

CLIMATE AND WEATHERING It's important that all of the materials you plan to use—including the mortar—are suitable for your climate. All grout joints will eventually fail, but a skilled mason knows that the best way to forestall the inevitable is to lay down an excellent subsurface, ensure proper drainage, and run the predominate number of joints parallel to the slope of the paved area. Consider using porous joints or caulk that is particularly resistant to temperature shifts.

It's not surprising that exterior mosaics last longer in climates with minimal freeze-thaw cycles or in protected locations. Rock salt and snowplows are anathema to mosaic or pattern paving and should never be used. Make do with sand or another safe substitute and always use extreme care.

INSTALLATION AND MAINTENANCE Mosaic and pattern pavements require precise masonry work, so if more than one mason is working on a project, it is best if they shift positions regularly so that their individual styles of setting blend together.

Tesserae, or pattern components, can be set in situ, using a wet cement base or by first applying the tesserae to panels or mesh and then setting them in place. For complicated patterns, consider a full-scale drawing template.

As in brick and stone paving, all mosaic paving not mortared to a concrete base must include a restraining edge to prevent drifting. Consider stone or brick edging that complements the general field color or ¼-inch steel edging powder coated to blend with the paving.

The most aesthetically pleasing mosaics use materials in a variety of sizes and shapes, fit together with minimal gaps and no long-running joint lines. The quality of the setting and pointing of mortar joints is critical in mosaic paving because there are so many joint lines. Unless the area can be protected from the elements, work only when the temperatures are mild, the wind is minimal and there is no rain in the forecast. All joints must be pointed with mortar within four hours of their initial setting.

18. Beach pebbles set in sand in Cordoba, Spain.
19. Granite sets zigzag through the streets in Dresden, Germany.
20. Terra cotta and river rock create a checkerboard pattern in Antigua, Guatemala.
21. Alternating black and white rectangles of marble in Jodhpur, India.
22. Multiple colors of inlaid marble create a refined pattern at the Lake Palace in Udaipur, India.

18

19

20

21

22

❋ *Paving Made of Stone* ❋

Stone paving was first used for building roads. In 1994, research geologists James Harrell and Thomas Bown discovered what is thought to be the world's oldest paved road, dating back to somewhere around 2500 BC. Located 43 miles from Cairo, the road—7 ½ miles long, 6 ½ feet wide and constructed of sandstone, limestone, and petrified wood—is thought to have linked a basalt quarry to the site of the pyramids at Giza.

Every civilization that followed constructed stone roads. In Crete, a road more than 30 miles long and 12 feet wide traversed mountains over 4,300 feet high. It was made of sandstone bound together by clay-gypsum mortar.

The most extensive early road system was begun by the Romans circa 500 BC. In *De Architectura*, the Roman architect Vitruvius (born around 80 BC) elaborated on proper construction of roads and pedestrian pavement, stating that roads should be surfaced with square or polygonal stones or lava, whereas pavement was to be surfaced with marble or mosaic. With the collapse of the Roman Empire, advances in road and pavement construction stagnated in Europe until the ninth century, when the Moors began to create sophisticated stone work in southern Spain. In addition to roads, they laid beautifully paved courtyards of alabaster and marble in palaces and gardens.

During the Middle Ages, stonework was highly prized and confined to functional areas, such as the cloisters of monasteries. Highly skilled masons used material from local quarries to design and install patterns of surprising intricacy, considering they had only one type of stone at their disposal.

During the Renaissance, gardens included extensive terrace areas connected by paths paved in stone—some of it was quarried and some "liberated" from important Roman sites, such as Hadrian's villa. From that time forward, garden design has always included paved areas, the material varying from country

1. Irregular pieces of marble are painstakingly set together in a masterful example of "crazy paving" found in Jaipur, India.
2. Granite cobblestone setts are banded by large slabs of granite in the gardens at Insel Mainau in Germany.
3. In Japan, large granite rocks create stepping stones through the uneven surface created by the smaller ones.
4. Indiana limestone is laid in an ingenious pattern at Dumbarton Oaks.

5. Granite stones set in moss create a checkerboard pattern at Tofuku-ji in Japan.
6. This overall radial pattern uses stones set on edge within bands of irregularly sized rectangles.
7. Granite and limestone squares and rectangles in a random pattern.
8. Crazy pattern stones set in mortar with alternating patterns of turf give a path rhythm at the Jardins d'Eyrignac.
9. Irregular blocks of granite are interspersed with cobblestones in Frankfurt, Germany.

to country, based on what was available locally.

In the last thirty years in the United States, the fashion has run toward extensive terraces in an astonishing array of materials. Imported stone is the norm and surprisingly affordable, but the cost of quality installation and masonry can be prohibitive, beginning with the cutting of the material. To keep this cost under control, its best to plan ahead (and very precisely) and have the stone cut to your specifications at the quarry before shipping.

If possible, use stone that is mined locally. Local stone holds within it the story of your regional geology, and is bound to respond well to your specific climatic conditions. That said, if yours is a small, urban garden, don't be afraid to take some chances with more exotic materials and patterns.

In large, public areas, stamped concrete reinforced with wire mesh is the most cost effective and durable. It is best to dye the stamped concrete to give it a more finished look, despite the fact that it will eventually effloresce and fade.

Concrete paving, particularly when dyed and/or textured, should be used judiciously in private gardens, however, as its repeating patterns can look artificial. Aggregate-concrete pavement, with a predominance of aggregate, or bush-hammered concrete are good substitutes.

New paving materials that incorporate recycled glass to add texture and color can be an interesting option. Many successful designs combine concrete with bands of natural materials such as brick, stone or stone chips embedded in the concrete.

DESIGN Natural stone is rarely uniform in color or texture, so don't be surprised if you find variations from piece to piece. When ordering, specify premium-select grade of one color range rather than mixing the full variety of the stone's colors. (For example, flagstone comes in ranges of green, blue, red, and buff; choose one and stick with it.) Reject stones that are marred by iron oxide staining or excessive flaking. If you want to avoid the process of rejecting unusable stones, you can select them yourself at the quarry for an additional charge.

10. In South Carolina, a concrete driveway features a central band inlaid with bricks and large pebbles.
11. Concrete stepping stones create a path at the Lodhi Gardens in New Delhi.
12. The introduction of brick adds color and pattern to a path of concrete pavers.
13. Stamped concrete pavers in Antigua, Guatemala.
14. Squares of concrete with two different surface treatments form a checkerboard pattern.
15. A compass inscribed on Pennsylvania flagstone.
16. Asphalt squares alternate with concrete and all are banded in brick to form this outdoor chess board in Bad Ragaz, Switzerland.

17. Impressive slabs of granite are surrounded by a sea of setts in Berlin, Germany.

18. Large irregular flagstones set in turf diminish in size as they near the side entrance to a house in Far Hills, New Jersey.

19. Random rectangular granite paving can be found in Sylvia's Garden at Newby Hall in England.

20. Crazy pattern stones separate as they give way to lawn.

21. Sandstone slabs are staggered as they move through the Gandhi Memorial Garden in New Delhi.

If the stones you select have striations, setting them in an opposing fashion will create a butterfly pattern that many find pleasing.

Avoid stones smaller than 12 by 18 inches. The larger your paving stones, the fewer joint lines you'll have and the larger your paved area will appear—but don't get carried away; stone is incredibly heavy and two strong masons can barely handle a 36 by 60 by 3-inch flagstone.

Almost all stone surfaces can be textured. Finishes can be thermal, honed, riven, hammered, punched, chiseled, combed, and more. Honed stone is slippery when wet, whereas punched stone holds water. Smooth, natural cleft and thermal finishes make for a natural look that is skid resistant and less likely to puddle.

Reclaimed stone has beautiful patina but is rarely uniform in size or thickness, making it difficult to create a level surface. Using it requires more cutting, so expect to incur higher installation expense.

In "crazy pattern" paving, stones of irregular size and shape appear to interlock as in a jigsaw puzzle. Although the result is delightfully intricate, fitting irregular stones together while maintaining a regular joint size requires the effort of a highly skilled mason. If necessary, groundcover can be planted in crevices to camouflage stones that don't quite fit together. This is preferable to filling the gaps with small stone "chinks" that can look amateurish. In any pallet of random stone, some won't fit the puzzle, so it is wise to assemble the stones at the quarry to avoid excessive waste.

CLIMATE AND WEATHERING Porous paving materials are unsuitable in freeze-thaw zones. To test a paver's porosity, place a sample in a bucket of water. If it bubbles for more than a minute, it is too porous to withstand freezing and should not be used. If you are importing your paving material, be certain that it has been used in climatic zones similar to your own.

Most stone types have been tested for temperature. For example, Pennsylvania flagstone has a surface temperature of 135°F in full sunlight, while limestone, sandstone, and brick remain at 95 to 97°F. Dark stones can become uncomfortably hot to the touch and in a southern exposure, they have a tendency to expand, cup, and separate from a concrete base. To avoid this, consider setting them on a nonrigid base and using a sand grout.

For northern exposures, select light-colored stone to increase reflected light. These will brighten dark areas and reflect heat but might cause glare in very sunny locations. Like dark-colored gravel, dark stone retains heat and hastens snowmelt.

Most stones with natural clefts tend to flake in freeze-thaw climates. Those with an absorption rate of less than 7 percent are the most durable. In moist climates, choose a finish that won't become slippery when wet or icy in freezing temperatures.

Limestone is susceptible to damage by acid rain and other atmospheric pollution and is very difficult to clean effectively. Acids will mar its surface and must never be used. Granite, on the other hand, is one of the most durable stones available and is rarely affected by climate or weathering—but it is very expensive and can be especially slick when wet.

As with brick paving, snow and ice should be removed from stone with care.

INSTALLATION AND MAINTENANCE Stone paving set on a rigid base can be as little as 1 inch thick, whereas a permeable base requires at least 2 inches.

Joint widths should be uniform throughout the paved area

22. Rectilinear pieces of granite are in-filled with unfinished stones in Kyoto.
23. Granite slabs set willy-nilly in the moss guide visitors toward a pond in Japan.
24. Random rectangular slabs of granite wind through the trees and moss at Saiho-ji in Kyoto.
25. A path of random rectangular coquina stone at Pinewood in Florida.

and a straight joint line should rarely exceed 6 feet in length or cross at a perpendicular (so that four corners line up). Joints between split-edge stones, regardless of pattern, should be at least ½ inch wide, whereas the joints between sawn-edge stones should be a minimum of a ¼ inch wide. All brick joints should be ⅜ inch wide. Expansion joints should be located adjacent to all edge restraints and long or wide areas of paving. Caulking with epoxy is an art and should only be done by someone with experience.

Limestone, sandstone and other porous stones stain easily —red wine is lethal. You might be tempted to use sealant, but we discourage it, as it requires continued reapplication and provides only limited stain protection. To clean porous stone, use a low-pressure power washer with diluted Murphy's Oil Soap. Be sure to soak and spray the leaves of all plants in the surrounding area first.

Never use limestone near chlorinated pools or hot tubs as the chemical will etch and stain the stone. Additional advice on keeping your stone paving functional and attractive can be found in the section on maintaining brick paving.

26

27

28

29

26. Reflective stones set in turf are cool to bare feet, making them a good choice next to a swimming pool.

27. Rectangles and squares of concrete alternate with river rock set with mortar in Ranakpur, India.

28. Contrasting colors and shapes can alleviate the monotony of an expansive concrete surface.

29. Alternating bands of turf and concrete create a pervious surface that keeps stormwater runoff under control.

PERGOLAS

Sitting in your garden is a feat to be worked at with unflagging determination and single-mindedness—for what gardener worth his salt sits down? I am deeply committed to sitting in the garden.

MIRABEL OSLER

1. A pergola supporting grape vines is tucked into the corner of a lush garden in Buffalo, New York. Square columns support a pair of lintels topped with rafters featuring decoratively carved tails.
2. The Roman settlement in Merida, Spain, dates to 25 BC and includes monumental architecture as well as compact urban villas. This spacious pergola with columns of Roman brick was restored in the mid-twentieth century, along with much of the site.
3. At Dumbarton Oaks, grapes are ripening on the vine atop the strong, natural wood rafters of this freestanding pergola.

As described in "The Gardens and Ponds of Ancient Egypt" by Jimmy Dunn, "It was not uncommon to find a pergola bordering the main alley along the axis. Fruit trees have their leaves and branches supported on the trelliswork of pergolas." The term pergola comes from the Latin word pergula, which means "projecting roof." Vitruvius described a pergola in the garden at Villa of Diomedes in Pompeii as "a platform over which vines were trained on a wooden framework supported by six columns of stucco."

Pergolas have been a part of Italian gardens throughout the centuries. After the fall of the Roman Empire, many that had been built in cloisters and residential gardens were maintained, cherished for the fruits always within reach of their shady and inviting interiors. One of the original pergolas in the gardens of the fifteenth-century Villa del Trebbio near Florence still stands today.

In 1494, the army of Charles VIII of France invaded Italy and the French troops were fascinated by the gardens they found there. Many of the design elements they admired—including pergolas—found their way into French gardens both modest and grandiose. The pergola's function remained the same: to provide shelter and support fruiting plants.

It was much later in garden history that pergolas came to support ornamental vines. Edwin Lutyens and Gertrude Jekyll,

British garden designers at the turn of the twentieth century, were influential in reinterpreting the Mediterranean pergola to suit the local climate and gardening style. They began to use the small shelters as connectors, focal points, terrace shading, architectural ornament, and frames for garden vistas. Because they were masters at both design and construction, their work endures and will likely survive for generations to come.

Pergolas became de rigueur in the United States around the turn of the century as well, in "Golden Age" gardens inspired by the grand ones of Europe. In recent years, pergolas have become increasingly popular again, as people look for new ways to inhabit and enjoy their gardens and punctuate open spaces with inviting shelter. Today's lush structures combine architectural and horticultural elements, while providing gardeners with an opportunity to experiment with a variety of climbing plants.

DESIGN Pergola columns may be made of wood, metal, concrete, brick, stone, or fiberglass. The rafters are usually wood but can be metal, and may feature a decorative profile on their ends.

Gertrude Jekyll wrote that the minimum height clearance of a pergola should be 7 feet 2 inches to prevent "scratching

4. Gertrude Jekyll and Edwin Lutyens designed and built this pergola at Hestercombe in England between 1904 and 1908. Alternating square and round columns of local stone support rafters crafted with a subtle arch meant to lift the eye.

5. A semicircular pergola with trellis walls at Dumbarton Oaks has a teak-topped bench built into its interior perimeter wall. Originally, the pergola overlooked a tennis court—but the site was repurposed as the Pebble Garden in 1959.

6. At Harkness Park in Connecticut, originally named Eolia, Beatrix Farrand designed additions to the gardens in the 1920s, including this pergola overlooking Long Island Sound.

7. The curved Rose Pergola at Bodnant in Wales boasts superbly crafted rafters and columns of trelliswork.

8. Stone columns support rafters completely hidden by a profusion of roses under-planted with Alchemilla mollis (lady's mantle).

9. In a private garden in Far Hills, New Jersey, a pergola built against a wall features round brick pillars supporting rafters smothered with wisteria.

10. A pergola of soaring height towers above a lower one in this unusual configuration at Arlington National Cemetery in Virginia. The two structures are differentiated by their column designs but united by the wisteria that covers them.

11. The Roseraie in Le Bagatelle in Paris uses pergolas to display some of the climbing roses in its vast collection.

12. A wide path is embraced by a pergola with stone columns, as wisteria pods dangle overhead.

13. The ruins of a courtyard have been transformed into a pergola in Antigua, Guatemala.

14. A pergola attached to a house in McLean, Virginia shelters an outdoor dining area.

a bald head." Today's bald heads sit on taller frames, so an 8-foot minimum might be safer. Columns should be overproportioned so they appear strong enough to support the mass of overhanging vegetation.

In selecting materials and design details for a pergola, you will naturally want to take the style of the house into consideration and keep the two structures harmonious. This is particularly true in one-vista gardens but is always a good idea.

The design of a pergola should defer to the forces of nature and the exigencies of maintenance and time. Keep in mind that the structure will ultimately be covered with plants, so design details may be hidden and structural repair and maintenance will be tricky.

Which climbing plants should you choose? This is your most significant decision. Some plants you love might not be suitable, yet others you haven't even considered might work beautifully. Gertrude Jekyll believed that roses were unacceptable for use in pergolas because their blooms reach upward and only the naked, thorny stems can be seen at eye level. But recent advances in rose hybridization make it possible to find varieties that might work. Plants whose flowers naturally hang down, such as laburnum, can be lovely but require greater height clearance.

The clever gardener avoids vines and fruits that attract stinging bees and other bothersome insects. These include grape vines, clematis, and Lonicera (honeysuckle). Be aware, also, that vines such as Chinese wisteria, Oriental bittersweet, and Japanese honeysuckle are extremely invasive, making them unsuitable for the confines of a pergola. Finally, consider the growth habit of the vine. Some are light and airy; others appear heavy and dense. Choose one that is likely to produce the effect you want.

Do not expect your lawn to thrive under the pergola unless you make a special effort to ensure that the soil is well drained and there is ample filtered sunlight.

Just like gazebos, sheds, and other outbuildings, pergolas are classified as permanent structures and must adhere to local building codes. Be sure to secure the necessary permits before beginning construction.

CLIMATE AND WEATHERING Because pergolas are meant to serve as a shelter from the sun, there is little point in situating them on the north side of a house, where they will remain cool, damp and uninviting while blocking precious light from reaching the rooms on that side.

In cold climates, pergolas are often built against a wall that blocks northerly winds, retains solar heat, and faces the sun to the south or west. Thus situated, a pergola might incorporate a fireplace to encourage use on chilly evenings and extend the season when it can be used.

In temperate, sunny climates, the crossbeams should be set perpendicular to the building with a minimum of overhang. This filters the sun's rays and allows for maximum solar exposure in the winter.

In arid areas with intense light and low winter sun angles, crossbeams are best set parallel to the building with a deep overhang and additional crossing purloins on top.

Lutyens and Jekyll expressed a preference for stone or brick columns topped by simple wooden rafters and purloins. They believed that freestanding pergolas should curve slightly upward in the middle to counterbalance the appearance of sagging created by overhanging plants.

INSTALLATION AND MAINTENANCE Take care in selecting the type of wood for your pergola, considering only the densest grades of decay-resistant hardwood, such as oak. Soft woods, such as redwood, cypress, cedar, pine, and fir, are rot resistant but make attractive nesting sites for carpenter bees. Pressure-treated wood is less susceptible to bees and boring insects but is infused with toxic chemicals and has a tendency to twist and crack. While painting wood can guard against carpenter bees,

it is not recommended for pergolas because maintenance is difficult once the structure is engulfed in plants. Painting among vines rarely produces satisfactory results and is time and labor intensive. Your best bet is to choose a hardwood and stain or seal it before construction.

If you do end up with an infestation, spray the tunnel with pyrethins or spread a layer of boric acid powder, using a syringe that will puff the powder into the hole. Wait 24 hours and seal the hole with a dowel, wood putty, or other suitable material. If you'd prefer to use chemical insecticides, follow the manufacturer's instructions for application.

Because the failure of a pergola post will bring the whole structure down, wooden posts are a risky choice. Columns of stone, metal, or brick are more durable. Fiberglass columns can be made to resemble stone in look and feel by painting them and filling them with sand. Precast concrete columns will fade and chip and inevitably look like concrete. What's more, when they are cast in sections, their epoxy joints tend to vary in color from the concrete, making it even more obvious that the columns are only masquerading as stone.

Allow iron to oxidize or powder coat it prior to construc-

15. Rectangular brick columns placed on a diagonal form this unusual pergola.
16. A pergola of rustic wooden columns, flanked by congenial topiary on one side, spans over path and into a flowerbed.
17. A circular pergola marks the entrance to Schloss Branitz while a linear one, referred to in earlier times as "the Italian wall," follows the facade of the house and connects it to an outbuilding which now houses a museum.

tion. It can then be waxed periodically to prevent rust stains from forming on the paving below.

All wood members should be notched together. Any fasteners should be galvanized or, preferably, made of stainless steel. The exposed topside of the crossbeams and purloins can be protected from weathering by capping them with lead or zinc sheathing.

Rot sets in when wooden posts come in contact with moist soil, so it is important to place them on stone sets with footings that extend below the frost line.

Many plants are adversely affected by contact with copper or freshly cut black walnut trees. These materials should be used with caution in the construction of a pergola.

18

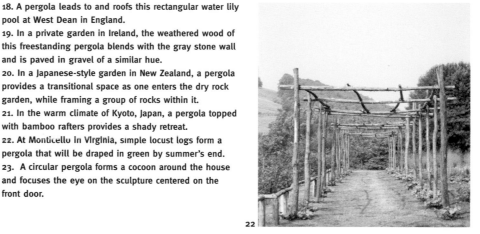

22

18. A pergola leads to and roofs this rectangular water lily pool at **West Dean** in England.
19. In a private garden in **Ireland**, the weathered wood of this freestanding pergola blends with the gray stone wall and is paved in gravel of a similar hue.
20. In a Japanese-style garden in **New Zealand**, a pergola provides a transitional space as one enters the dry rock garden, while framing a group of rocks within it.
21. In the warm climate of Kyoto, **Japan**, a pergola topped with bamboo rafters provides a shady retreat.
22. At **Monticello** in Virginia, simple locust logs form a pergola that will be draped in green by summer's end.
23. A circular pergola forms a cocoon around the house and focuses the eye on the sculpture centered on the front door.

19

21

20

23

PLANTERS

Flowers are beautiful hieroglyphics of nature, with which she indicates how much she loves us.
WOLFGANG VON GOETHE

1. A sequence of colorful glazed planters set on a balustrade of stone piers draws the eye to a view of Lake Konstanz, at Insel Mainau, and frames the garden below.
2. An enormous olive oil jar becomes a sculptural accent. These graceful vessels have been used as planters for centuries and their form has inspired countless reproductions.
3. At home among the fascinating sculptures at the Parco dei Mostri is a planter in the form of a carved stone bust. It nurtures thriving but untamed greenery.
4. Stone boxes planted with laurels punctuate the terrace balustrade at Mount Stewart in Northern Ireland. The nearby flow of the Gulf Stream has created a microclimate favorable to plants that would normally be unsuited to the latitude.

Accounts of the Festival of Adonia in ancient Greece provide one of the first descriptions of the use of garden planters. The participants in this unique ritual were women mourning the death of Adonis, Greek god of beauty and desire. They planted the seeds of fast-growing plants, such as lettuce and fennel, in pots and placed them around a sculpture of Adonis in a hot sunny location, usually on a rooftop. Beautiful seedlings would quickly sprout and grow but would soon wither and die, reminding everyone of the short life of the handsome god—and of all of us.

The Egyptians were avid users of container gardening. According to paintings and hieroglyphics adorning the pyramids and other ancient ruins, they were among the earliest cultures to decorate planters, fill them with their prized plants, and place them in gardens. Aside from their beauty, the planters also conserved valuable water in Egypt's desert climate.

In his *Naturalis Historia*, written in the first century AD, Pliny the Elder expressed his appreciation for the window boxes of Rome, which he called "miniature gardens that bring the country into the city." Potted plants could also be found in Pompeii and Herculaneum, around pools and along colonnades. The Moors planted trees and shrubs in containers to fill their outdoor living spaces and courtyards with foliage and fragrance.

In Japan, plant containers have always been used primarily for bonsai, the carefully cultivated miniature plants and trees that have been an art form in Japanese culture for over a thousand years. The art of training bonsai is considered a kind of meditation: the creation of "heaven and earth in one container." Bonsai planters are shallow in depth (to help contain roots) and simple in design. American bonsai master and Cistercian monk Father Paul Bourne (1908–1995) cautioned, "If one notices the pot before the tree, there is lack of harmony."

The Italian Renaissance brought elaborate interpretations of the once simple clay pot or jar. During Greece's occupation of Italy, between the seventh and second century BC, Greek vessels and their Roman counterparts were used for practical purposes, such as food, oil, and wine storage, but were eventually adapted for use as plant containers. These ancient designs and shapes were studied by Renaissance craftsmen who copied them in carved stone. The planters were placed symmetrically on balustrades or walls of the same stone and filled with citrus, jasmine, and oleander.

In sixteenth-century Europe, as interest in horticulture burgeoned, people began to import tender plants, such as pineapples and citrus from tropical climates. They were kept in containers so that they could be moved to glass houses during the winter months. The weight of the larger plants proved problematic but a solution was soon devised: wood containers. Louis XIV, desiring to have access to fresh oranges year round, kept hundreds of orange trees in wooden "Versailles boxes." The hinged sides of these decorative containers were removable and inside was a metal liner with brackets into which strong wooden slats could be placed, allowing two men a sturdy grip for transporting the trees to the Orangerie. The Versailles box, along with the sophisticated pruning and fertilizing techniques of Louis's gardeners, made it possible for the monarch to fulfill his wish for a constant supply of the fresh citrus fruits.

During the same period, vases *d'Anduze* were being made in southern France. These planters, whose shape was inspired by Renaissance Italian stone planters, were made from the very dense local red clay and glazed in subtle shades of green, brown, and honey yellow. Many were quite large so as to accommodate citrus trees, but they were porous and not meant to be left in the garden during freezing temperatures. Extant examples show evidence of

5. The courtyard of the Orangerie at Versailles is home to a multitude of citrus trees and palms. It was built between 1684 and 1686 with the specific purpose of protecting some one thousand trees during the cold season.

6. An example of the patented Versailles box currently made by Les Jardins du Roi Soleil. This authorized reproduction is true to the original design of LeNôtre but with added structural reinforcement.

7. This interpretation of the Versailles box is fixed in place and lacks the hinges necessary to disengage its sides.

8. An understated, custom-made lead planter with rolled edges.

9. This elegant lead box with a stamped design and restrained planting is slightly elevated on a stone base and set off by the backdrop of a rich clipped hedge.

10. A distressed reproduction of a vase d'Anduze, designed around the same time as the Versailles box.

11

11. This acanthus-patterned planter may be made of Coade stone. Set on a pedestal, it marks the spot of a barely noticeable exit in the hedges at Sissinghurst.

cracking and flaking of the glaze from weathering.

The first lead planters originated in England in the seventeenth century and were often gilded or painted to resemble stone, their surfaces stamped with patterns and emblems. Planters of lead proved durable and inexpensive to produce, but were too heavy to be moved and offered no insulation for plants' roots in extreme temperatures.

In 1769, Eleanor Coade opened a factory in London that produced garden and architectural ornaments made of what she called Coade stone. These decorative elements, molded in the designs of local master stone carvers, were made from a substance of Mrs. Coade's own invention, a combination of china clay, sand, and finely ground stoneware fired at high temperature. Unlike terracotta, Coade Stone was frost-proof, more durable than stone, impervious to pollution, and could be mass produced. This ingenious form of artificial stone was as beautiful as the real thing—but when Eleanor Coade died, she took her secret recipe to the grave. Several companies in England believe they have re-created it, but the original molds are long gone.

In the early nineteenth century, cast-iron planters came into fashion, prized for their durability, detail, and relatively low cost. These planters were usually painted—black or white—to seal and protect them from inevitable exposure to water.

Plant containers in a wide variety of new forms and substances have entered the market in recent years, driven by demand from those living with limited garden space. Planters make it possible to create an inviting garden on a balcony, front stoop, porch, terrace, or deck. Most contemporary models are lightweight and keep roots well insulated. Some come with self-watering reservoirs, lighting, or even stereo speakers.

DESIGN Plant containers should be harmonious with their surroundings—ideally in a style and material that blends with the house or adjacent walls. If painted or stained, they should match or blend with exterior house colors.

12. The entrance court at Sissinghurst includes sculptural cast-iron planters set on wooden blocks to preserve their iron bases. They are subtly planted with Helichrysum petiolatum, sometimes called Trailing Dusty Miller.

13. This ornate cast iron planter made in two pieces, urn and pedestal, features a pattern of morning glory vines. It was made by J. L. Mott Iron Works in the late nineteenth century.

14. A wall planter in the shape of a tree holds many small terra cotta pots, making it lovely but difficult to maintain.

15. "BioHavens" such as the ones floating on the Avon River in Christchurch, New Zealand, are porous mats made from recycled plastic, meant to mimic naturally occurring floating wetlands. They have many practical environmental applications in addition to their ornamental interest.

16. A corrugated aluminum drainage pipe has been repurposed as a large planter at the North Carolina Arboretum.

17. Stacked and staggered concrete pipes create a wall of planters of varying heights at Insel Mainau.

18. Terra cotta planters blend well with the paving, stucco and tile work at Pinewood in Florida.

21. Rectangular boxes with applied lattice are laden with fuchsia blossoms. Note the liner just barely visible above the upper lip; this will add years to their life!

22. A grouping of terra-cotta pots in an assortment of styles fills the corner of a terrace.

23. An unusual glazed antique hedgehog planter, meant for crocuses, carries a Wedgewood stamp beneath.

24. This highly ornamented cast-iron planter, made by the Kramer Brothers Foundry circa 1900, is made in two pieces. The urn, encircled by vines with handles in the shape of winged griffins, sits on a pedestal base of ogee design.

25. The trailing plants seem to favor the indentations formed by the scalloped edges of this planter.

26. A copper vat used as a planter by Vita Sackville-West at Sissinghurst is adorned only by its lovely patina. It marks the intersection of two paths.

19. The circular shape of these oversized barrels complements the curve of the walls, and their size provides ample space for roots.

20. The tapered sides of this wooden planter, made in Pennsylvania circa 1910, are decorated with raised diamond patterns that anchor helpful handles. It is planted simply with evergreen boxwood.

Wood is lightweight, a good insulator, and affordable. You'll find many nicely designed wooden planters on the market. Their drawback is that unless they are made of the most durable wood and include carefully crafted joints and a protective liner, they may not last long.

Terra-cotta is the most widely used material for plant containers, as well as the least expensive. Planters of this ubiquitous substance insulate plants' root systems and aren't too heavy. The downside here is that, due to their porosity, they tend to freeze and crack in temperate climates and dry out quickly, requiring more frequent watering. An impenetrable glaze applied to the outside slows down the rate of evaporation.

Precast limestone planters are porous as well, but keep roots cool and moist and are more durable than terra-cotta in temperate winters. Just be sure to provide proper drainage for best results.

Metal (lead or cast iron) containers are expensive, heavy, and do not insulate root systems. On the plus side, they are durable, safeguard against rapid evaporation, and come in many designs and sizes. Because they have the thinnest walls, they also provide more space for roots to spread out.

27. A piece of granite is chiseled and hollowed out to become a small but rugged planter strong enough to withstand winter temperatures in Buffalo, New York.

28. A horizontal planter made of local coral stone acts as a finial on a pier of the same stone at Vizcaya in Florida.

29. An elegant cast-iron urn, circa 1860, is guarded by owls originally used in barns to scare off unwanted vermin.

30. Raised trough planters are often used to provide the proper growing conditions for plants with special drainage or pH requirements.

31. Undulating planters thread their way through the courtyard at Casa Popenoe in Antigua, Guatemala.

32. The walls of these planter beds in a Vancouver public garden invite visitors to sit amidst the flowers.

33. Shallow stone trays on carved pedestals at Vaux-le-Vicomte echo the low hedges surrounding them.

Stone is the most expensive and heaviest of all planter materials. It is a great insulator and, if impervious, will not freeze and crack even in the coldest temperatures. Most stone ages well, though some, such as limestone, tend to stain and are sensitive to the acidity of pollution.

Concrete makes a poor choice for planters as these tend to crack or chip and the dyes used on them typically fade. They are also quite heavy, making them difficult to move.

High-quality resin and fiberglass planters are readily available, lightweight, and inexpensive. Both resin and fiberglass fade in sunlight and scratch easily, but these problems can be ameliorated with a coat of bronze or lead paint. You might be disappointed in their hollow feel, so examine them in person before making a purchase.

Before you select a shape for your planters, map out exactly where you intend to place them. Round and polygonal containers do not fit comfortably into square corners.

Planters can be large enough to provide seating and an adequate root zone for a small tree or small enough to enliven a niche or decorate a tabletop. The larger varieties are sometimes used in place of bollards, as security barriers or deterrents to foot or vehicular traffic.

Although it can provide a pleasing look, you might want to avoid grouping many small pots together in place of one large one. Smaller vessels require more maintenance; in temperate or arid climates, any pot less than nine inches in diameter will dry out quickly and may even need watering more than once a day in hot weather.

Window boxes and planters should not form the primary focus of your garden or the terminus of a main walk, unless you select plants that perform throughout the seasons and are committed to year-round maintenance. Well planted and maintained window boxes and planters do add an aspect of interest to a multifaceted garden.

Most container plants have fibrous roots that reach no deeper than 18 inches. It's best to avoid containers that are vertical in shape or narrow at the top, as they may appear top heavy even with low plantings.

Gertrude Jekyll, master gardener of early-twentieth-century Europe, believed that plants should be embedded within gardens pots and all. She herself cultivated "spare" flowering plants in pots and when there was a dull gap in her flowerbeds, she would plant them intact in that space. In that way, she could maintain a fully blooming, fragrant border throughout the season.

No matter what size, shape, or material you select, it is crucial for both the plant and container that all planters provide excellent drainage.

CLIMATE AND WEATHERING In temperate climates, porous stone and terra-cotta planters should be emptied and stored before winter sets in. Wood, concrete, stone, metal, and fiberglass planters that are to be left out should be strong enough to withstand the pressure from expanding frozen soil. If you live in a cold or rainy climate, use soil that drains quickly to guard against root rot.

The roots of most container plants are stressed by extreme temperature changes. Direct sunlight heats up the soil in containers faster and earlier in the spring and stays warmer later in the fall, so container plants tend to come into leaf and flower earlier than garden plants. This makes them susceptible to damage from a late spring frost and apt to produce tender, new growth late in the season that may be nipped by frost. Containers should be set on pedestal feet and not directly on paving, which can get excessively hot. Larger planters provide more insulation for roots and dark-colored planters absorb solar heat, whereas lighter ones reflect it.

Fluctuations in moisture level are also highly stressful to container plants. Repeated wilting because of insufficient water or, conversely, waterlogging from sitting in a saucer full of rainwater for extended periods, will lead to disease, insect problems, and possibly root rot.

In rooftop gardens and other exposed or windy locations, tall plantings should be secured with stakes. If you intend to keep your containers in place permanently, your plant choices are somewhat limited as they must be capable of surviving in a hardiness zone two zones colder than your own. Broadleaf evergreens should be protected from the harsh winter winds and sun that will hit them when surrounding trees have dropped their leaves. These elements may dry them out and cause "winter burn." It is also essential to keep the roots watered through the winter, or until they have frozen solid. The root mass of a broadleaf evergreen is often larger than its leaf spread so it is important to note that the container must be large enough to accommodate the roots.

43

44

34. A cast-iron plant stand hosts a proliferation of geraniums in glazed pots. The glazing slows the evaporation of water.

35. A three-tiered wood plant stand holds a grouping of rectangular planters large enough to retain moisture.

36. A wood plant stand with sweeping legs is elegant, but the small terra-cotta pots it contains require constant monitoring of moisture levels—even when planted with the somewhat drought-tolerant thyme.

37. Terra cotta oil jars filled with bougainvillea mark each pier of the stone balustrade surrounding a terrace at Cà d'Zan in Florida.

38. A copper window box blends with the color of the surrounding brick wall but seems a bit skimpy in proportion.

39. An elegant, elliptical window box suspended from a low sill blends nicely with the surrounding architectural details.

40. Wire mesh inserts connect cast-iron ribs, creating visual interest as well as providing excellent drainage for this planter set on stone paving.

41. This unusual aluminum planter in the shape of a chaise longue is in direct contact with the paving, making drainage difficult. The elevated planters that surround it have no such problem.

42. This copper cache pot (literally, "pot hider") shows a fine level of craftsmanship in the detailed interweaving of the metal.

43. Rows of terra-cotta pots hold lemon trees and hibiscus that can be overwintered indoors, protecting both the plants and pots from freezing temperatures.

44. Plants placed in containers of good size with generous walls can be watered less frequently.

45. Cast-iron feet protect this planter from rust, improve its drainage and protect the plants from heat absorbed by the surrounding paving.

46. Wooden planters require high-quality liners that protect the wood and allow for proper drainage.

45

46

INSTALLATION AND MAINTENANCE To reduce the need for maintenance, stain rather than paint wooden planters. Metal containers should be undercoated with zinc and powder coated. Never consider sealing stone, concrete, or porous materials unless you intend to remove all plantings and soil and reseal the containers every three to seven years, depending on the material.

Unlined planters made of nondense and nonresistant wood have a very limited life span. Never put edible plants in wooden containers that have been treated with an unstable preservative or made of pressure-treated lumber because of the possible leaching of chemicals.

Terra-cotta pots should be soaked before planting to prevent the material from drawing moisture out of the soil and stressing the new transplants.

Many planters have built-in reservoirs that allow for self-watering. If you have no intention of moving your planters, irrigation, lighting, and speaker sleeves may be inserted through their bottoms. (The latter are fairly high-tech options and are used mainly in commercial settings.)

Consider irrigating your planters with collected rainwater rather than chlorinated tap water. Fertilizing with either slow-release granules or liquid fertilizer is essential, but too much fertilizer can result in spindly, nonflowering growth and increased salt concentrations in the soil. Water- and nutrient-releasing polymers may be mixed into the soil to decrease the need for watering, but these additives should not be used with edible plants. In any case, the soil in all planters should be changed at least once every three years.

47

48

49

50

47. Each of these modest-sized terra-cotta pots is attached to a fairly inconspicuous irrigation system, making it feasible to maintain the health of such a large configuration of container plants.
48. Sturdy wrought-iron handles make it easier to move these tender plants to shelter for the winter.
49. A carved stone wellhead has been repurposed as a planter and forms the focal point of this terrace.
50. Second-story window boxes lift the eye and increase the sense of space in a narrow corridor between two houses in Antwerp, Belgium.

PORCHES, DECKS & TERRACES

The best kind of friend is the kind you can sit on a porch swing with, never say a word,
then walk away feeling like it was the best conversation that you ever had.

ANONYMOUS

1. Built in the 1860s, Ohinetahi is an example of New Zealand's colonial architecture. Made of local Oamaru sandstone, it features a wraparound porch with square posts connected by brackets to create a series of arches. Sadly, Ohinetahi was severely damaged during the earthquakes that struck the island in 2010 and 2011 and is in the process of a reconstruction that will preserve the porch design but modify the upper portions of the house.
2. Corinthian columns surrounding the canal in the Canopus at Hadrian's Villa lead to the recessed Serapeum and define its space as an outdoor room.

Well-designed porches, porticoes, verandas, balconies, loggias, decks, terraces, and patios provide graceful transitions from indoors to outdoors. As an extension of the interior living space, they offer many of the comforts of the house, while providing access to the open-air pleasures of the garden. Over the centuries, the basic configuration of porches and porticoes has remained constant but their function and placement have varied from public use in conjunction with civic buildings and churches to strictly private use as part of home gardens.

The words *porch* and *portico* both derive from the Latin *porticus*, a roofed entryway supported by columns. In Greece, porticoes were meeting places for philosophers, often richly ornamented additions to temples, such as the Porch of the Maidens at the Erechteum (built 421–26 BC). In this ingenious structure, beautifully sculpted figures of young women served as columns that camouflaged a supporting beam.

In ancient Rome, porches or porticoes provided shelter for markets and served as civic gathering places. In today's terminology, the number of columns supporting the portico is noted in its name: a tetrastyle portico has four columns, for example; a hexastyle has six, and so on.

J. C. Cooper (1905–1999), an expert on the Taoist gardens of China, wrote that during the time of the Six Dynasties (AD 220–589), "The garden was for all seasons with their changing moods and colors, flowers and trees, so an open gallery was necessary for enjoyment in the heat of summer or the cold of winter and became an integral part of the scenery. Even in winter, one sat out in the open gallery to admire the beauties of the snow and to watch the budding of the almond and plum blossom. A portable brazier of glowing charcoal kept one warm and a large brazier was used to melt the snow to make tea."

During the Middle Ages, cathedrals included porches that served as vestibules where worshippers could gather to socialize before or after a service. Although porches were not widely incorporated into residential architecture in Europe until later, European explorers traveling in Africa in the fifteenth and sixteenth centuries encountered dwellings built above ground level, with roofed extensions open on three sides. These shel-tered exterior spaces provided welcome relief from hot interiors for performing domestic chores or relaxing, while offering protection from rain and crawling creatures.

As European settlements were established in places with warm climates, such as the islands of the Caribbean, the porch became an increasingly popular architectural element, incorporated into various styles of colonial architecture.

American architecture has been influenced by a myriad of cultures and this can be seen clearly in the evolution of the porch. Not surprisingly, the feature first caught on in the Deep South. During the eighteenth century, southern architecture included features of the French Colonial style left over from the French occupation of Louisiana, as well as African vernacular from the influx and efforts of the slave population, who built porches onto their simple shacks in an attempt to seek comfort during the long, stifling summers.

The front porch became ubiquitous in nineteenth-century American residential architecture, which was an explosion of

3. Shisen-do was built in 1641 by poet Ishikawa Jozan (1583–1672) as a retreat. The tatami room was for contemplative viewing of the garden.

4. This tea house, built in 1640 at Ritsurin Koen in Takamatsu, Japan, provides a view to a *karesansui* (dry garden) filled with many symbols awaiting personal interpretation.

5. An amalgamation of neoclassical details and groupings of Corinthian columns create multiple grand porches in an architectural tradition upheld throughout the Deep South.

6

6. This small-scale porch is large enough to provide some seating in addition to a protected entryway to the house.

styles including Greek Revival, Gothic Revival, Italianate, Second Empire, and Queen Anne. The introduction of the balloon frame in the 1830s (a new form of house construction that replaced heavy beams and mortise-and-tenon joints with precut 2- by 4-inch studs and nails) made porch construction easier, cheaper, and less dependent on skilled carpenters. Innovation and diversity followed and an amazing array of front porch details appeared: square or round columns, an assortment of rooflines, simple Y brackets or ornate filigree, railings with turned posts or plain slats, double porches with an upper-story view, and more.

In practice, the front porch became the locus of "social networking," families and neighbors gathering to enjoy one another's company and exchange news and gossip. The "front porch campaign" proved a successful political strategy for President William McKinley, during his run for the presidency in 1896. Rather than traveling the country making speeches,

he received the public on his own porch in Canton, Ohio. It is said that about 750,000 people visited over the course of his campaign.

Situating a porch at the front of the house was practical as well as convivial, since the "necessaries" of living, including the outhouse, laundry, and perhaps a few chickens tended to occupy the backyard. In the 1930s, as indoor plumbing and washing machines became more common, the popularity of the front porch declined. Families spent more time in the backyard, which offered privacy and greenspace. House design became more horizontal, featuring fewer embellishments, and front porches grew rare in new construction. But design is a cyclical thing. By the late twentieth century, porches had regained a foothold as people renovated lovely older homes or built new ones based on historic designs. The pleasures of porch-sitting were rediscovered and cherished anew.

The veranda has its roots in India, its name deriving from

the Hindustani word *baranda*: an outside space under a roof, partially enclosed by a railing and usually attached to a small one- to one-and-a-half-story house. The *baranda* was a common feature of Bengali residential architecture of India, described by Portuguese explorers as early as the sixteenth century. British colonists referred to these Bengali houses as "bungle houses" and eventually they became known as bungalows. In the United States, the bungalow became a popular iteration of the arts and crafts style (1890–1910), sometimes referred to as the Craftsman style. These small houses were a reaction to the ornate Victorian aesthetic. Simple in design, with little ornamentation, they were tastefully built, using natural, high-quality materials. The veranda was a signature feature, usually set low to the ground, generous in proportion, and shaded by overhanging eaves. The bungalow style became so popular that by 1908, Sears and a few other companies were offering mail-order kits for the homes. By 1920, dozens of other companies had joined them. Bungalows remain popular today and can be found in historic neighborhoods throughout the United States.

A balcony (the word comes from the Italian *balco*, meaning "scaffold") is a platform with a railing projecting from an upper story of a building. Evidence indicates that these have been around since the dawn of the common era: Pliny the Younger (AD 61-112) wrote in one of his many letters that he was thrilled to be able to fish from the balcony of his villa on Lake Como. In cities, balconies may take the place of gardens, providing a small space in which to enjoy the outdoors and, depending on the exposure, grow some plants. They may be fully or partly recessed, offering shade and shelter from wind and rain.

Loggias are covered, open-air spaces usually found along the side of a building rather than adjacent to a main entrance. The term is thought to have derived from the medieval Latin

7. The roof of this bungalow gracefully extends to cover an elegantly conceived porch set on two widely spaced piers connected by a segmental arch.

8. A balcony at Pinewood Estate in Lake Wales, Florida, features a wrought-iron railing and tile floor carefully secured to the wall by flowing iron scrollwork.

9. On a narrow street in St. German, Puerto Rico, a series of covered balconies provide room to enjoy the outdoors, rain or shine.

10. A curved balcony encircles the corner of a building in Prague. Its stone floor is supported by fluted brackets with carved apples and its wrought iron railing is a mixture of exuberant scrolls painted a warm red in contrast to the stone.

11. The central, pedimented structure of Palladio's Villa Maser is flanked by symmetrical wings fronted with loggias. The wings once housed barchessas used for storing grain and making wine. They terminated in elevated dovecotes surfaced with sundials.

word *laubia*, meaning "arbor or porch." Loggias are conceived as gallery-like outdoor sitting rooms, very architectural in design, often featuring a succession of arches. Occasionally, they are accessible only from the interior of the building. In another letter from Lake Como, Pliny the Younger described views framed by the columns of loggias.

Renaissance architect Andrea Palladio (1508–1580) is well known for his classical building designs that often featured loggias.

The first decks were found on ships, the word coming from the fifteenth-century Middle Dutch word *dec*. It referred to a wooden roof that enclosed the lower compartments of a vessel and could be walked upon. The term soon evolved to signify open, roofless structures typically enclosed by a railing and usually adjoining a building.

In Japan, decks have been used for centuries to provide a place to view the garden or as a quiet place for meditation, sometimes overhanging a pond.

In his book *Gardens Are for People* (1955), landscape architect Thomas D. Church (1907–1978) writes: "Balconies of 18th-century European design were forerunners and porches and verandas of the Victorian Era were ancestors. But porches have become detached from houses and wander freely around the property—sometimes jutting out over it, providing the illusion of level spaciousness on a sloping hillside lot. These wandering porches, which, in one form or another, have been with us for a long time, are now what we call decks." "Tommy" Church designed many decks with the purpose of safeguarding the existing environment—trees, sand dunes, and other natural features. The popularity of the deck has risen steadily since the publication of his landmark book.

Porches, decks, and verandas are sometimes referred to as terraces, although they can be described more precisely as paved or planted areas adjoining a house. The term derives from the Old Latin word *terracea*, meaning "earthen" or "beaten earth."

An important part of formal garden design dating back at

12

14

16

12. A deck hovers over a pond, connecting visitors to the water.

13. A beautifully crafted deck with floorboards of contrasting sizes and elegant low rails is positioned for viewing near and distant views.

14. Thomas Jefferson designed L-shaped wood "terraces" with chinoiserie railings to provide a seamless flow from the interior of Monticello to the outdoors, a feature quite unique in house design of the time.

15. The shape of a low, painted-wood deck in Los Angeles accommodates the bay window of the house and marks its border with boxwood rather than a railing.

16. A house whose back door is set in the tree tops is connected to the street by a wood deck that floats above ground level.

17. A flagstone terrace with comfortable furnishings becomes an outdoor living room.

18. Cloud shaped yews and pots of lilies frame a gravel terrace. The table and chairs, protected by an umbrella, transform it into an outdoor dining room.

13

15

17

18

19. A brick terrace designed with a planting bed enhances the flow between terrace and garden.
20. The Arbor Terrace at Dumbarton Oaks is paved with a rare type of stone from Tennessee called Crab Orchard Stone. Beatrix Farrand designed the double benches of teak, oak, and iron that provide a balcony view to the gardens below.

21. This pleasant resting spot on a gravel terrace outside the orangery at Dunham Massey in England is surrounded by espaliers and topiaries.
22. Tree trunks have limited room to grow as they emerge from a courtyard in Spain paved with pebble mosaics.

23. The Cloisters in New York City was created in the 1930s, using architectural elements from abbeys dating to the late thirteenth and early fourteenth centuries. The design of the courtyard and layout of the garden are true to the medieval period.

least as far as construction of the Persian gardens at Pasargadae (550–30 BC), terraces may be paved with brick, stone or gravel or simply turfed. The Greek writer Xenophon wrote about these ancient gardens and their terraces and they became models for Greek, Roman, and eventually Renaissance garden design. In Italy, terraces were created to tame the hilly topography and connect the gardens to the architecture. In France, renowned landscape architect André Le Nôtre (1613–1700) cleverly manipulated the views within a vast, flat area by designing terraces that revealed successive surprises as visitors proceeded along. His English counterpart of a half-century later, Capability Brown, incorporated terraces as well, while maintaining the natural feeling of the landscape as much as possible. American colonial gardens at Williamsburg, Mount Vernon, and the Paca House in Annapolis, Maryland, all include terraces.

The word *patio* is most likely a derivation of the Latin word *patere* ("to lie open"). In broadest terms, it is a paved area next to a house that is used for dining or lounging. In Spanish architecture, however, *patio* often refers to an interior courtyard. These courtyard patios, inspired by Islamic architecture, could be quite grand, enclosed by alabaster columns topped with panels of intricately carved stone and incorporating a cooling fountain at the center. Beautiful examples, built by the Moors, can be seen at the Alhambra and the Generalife in Grenada. Courtyards remain a quintessential feature of Spanish-style architecture in Mexico, Central, and South America and the western United States.

Diverse cultures throughout the ages have created comfortable and useful outdoor spaces that provide shelter and comfort along with the experience of outdoor living. Porches, porticoes, verandas, balconies, loggias, decks, terraces, and patios are simply variations on the "outdoor rooms" prized for bringing us closer to the natural world around us.

DESIGN The local climate—sun, wind, temperature, and so forth—is the first thing to take into consideration when considering the form an "outdoor room" should take. Personal taste, existing architecture, available space, topography, privacy, views, budget, and local building codes factor in as well. And it is important to think about the intended function of the space: will it be a family room, entertaining area, outdoor kitchen, private nook, street-side greeting place, or simply a sheltered entryway? The probability is that it will serve more than one of these uses.

Your personal taste may have attracted you to a house that already includes a loggia, courtyard or the like. These are most often included in the original building plan. When adding a porch, portico, deck, balcony, or veranda to an existing structure, it is important to consider the architecture of the house. Not only should the design and material of the addition be complementary, but its height, shape and placement should not interfere with existing windows, roof lines, gutters, or downspouts.

Porches, porticoes, verandas, and loggias have foundations, floors, roofs, and supporting elements. These supports may be columns or piers connected by a railing or balustrade. Each of these elements should relate to the existing house in design, architectural style, material, and color.

24

25

28

26

27

29

24. A color scheme successfully connects this Asheville, North Carolina, house with its porch and terrace-level planters. Note the unusual configuration of square columns recessed within the surrounding metal rail and the use of a sturdy bracket design known as the Montford bracket.

25. A rustic bungalow with poplar bark siding built by Nan and Saul Chase in 2008, just outside downtown Asheville, North Carolina. Edible landscaping surrounds the first-floor porch that wraps around two sides—a perfect spot for entertaining—while the upper porch has gorgeous views.

26. A porch featuring elegant woodwork wraps around the side of a house with two entrances and two stairways, providing free-flowing inside-outside circulation and easy access to the lawn area. Ceiling fans add comfort during the hot summers in Beaufort, South Carolina.

27. A Tudor revival cottage with a screened-in porch designed by Charles N. Parker in Asheville, North Carolina, in 1915, an era when the area was popular for the healing qualities of its clean mountain air.

28. Towering fluted Corinthian columns increase the sense of volume and airflow and contrast with the low balustrade that can be used for seating.

29. This brick loggia features triple arches and stone columns that reflect the stone quoining of the house.

The floors of porches, porticoes, verandas, and loggias can be made of wood, composite, stone, brick, concrete, or tile. Once you've chosen the material, you'll want to select a design and color that blend well with the surrounding garden, the interior of the house, and its architecture.

Building codes tend to be very specific regarding railings—right down to the amount of space between spindles—so it is essential to determine your local constraints. The most common minimum height requirement from the ground to the top of a railing is 36 inches. Railings on older houses tend to be lower than this, the top of the rail lining up with the lower sill of the front windows. In many municipalities, these railings are allowed to remain as long as they are kept in good repair. But if the homeowner chooses to replace them, the new railings must comply with the current regulations. Unfortunately, the design of a facade may be compromised by the new, probably higher railings, but careful choice of style and materials can ameliorate the impact. Railings can sometimes be omitted altogether when the structure is close to the ground. A porch of this design is called an open porch.

Although often made of simple wood pickets, railings provide an opportunity to add ornamental interest. They may be handsomely turned wood balusters or an artfully joined Chippendale pattern. Horizontal designs should be avoided, particularly in households that include young children, because of the temptation to climb the crosspieces like a ladder. Ornamental metal railings and stone balusters enjoy a long tradition and can be apt choices for some structures.

30. Originally named the Beaufort Lodge, the Queen Anne-style Beaufort House Inn in Asheville, North Carolina, was designed in 1894 by A. L. Melton. Its comfortable porches offer beautiful mountain and sunset views.

31. Random rectangular flagstones enclosed by a wood railing in an open lattice pattern create an elegant, elevated side terrace with a serene view. If wood had been used instead of flagstone, this would be considered a deck—and would not be as well suited to the brick construction of the house.

32. Drayton Hall in South Carolina was built between 1738 and 1742. Its entrance porch is paved in a checkerboard pattern of contrasting sandstone.

33. Curved brackets turn rectangular openings into arches. They are enclosed by a railing in a Chippendale pattern set above a low, clipped hedge of Teucrium chamaedrys, also called germander.

34. A contrasting paint scheme draws attention to the architectural details of the balustrade, piers, and column of this porch.

35. Cord Asendorf, a merchant in Savannah, Georgia, built this house with elaborately detailed double porches in 1899, applying fine carpentry to an assemblage of ready-made spindles and millwork. It is considered a very good example of "Steamboat Gothic" architecture and locally referred to as the "Gingerbread House."

36. This house with poplar bark siding has posts and rails of peeled natural locust in contrast with the floor of composite decking.

37. Built by the owner of Kehoe Ironworks of Savannah in 1892, this entire porch and all exterior trim work are made of cast iron.

38. A porch with a hipped roof made of corrugated metal with ornamental beading at the seams overlooks Lyttleton Harbor in New Zealand.

39. Savannah's Forsyth Ward house, built in 1897, has a porch with symmetrical, copper-roofed gazebos that create two separate outdoor spaces.

40. Built in 1893 by E.A Scheper, this house in Beaufort, South Carolina, originally had a Victorian exterior. In 1938, it was renovated in the "Antebellum Revival" style, with a columned front porch two stories tall surmounted by a pediment.

Solid rails made of shingles or wood siding are called knee walls. More recent innovations, tempered glass and cable railings, provide enclosure without obstructing the view. It is important that railings not be too tall, as this creates the feeling of being in a cage.

Columns, posts and piers are usually made of wood, stone, brick, cement, fiberglass, or ironwork. An assortment of composites is available as well. Whatever material you choose, it must be strong enough to support the roof. Proper spacing of these elements is essential to structural integrity and, as always, their design and proportion should relate to the existing architecture and comply with local requirements.

The most common design styles for the roofs of outdoor rooms are shed, gable, hipped, and gazebo. A shed roof is the simplest, often appearing flat while sloping gently away from the house to direct rainwater. A gable roof appears triangular, with two sloping sides joined in the center. A hipped roof has three sloped sides that readily shed rain and snow and are self-bracing and self-supporting. This design makes a good choice for places where the weather can be inclement. A gazebo roof has an elevated center ceiling and is often placed at the end of a shed, gable, or hipped roof porch as a focal point. Porch roofs may be finished with shingles, metal, tile, or slate.

Porches that envelop a house on more than one side are called wraparound porches. They offer added vantage points from which to view the garden and a variety of exposures for those seeking to follow the shade (or sun) throughout the day. They also provide extra shade for inside the house, keeping it cooler. Some wraparounds include an area that is open to the sky.

Two-story "double porches" offer outdoor access from more than one level and provide elevated views of the surrounding landscape. These are popular in the South, where the upper story, often accessible through a bedroom, might be designed for sleeping.

Open to the sky, decks are usually attached to a house but can be freestanding. If the structure is to be built close to the ground, a terrace might be a better alternative: terraces are more durable, require less maintenance, and yet are comparable in cost. Decks are the best option when the house is on a hillside or when tree roots might be damaged by terrace construction. An elevated deck provides a better view of the sur-

rounding landscape, and in some cases, might even evoke the sense of being in a tree house. Some decks feel like self-contained living spaces, especially when projecting over a stream or pond. In conceiving outdoor living areas, many opt for decks simply because they prefer the texture, warmth, and color of wood.

A deck should be generous enough in size to accommodate whatever activity you plan to engage in there. A good way to visualize its footprint in the landscape is to stake out its outline on the ground and cover the area with a tarp. As you assess the effect, think about the furnishings, potted plants, and other items you plan to place on it. Evaluate the views at the chosen elevation and make sure you won't be looking at anything unsightly or breaching your neighbors' privacy. Confirm that you won't be encroaching on any underground utilities, light wells, or septic tanks. Even the underside of the deck should be considered: Be sure to leave crawl space to make future maintenance easier. If the deck is relatively high off the ground, give some thought to screening the area below it to discourage animal activity.

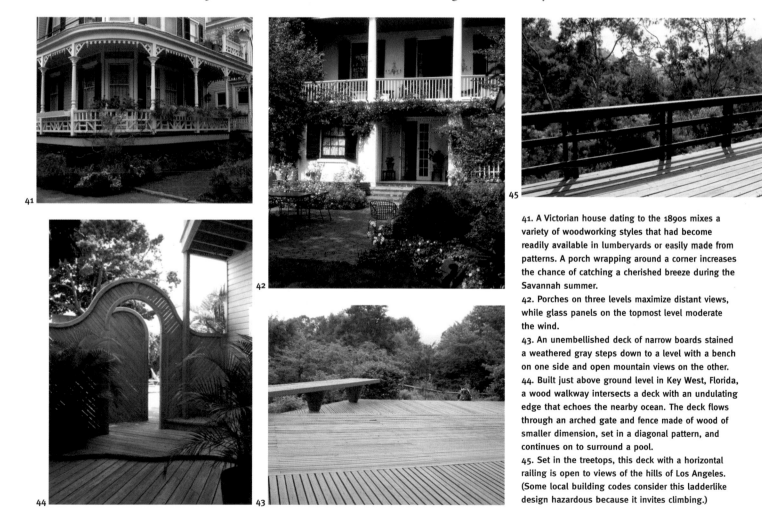

41. A Victorian house dating to the 1890s mixes a variety of woodworking styles that had become readily available in lumberyards or easily made from patterns. A porch wrapping around a corner increases the chance of catching a cherished breeze during the Savannah summer.

42. Porches on three levels maximize distant views, while glass panels on the topmost level moderate the wind.

43. An unembellished deck of narrow boards stained a weathered gray steps down to a level with a bench on one side and open mountain views on the other.

44. Built just above ground level in Key West, Florida, a wood walkway intersects a deck with an undulating edge that echoes the nearby ocean. The deck flows through an arched gate and fence made of wood of smaller dimension, set in a diagonal pattern, and continues on to surround a pool.

45. Set in the treetops, this deck with a horizontal railing is open to views of the hills of Los Angeles. (Some local building codes consider this ladderlike design hazardous because it invites climbing.)

46

47

48

49

46. Mirrors bring both light and images of surrounding trees on to a porch enclosed by freestanding columns surrounded by balustrades.

47. A terrace of mosaics becomes a unique garden room with built-in seats and table in "Emile Dancing with her Tutu as a Table" at the "Giant's House" in New Zealand.

48. Herbs overflowing from the joints and crevices of a flagstone terrace surround a welcoming array of furnishings. The plants exude softness and fragrance as one brushes against them.

49. A fine example of a stone terrace in the crazy pattern at Mt. Stewart in Northern Ireland. Planting beds with lavender break up the expanse of stone enclosed by planters of the same material that hold topiaries of Laurus nobilis and clipped hedges of Cupressus macrocarpa at the far end.

50

51

50. An open wrought-iron railing with an attached floor creates a balcony overlooking the Pebble Garden at Dumbarton Oaks. Originally a tennis court, the garden was designed in 1959 by Ruth Havey and Mildred Bliss, featuring Mexican pebbles and low planting beds of swirled limestone.

51. The circular terrace in the *hui marae*, or meeting place, at the Ora Garden in Taupo, New Zealand, is paved with local Hinuera sandstone in swirling patterns symbolic to Maori culture.

A deck must be strong enough to support heavy loads, so it is wise to consult an engineer or architect before beginning construction. It is always better to overbuild than cut corners, and special attention should be paid to the fasteners, which must be rust resistant. Screws are far superior to nails, which may pull out under pressure. Railing designs for decks vary as widely as those for porches and can incorporate built-in seating, storage, planters, or trellises for growing plants.

Terraces are constructed of stone, brick, gravel, concrete, mosaics, grass, or combinations of these materials. To avoid monotony, the paving adjoining a house should not be of the same material as the facade but be complementary in color and style. The further removed it is from the main house, the more leeway you have. A terrace next to a pond in the "back forty" might have a character all its own.

A well-designed terrace or patio may actually improve the

topography of the area surrounding the house, making for a seamless flow between house and garden. Terraces built into sloping land (by cutting or filling as necessary) effectively increase the usable space in the garden. These must be kept in place by retaining walls of stone, brick, wood, or compacted earth.

A terrace should be either larger or smaller than the planting area of a garden, never the same size. In one-vista gardens, it is best to use a single paving material and vary the patterns rather than introducing more than one material. If you prefer more contrast, you can vary the color range or surface finish, while confining yourself to one kind of stone. If your garden and terrace are spacious enough, variations in material and pattern can help delineate areas of the terrace designated for different uses.

A free-standing terrace placed well away from the house can direct visitors to the nicest views, function as a discrete garden room and act as a substitute for lawn or plantings, thus reducing garden maintenance.

CLIMATE AND WEATHERING Terraces and decks are fully exposed to rain, snow, wind, and sun. In sunny areas, UV rays fade concrete quickly and may cause wood to crack. Direct sunlight might also damage mortar joints in paving. Porches, although somewhat protected, are still subject to shifts in temperature and humidity.

Algae and moss thrive in shaded, cool, or damp areas and can be as slippery and treacherous as ice in the winter. Fallen leaves from overhanging deciduous plants can pose the same danger and should be cleaned up regularly.

It's important that the flashing between the porch and house remain sealed so as to prevent rain from seeping in and causing leaks and damage. Check it seasonally.

A solid knee wall will help reduce snow accumulation on a porch. Snow should never be allowed to pile up on decks or porches as its weight and moisture can wreak havoc over the long term. And, particularly if you don't have screening below, it is wise to check underneath porches and decks to make sure no animals have taken up winter residence.

Composite decking will weather and change color at first, because of its natural wood fibers—but after a few months the color should stabilize. When selecting your decking, try to look at examples that have been in place for a while, to be sure that the ultimate color suits your taste.

52

53

54

52. Double porches with louvered shutters that can be adjusted for privacy, sun exposure and air flow are surrounded by a terrace enclosed by a balustrade that is joined with sturdy square-paneled piers.

53. A solid "knee wall" with recessed panels painted to emphasize their architectural detail serves to reduce accumulation of blowing snow.

54. A composite deck set low to the ground on a base of large gravel is scored with grooves for sure footing in wet conditions.

INSTALLATION AND MAINTENANCE The foundation is the workhorse of any structure and must be carefully laid. Climate, geology, the slope of the site and local building codes all factor in to proper construction of a foundation; professional consultation is highly advisable.

Wood is the most common flooring material for outdoor rooms, particularly porches and verandas. We recommend tongue-and-groove joining as it creates a strong joint that can accommodate fluctuations in temperature and humidity without gapping. Pay careful attention to the selection of nails, screws, bolts and fasteners, as their failure might compromise the structure to the point of collapse.

Installation details for wood decks should be suitable for fully exposed areas. Many of the fine details that are recommended for the protected environment of a porch (including tongue-and-groove joinery) are best avoided because they tend to hold moisture when directly exposed to rain and this encourages decay.

Southern yellow pine (SYP) is one of various woods suitable for flooring. It is a budget-friendly choice that may be painted or stained, although lumber from different batches may absorb the coating differently, so it is wise to draw from a single batch if that is your intention. Another popular choice, ma-

hogany, is dense and has few knots. It is rot resistant but has the tendency to swell in humid areas and this should be considered when spacing the boards. Western red cedar is imbued with natural oils that repel insects and decay, and may be stained or allowed to weather naturally. Ipe, a tropical wood particularly in vogue right now, is so dense that premium carbide blades should be used to cut it and stains will not penetrate it. On the plus side, it is resistant to insects, decay, mold, and even fire. Redwood rarely shrinks or warps and may be finished or left natural. (For more on the various types of wood used in garden construction, see the "Fences" chapter.)

Composite decking, made of recycled wood and plastic, is an environmentally friendly choice. It costs about 20 percent more than treated southern yellow pine but contains no toxic preservatives and is resistant to rot and insects. It doesn't splinter, crack, or fade and tends to be slip resistant. A number of manufacturers offer an array of colors and textures.

All flooring should run perpendicular to the house and be installed so that it slopes outward to direct potentially damaging water away from the main structure. And don't forget the ground under the floor: it, too, should be graded to direct runoff away from the foundation.

A moisture barrier placed on top of exposed soil will reduce

55

56

57

55. A stone foundation provides solid support for a porch, both physically and visually.

56. A side porch provides a comfortable outdoor living room as well as tastefully concealed space for storage below.

57. Setting floorboards perpendicular to a building and on a gentle slope prevents puddling and protects both the porch and foundation. Note that the porch's ceiling is painted "haint" blue here, at the Reynolds Mansion in Asheville, North Carolina.

the dampness that rises from it. It is best to finish the area with a "skirt" for aesthetic reasons and to provide a barrier to wildlife that may seek shelter. The skirt should be an open design that allows air circulation and keeps moisture from building up. But be sure the lattice pattern you choose has relatively small openings so that leaves and other debris can't penetrate and pile up under the floor.

For detailed information on the installation of terraces made of brick, concrete, gravel, pattern and mosaic, and stone, see the "Installation and Maintenance" section of the "Paving" chapter.

All outdoor rooms demand regular maintenance to ensure their safety and longevity. All floor surfaces should be cleaned at the end of winter and summer to guard against algae, moss, and mildew growth. Avoid using strong pressure washers, though, as they are apt to erode finishes and mortar joints. Powdered, oxygenated bleach is friendly to the environment, gentle on plants, and well suited to cleaning wood and masonry. An alternative is dilute liquid bleach. There are many deck-cleaning products on the market but be sure to read the directions carefully, as some are quite strong and may be harmful to skin or plants.

All structural components of decks and porches should be checked annually. Hardware, joints, and boards should be examined for rot, rust, and loosening; gutters and flashing should be inspected to be sure they are directing water properly.

Cracked mortar joints must be repaired to prevent damage from water's seeping under the terrace. Cracks in concrete paving should also be attended to before they get worse, although the repair might seem unsightly for awhile. Loose bricks and stones should be reset to avoid tripping hazards. Gravel terraces should be raked level regularly for the same reason.

Once you've created a lovely outdoor room, don't turn it into a utility closet or overflow storage area. This can cut into your enjoyment of both the porch itself and views of the house and garden it is meant to showcase.

58

59

58. Vertical slats conceal the area beneath this deck and camouflage the mechanical equipment housed there.

59. The Lover's Lane Pool at Dumbarton Oaks, shown here without water, is an elegant design for a stone terrace.

Thoughtfully select furnishings, decor, and lighting that suit the space, its function, your taste and budget. The proper scale, material, and placement will create a pleasing, inviting outdoor room you can use seasonally or all year round.

60. A thoughtful combination of comfortable furnishings, potted plants, sculptural accents and architectural elements overlook a lovely view— creating an enticing outdoor room.

61. Elaborately carved figures of musicians stretch their arms to support a balcony ornamented with railings of repoussé leaves in Prague.

60

61

REFLECTING POOLS
& PONDS

*A lake is the landscape's most beautiful and expressive feature. It is earth's eye,
looking into which the beholder measures the depth of his own nature.*

HENRY DAVID THOREAU

1. Sculpted turf terraces frame the Butterfly Lakes at Middleton Place in South Carolina, and the calm water mirrors the clouds and sky.

2. The canal called the Canopus at Hadrian's Villa in Tivoli, Italy (second century AD), is filled to the rim and reflects the surrounding columns and sculpture. Long thought to be a representation of the Nile River, it is now believed by some to depict the Mediterranean Sea.

3. This courtyard at the Alhambra is known by several names, including the Patio de los Arrayanes ("Patio of the Myrtles") referring to the surrounding hedge; the Patio del Estanque ("Patio of the Tank"); and the Patio de la Alberca ("Patio of the Pool"). The pool provides a looking-glass reflection of the surrounding architecture.

4. The water tank in the Jardin del Estanque at the Alcazar in Seville, Spain, was originally used to collect water for irrigation but today, it is an ornamental pool. The Mercury Fountain at its center was designed by Diego de Pesquera in 1575.

Throughout the ages and across cultures, water has been revered as the source of life. It has been linked to the spiritual and valued for the many vital functions it serves. The containment of water in pools, ponds, lakes, and tanks is often simultaneously practical and ornamental.

As early as 2500 BC, the Chinese began gathering carp from flooded eddies by the river and relocating them to spring-fed ponds in which they also planted rice. Over the centuries that followed, they perfected the creation of eco-friendly ponds for the cultivation of frogs, turtles, crawfish, and freshwater shrimp, as well as carp. In 500 BC, a book called *Fish Husbandry*, by Fan Li, became the first textbook on aquaculture, mapping out methods that are still in practice today.

During the Sung Dynasty (AD 960–1279), the keeping of ornamental fish in ponds became enormously popular—so much so that eating them was strictly forbidden. Emperors throughout the Far East created large hunting parks with ponds that attracted geese and wild birds. Duck blinds were constructed on their banks from which they and their guests would hurl flying nets.

Gardens in Japan still include naturalistic ponds often meant to represent grander bodies of water, such as a sea or lagoon.

Early Egyptians of wealth used man-made ponds for the farming of fish, cultivation of the prized lotus flower, and growth of papyrus used for making paper. The large complex known as the Great Temple of Amun included a sacred lake with canals connecting its buildings. A painting discovered in the tomb of Sennufer, a fifteenth-century BC "overseer of the granaries and fields, gardens, and cattle of Amun," depicts a symmetrical garden featuring a series of rectangular pools.

The ancient Greeks revered water in its natural form and built gardens for worship around existing springs and pools. The Romans developed extensive tanks of both fresh and salt-water for bathing and cultivating eels and oysters. Eels, which thrive in manmade ponds, were a popular food and some Romans even kept them as pets. It is said that Antonia, the mother of Emperor Claudius, attached earrings to the fins of her favorite eel. At Hadrian's Villa, geometrical ponds were used for bathing, aquaculture, and as staging grounds for *naumachiae*, staged, small-scale naval battles. These ponds were the inspiration for the water parterres of the Renaissance.

5

6

5. One of three islands in the Golden Pond of Saiho-ji in Kyoto, also known as Kokedera, or Moss Temple. The pond is in the shape of the Japanese character meaning heart and is encircled by a strolling path. More than 120 types of moss can be found at Saiho-ji.

6. Deeg Palace was built in the mid-eighteenth century as the summer residence for the Raja Suraj Mai. The water tank served a number of purposes, including reflecting the moon, cooling the palace, and serving as a swimming pool. The platform in the foreground was used for diving.

The Persians and Moors built gardens with elaborate water features. The classic design included two intersecting canals that represented the four rivers of life: the Gihon, Pishan, Tigris, and Euphrates. Their junction often featured a pavilion or water tank, filled to the brim to represent paradise overflowing with life-giving water. The stillness of the water was meant to evoke a feeling of serenity, its crystalline reflection (often of an intricate facade) adding dimension to the view. The Persians also built water tanks within courtyards for ablution and cooling.

In medieval times in the Middle East, small, shallow, ornamental pools could be found within walled gardens. Knights involved in the Crusades visited the "paradise gardens" of Byzantium and Arabia and admired them for their beauty and utility. Upon returning home, they were instrumental in introducing the elements they'd seen into the gardens of Europe.

The maharajas of India constructed immense reservoirs near their summer palaces for drinking, bathing, and the cultivation of fish. They also built canals that flowed underneath their palaces for cooling—the first air conditioners.

Italian Renaissance gardens featured grand, elaborately

sculpted water parterres, geometric pools symmetrically arranged around a central basin. They were—and still are—valued for their reflections of the central fountain and the views beyond.

The French baroque gardens designed by André Le Nôtre featured immense formal canals stretching great distances. At Vaux-le-Vicomte, he designed a grand *bassin* sited to capture only the reflection of the château. German baroque gardens emulated French design on a very large scale. Vast formal beds featured water parterres, expanses of reflective water, and fountains.

Dutch gardens were designed with borders of geometric dikes and canals that were aesthetically pleasing, while pro-viding necessary drainage. In turn, this design was the inspi-ration for some formal gardens in late-seventeenth-century England that were dominated by canals and reflecting pools.

The designers of the British landscape movement rejected all formal water features. Instead they created understated, in-formal pools and naturalistic bodies of water connected by streams and waterfalls.

In the New World, Thomas Jefferson designed and built an ornamental pool west of the main house at Monticello and stocked it with fish and eels. Oval, 3 feet deep, sealed with mortar, and edged with brick, it offered a reflection of the house and can still be enjoyed today.

Renowned landscape architect Frederick Law Olmstead

7

8

9

10

11

12

13

7. The water parterre in the Quadrato at Villa Lante is separated from the central fountain, the Fontana dei Mori, to preserve its stillness and reflective qualities.
8. The grand reflective canals at the Château de Courances in France are sometimes attributed to Le Nôtre, though few historians concur.
9. At Vaux-le-Vicomte, Le Nôtre used vast sheets of water as "mirrors of infinity." He employed forced perspective (anamorphosis abscondita, or "hidden distortion") to visually enlarge the space.
10. Courances has been rightfully dubbed the Garden of Mirrors and Infinite Reflections." This particular mirror sits in front of "La Foulerie," an outbuilding once used to prepare flax for linen manufacture.

11. This Dutch water garden, laid out at Westbury Court between 1696 and 1705, is one of the few gardens of its type to survive the onslaught of the British landscape movement.
12. One of four lakes Capability Brown designed at Sheffield Park to reflect the surrounding landscape.
13. Thomas Jefferson designed his oval pond to be reflective and to provide a fresh supply of edible fish.

believed that city parks were the "lungs of the city." His designs for Central Park in New York City and the Emerald Necklace in Boston were greatly influenced by the English landscape movement and include expansive ponds, lagoons, lakes, and reservoirs with perimeter walks.

With the introduction of flexible liners, ponds have become more affordable and popular. Small, shallow ones are fairly easy to install and a variety of aquatic plants, pumps, and filter systems are available. Many companies specialize in constructing ponds and reflecting pools, so there is probably one in your area—but it is wise to get references.

DESIGN In her 1918 book *Colour in my Garden*, Louise Beebe Wilder describes the many virtues of reflective water: "A pool is the eye of the garden in whose candid depths is mirrored its advancing grace. . . . We do not require a great expanse of water to add this pleasure of reflections to the list of our garden joys. . . . Arrange the Cherry and Hawthorn, place our Irises and Lupines where the pool may mirror their fine designs, and leave the rest to the wind and clouds."

Pond shells may be made of gunite, concrete, or sodium bentonite (a natural type of clay) or liners of rubber or plastic and fiberglass. Gunite is a form of concrete applied under high pressure. It is the most expensive substance to use, but also

the most durable and maintenance-free. A gunite shell must be sealed or plastered to waterproof it. Select a flat or mottled black coating to make the pond appear deeper and enhance its reflective properties.

Concrete shells are less expensive but may crack and chip in temperate climates and must also be waterproofed. Clay is the best choice for larger ponds. Made with a layer of tamped clay and bentonite, they are the most economical. (There was a time when these were constructed by applying a layer of clay and then fencing pigs into the area to compact it!)

Flexible pond liners are available in many types, but should always be puncture-proof and UV resistant. EPDM (ethylene, propylene, diene, monomer) rubber pond liners are inexpensive and naturally UV resistant. They contain no toxins that might harm fish. Rocks can be stacked or epoxied onto them to conceal them and guard against punctures. Plastic liners are available in various thicknesses; the higher grades provide the most UV and puncture resistance and longevity.

Smaller ponds may be lined with prefabricated plastic and fiberglass shells. These are fairly easy to install and maintain but limited in size and shape. Pure fiberglass shells are expensive but very durable.

When designing your pond or reflecting pool, avoid complex shapes and acute angles. These make the feature difficult

14. The pond in Central Park, designed by Frederick Law Olmsted, was diminished in size by the construction of a skating rink in 1949 but still provides enough water to enjoy reflections from the deck of Gapstow Bridge.

15. A stone bust overlooks a small, still pond at Les Quatre Vents in Canada as images of waterside plantings float on the surface.

16. The shimmering reflections in the water-lily pond he created at Giverny, France, inspired Claude Monet to paint a series of some 250 oil paintings that have immortalized the spot.

17. This stone pool, though diminutive, is beautifully reflective.

18. A carved rock nestled in a planting of shrubs collects water to create a small mirror.
19. The rectangular lily pool at Villa Melzi on Lake Como draws the lake onto the terrace.
20. "A garden anchored in a lake of dreams" is how Edith Wharton described Isola Bella on Lake Maggiore. The small circular pond does indeed anchor the garden to the lake.

21. A gazebo overlooks a water view in New York's Central Park.
22. The stepping stones that traverse this long canal in the gardens of the Villa Ephrussi de Rothschild provide visitors with close-up views of the water's reflections.
23. A reflecting pool at the Pope John Paul II Cultural Center in Washington, DC, provides a mirror image of its surroundings.

to construct and impede the water from circulating evenly. The resulting eddies can trap floating debris.

The pond should fit into your overall garden design and be set on a level area that, ideally, can be seen from the best spots in the house and any outdoor rooms. Ponds may be formal or informal in design. In Western gardens, water features set close to buildings are usually quite formal, whereas in Asian gardens, they are more often naturalistic. In fact, is rare to see a formal pond anywhere in Asia; more common are simple basins of carved stone designed to entice birds and reflect the sky.

A distant body of water can be coaxed into the garden vista by placing a smaller pond in the foreground. The view of water leading to water will draw the eye outward and link the two, enlarging the overall sense of space.

Gazebos and pergolas are often placed near ponds, providing sheltered seating focused on the loveliest views. All struc-tural elements near a water feature should be scaled down to increase the perceived distance from the viewing point. A false bridge may be placed overhanging the far edge of a pond to give the illusion that it continues beyond.

A pond should be designed to present the greatest expanse of water from the primary view. Pools should be filled to the brim, increasing their apparent size and maximizing reflec-tions. If space permits, consider putting in two smaller ponds rather than one large one. This allows for more perimeter area and a greater perceived expanse. An island in a pond can make it look smaller and interrupt reflections, but if your pond is on the larger size, it might add visual interest and even be-come a picnic destination.

Before breaking ground, analyze what the water will reflect and whether a back planting might make the reflection more interesting. If you opt for this, specify only fine-textured plants so as to increase the perceived distance from viewing points.

Skimmers and light fixtures should be located as unobtrusively as possible and directed to avoid surface glare. Naturalistic ponds should never be illuminated with underwater lights.

Because moving water reduces the clarity of the reflection, it should be separated from the reflecting pool with a short rill. Ponds should adhere to county regulations concerning maximum depth, setbacks, and fencing—but ideally should not be shallower than 18 inches. The pond depth necessary to overwinter fish varies by location and type of fish. Koi require greater depths than do some other popular species.

Ponds can be edged in lawn, plants, stone, wood, or gravel. They can serve as wading or even swimming pools if the water is properly filtered.

Runoff from impervious paving and rainwater directed from roof downspouts can be used to fill ponds naturally. The collected water may then be used for irrigation. In rural areas, water from large ponds can be pumped to extinguish building fires and the cost of building the pond may be offset by a reduction in fire insurance rates.

CLIMATE AND WEATHERING Ponds placed close to windows and glass doors will reflect light into adjacent rooms. Placed directly to the west and east of primary views, ponds may produce glare at sunset and sunrise but this might be a worthwhile trade-off for dazzling midday reflections of floating clouds.

Ponds in full sun are susceptible to algae bloom and rapid evaporation, yet most aquatic plants require at least six hours of sunlight to bloom. The best solution for sunny ponds is to ensure that at least half the surface water is shaded with aquatic plant leaves. Algae is less problematic if pond water is aerated by floating fountains.

When siting your pond, keep in mind the direction of summer prevailing winds. Breezes will cool the downwind area but excessive wind will evaporate pond water quickly and introduce windblown debris, and the ripples of a windblown pond break up the reflection. In high-wind areas, it's best to locate the pond near some sort of shelter or plant or construct a windscreen.

Pond basins in temperate climates must be designed to

24. A long, narrow pool in Ireland shimmers beneath an overcast sky.
25. Water lilies are carefully constrained to allow a sharp reflection of the Pin Mill in the canal at Bodnant in Wales.
26. The pool at the Patio de la Alberca in the Alhambra is gently fed by fountains at each end engineered to maintain the still surface that reflects the portico and its seven arches topped with marble filigree.
27. Rippling water, valued for sound, is separated from still water, valued for reflection, in the gardens of Kenroku-en in Japan.
28. A series of weirs along the River Vartry at Mount Usher Gardens in Ireland ensures contrasting sections of still and running water.
29. Placed adjacent to windows, this canal bounces light into the house.

withstand the pressure of expanding ice or must be partially emptied. It isn't a good idea to empty the pool completely, as its shell may pop up due to hydrostatic pressure and the expansion of frozen soil. If a pond that contains fish is likely to freeze over, it should have a floating ice heater to prevent a lack of oxygen and the buildup of trapped methane from decaying pond debris. Never open air pockets by pounding on the ice, as this creates shock waves that can kill the fish. If, for reasons of practicality or choice, you opt not to aerate your pond, be aware that still water may be a breeding ground for mosquitoes and gnats. Fish can be beneficial in controlling the insect population.

INSTALLATION AND MAINTENANCE Be sure to locate all underground utilities before breaking ground.

Any gunite or concrete pool with a capacity of over 200,000 gallons should be designed and installed by professional masons or pool builders. While not essential, it is wise to take added precautions to avoid possible leaks, such as laying a continuous sheet of flexible liner between the concrete and the soil or gravel base and specifying waterproof cement.

The expense of building a pond is greatly reduced if the area is accessible to machinery, located near existing electric lines, and the excavated soil may stay on site.

Blasting out bedrock or replacing unstable soils can be very costly. In rocky or unstable areas, the proposed pond location should be bore tested for levels of bedrock and stable compacted soil.

Ponds that are gravity-fed by streams should be designed with an intercepting sediment pond that is accessible to machinery for periodic dredging. Most small ponds should be emptied and thoroughly cleaned out every spring.

Flexible liners can be punctured by animals and the aggressive roots of plants such as *Salix* (willow) and *Phyllostachys* (bamboo). They should be protected with a setting bed of sand or geotextile fabric.

The water in a small fish pond should circulate through a filter at least once every five hours. Pumps and filters last longer if sheltered from the elements and not submerged in water. The best course is to hide them from view with plantings, along with any skimmers and lights.

Surface water around ornamental ponds should be directed away from the pond to decrease the chance of sediment, fertilizers, and contaminants seeping into it. Avoid planting trees and shrubs with "messy" leaves, flowers, or fruits that might end up in your pond or pool. Besides being unsightly, some plant droppings, including *Taxus* (yew), *Ilex* (holly), *Kalmia* (mountain laurel), *Salix* (willow), and *Rhododendron* are toxic to fish. During the autumn, ponds can be netted to prevent falling leaves from settling on the bottom.

30

31

32

33

Nonmigrating geese can be quite a nuisance. Deterrents include swans, herding dogs, and self-propelled artificial alligator heads (yes, these exist!). More radical options are to install a 2-foot barrier or a series of pulsating lawn sprinklers around the pond, crisscross the water surface with fishing line or leave a 20-foot strip of unmown lawn around the pond.

Green pond water indicates the presence of single-cell algae, which can be deterred by the introduction of submerged oxygenator plants or other items readily available at garden centers. Barley straw or liquid and UV sterilizers are good options. Avoid overstocking the water with fish as this encourages algae growth.

Rocks placed on the bottom of the pool are most attractive and natural, but their crevices can collect debris, making maintenance more difficult.

Reflective bodies of water, large or small, add elegance and unparalleled visual interest to the garden. When well planned and maintained, they enrich the ecosystem of the garden by conserving water and attracting wildlife. They are well worth the added effort and expense they demand.

34

37

30. This stone garden pool at Linderhof has survived the harsh winters of the German Alps since the second half of the nineteenth century.

31. A circular garden pool at Chiswick House in London, designed by William Kent in the early eighteenth century.

32. An oval pool set into the lawn at Les Quatre Vents in Canada.

33. This natural quarry pool at Opus 40 in Saugerties, New York, was created by Harry Fite, who worked alone on the site for more than thirty-seven years to create what has been called an "environmental sculpture," 6.5 acres in size.

34. A serene stream lined with locust logs meanders through the lawn at Buck Gardens in New Jersey.

35. The Lovers' Lane Pool at Dumbarton Oaks, built on the site of a natural pool, provides lovely reflections of the surrounding trees. Surrounded by brick seats built into the hillside, it once served as an intimate outdoor theater when not filled with water, though it is rarely used this way now.

36. Moving water is skillfully harnessed by terracing to allow both the sense of motion and the stillness necessary for reflection.

37. The loveliness of the stone folly ruin is reflected in a "table" of water at Chanticleer in Pennsylvania.

36

35

38. Beds of daffodils are twice as charming for being planted next to a still pond in Holland.
39. An unobtrusive, tranquil canal adds light, depth, and elegance to an already stunning setting.

38

39

SCULPTURES &
STATUARY

I saw the angel in the marble and carved until I set him free.
MICHELANGELO

1. An explosion of azaleas envelop Adam and Eve, while out of sight is a stand of apple trees. Mischievous Adam holds two apples behind his back. Ladew Gardens.

2. Obelisks at Dumbarton Oaks in Washington, DC, were probably inspired by the ones Gertrude Jekyll featured in her 1918 book, *Garden Ornament*. Note the pyramidon on top, reminiscent of traditional obelisk design.

3. A grotesque figure carved from living rock, dating to the sixteenth century, at the Parc dei Mostri or "Garden of the Monsters" at Bomarzo in Italy.

Egypt's Great Sphinx of Giza dates back to the third millennium BC and is considered one of the oldest examples of monumental landscape sculpture in existence. The word *sphinx* was probably a Greek corruption of the Egyptian term *shesep-ankh*, which meant "living image." It referred to statues of "living rock," or rock carved where it was found rather than brought from another location. Smaller-scale statues of gods were an important part of Egyptian temple gardens. Obelisks carved from a single piece of granite ranged in height from 3 to 100 feet and were tributes to the sun god, Ra, the gold-plated *pyramidons* at their tops representing the sun's rays. In addition to their aesthetic appeal, sculptural earthenware vases proved an efficient way to grow plants in Egypt's arid climate.

The earliest Greek sculptures were religious in nature as well, created to adorn temples and sacred groves, pay homage to the oracles, and mark graves. They most often depicted Greek gods in an idealized human form, manifestations of beauty, piety, and heroism. With the conquest of Alexander the Great (336–323 BC) came the influence of Eastern and Buddhist art; by the second century BC, Greek sculpture had become more naturalistic. Men, women, children, and animals were depicted in earthier, more realistic terms and the wealthy commissioned such sculptures for their gardens. As Hellenistic cities developed in Egypt, Syria, and Turkey just before the Common Era, Greek sculpture spread and became an industry. Classical subjects remained popular but new techniques were developed, including refinements in bronze casting that made it possible to create larger figures. A new aesthetic principle referred to as *contrapposto* involved depicting the weight shift of a human torso to produce a more relaxed and natural look. Much of the surviving Greek sculpture is from this era.

The Romans brought Greek statues home from their conquests and often copied them. Although they renamed the deities (Ares to Mars, Poseidon to Neptune, and so on), they retained the figures' underlying attributes. In Rome, statues of the gods were considered decorative rather than religious and were placed in settings befitting their characters. Neptune, the god of the sea, was most often sited near a pool or fountain, for example.

Nero's Villa Poppaea, near Mt. Vesuvius, was covered in volcanic ash in an eruption around AD 49. It remained hidden and well preserved until 1964, when excavations revealed forty-four statues placed around the pool and in the courtyard. Some were quite whimsical, including a boy holding a duck, while others expressed more conventional classical themes. Roman sites as far afield as Flavian's palace near Fishbourne, England (AD 72), corroborate the Romans' use of sculpture as decoration.

Buddhism was introduced to Japan in the sixth century, giving rise to outdoor sculptures depicting the Buddha. Stone was scarce, so these were most often carved from the wood of a single tree, then painted in bright colors, lacquered, or gilded. Likenesses of the Buddha were also cast in bronze or other metals.

As Christianity overtook the old world during the fourth and fifth centuries, many "pagan" statues of Greek and Roman deities were destroyed. Those made of bronze or lead were melted down for reuse. By the start of the Middle Ages, the creation of sculpture had been banned altogether; the practice would not reemerge until the eleventh century, at which point the art form had sunk to a rudimentary level, lacking proportion and representational quality. The evolution of sculpture had to begin anew, continuing through the Romanesque and Gothic periods.

4

4. Hadrian was a student of Greek history, architecture, and design as well as a well-traveled commander of the Roman navy. Here in the Canopus garden at Hadrian's Villa, the Greek influence is most evident in the caryatids on the right.
5. A bronze figure of Buddha resting on a lotus flower in Nara, Japan.

5

6. Renaissance "River Gods" were meant as a tribute to the forces of water, without which the garden would not exist.

7. Villa Adriana, or Hadrian's Villa, was a favorite site for Renaissance architects and designers to study—and soon became a source for sculptures and other materials they could pilfer for their own use.

8. A river god at Vaux-le-Vicomte in France.

9. A trio of cherubs holding a basket of fruits and flowers at Vaux-le-Vicomte.

10. William Kent (1645-1748) designed the urn as well the loggia, called the Praeneste, at Rousham in England.

11. A replica of the Farnese Hercules stands watch over Vaux-le-Vicomte, as specified by Andre Le Nôtre.

The Renaissance brought a renewed fascination with the classical world of the Greeks and Romans. Archeological excavations, such as those at Hadrian's Villa, unearthed statues, vases, and urns, many of which were absconded with and placed in Renaissance gardens. Classical forms inspired much of the art of the time and sculpture became an important element in garden design—so much so that many sculptors were pressed into service as garden designers as well.

André Le Nôtre's vast seventeenth-century gardens at Vaux-le-Vicomte and Versailles were defined as much by their architectural features and ornaments as anything. The sculptures, urns, and vases he so thoughtfully arranged had a profound effect on the use and design of garden ornaments throughout northern Europe.

In 1677, John Worlidge of Hampshire, England, wrote in his book on gardening, *Systema Horticulturae*, "To buoy up their hopes of another spring, many have placed in their gardens statues and figures of several animals of great variety and other curious pieces of workmanship that their walks might be pleasant at any time." An interest in garden sculpture was blossoming at the time and British craftsmen were sent to Europe to refine their techniques while talented European craftsmen immigrated to England. Many ornaments of the period were made of native stone or lead. Original designs stood beside copies of such classical pieces as the *Venus de Medici* and the *Farnese Hercules*. Reproductions of many of Le Nôtre's works were also common.

The eighteenth century brought an emerging fascination

with the concept of *arcadia* and garden designers strove to create idyllic settings of rustic simplicity and pastoral contentment. Employing sculptures of the forest god Pan alongside frolicking shepherds and shepherdesses, they transformed the local landscape into an arcadian paradise.

As the century progressed, Capability Brown espoused the landscape movement, defined by a simpler, more natural approach to garden design. Statues, vases, and urns had no place in this aesthetic and fell into disfavor, replaced by artfully placed bridges, temples, and other architectural elements.

The romantic movement followed, and gardens of this period were termed "picturesque." Brown's concepts were deemed placid, uninspiring, and lacking the wilder qualities of nature. Rustic cottages, ruins, and irregular groupings of rocks began to dot the landscape as a form of ornament. Urns reemerged as purely ornamental features, never planted.

12. A pastoral figure holds a sheaf signifying abundance.
13. Romantic ruins at Willhemshohe in Germany provide a destination within the larger garden.
14. The ruins at Scotney Castle in England are both a sculptural folly and a protected, walled garden.
15. A shepherd and shepherdess look to the fields beyond this private garden in Connecticut.
16. Many urns and vases can be found throughout the gardens at Dumbarton Oaks. Some (including this one, known as the Newell Vase) were designed or selected by Beatrix Farrand and others were added later by Ruth Havey.

17. The lake and its surroundings at Stourhead in England exemplify the way that garden elements were used at the height of the landscape movement. The shape and size of the lake, the plantings and paths around it, the bridges crossing it and the well-placed pavilions are sculptural focal points.
18. One of a pair of limestone urns designed by Beatrix Farrand for the Green Garden at Dumbarton Oaks.

Early American gardeners looked to England and Europe for inspiration. Formality and geometry were valued for their contrast with the vast, untamed countryside, and the use of sculpture reflected this ideal. Statues of gods, goddesses, nymphs, satyrs, and busts of Roman emperors were imported and incorporated into American gardens. In 1841, Andrew Jackson Downing gave voice to a distinctly American interpretation of garden design when he wrote, "The eye, instead of witnessing the sudden termination of the architecture at the base of the house, where the lawn commences as suddenly, will be at once struck with the increased variety and richness imparted to the whole scene, by the addition of architectural and garden decorations…the amount of enrichment bestowed on exterior decoration near the house should correspond to the style of art evinced in the exterior of the house itself.… There can be no reason why the smallest cottage should not have a terrace decorated in a suitable manner." Downing particularly appreciated the use of vases and urns placed on pedestals as a way to unite architecture and garden.

The Victorian era in the United States and abroad (1837–1901) brought out an exuberant array of eclectic styles. Renaissance design experienced a revival, as large and lavish gardens featured balustraded terraces overlooking elaborate parterres. Flower gardens were enlivened by statues of gods and heroes. As the innovations of the Industrial Revolution ushered in the era of mass production, a dizzying array of

19. A bronze Diana, as sculpted by Gleb Derujinsky in 1925 and placed in Brookgreen Gardens in 1935.

20. Limestone garden sphinxes came into vogue in late nineteenth and early twentieth centuries. Sometimes the face was carved to be a recognizable likeness.

21. Baskets of flowers, made of limestone and lead, were a collaboration between Beatrix Farrand and Albert Rateau.

22. A boat-shaped basket with turtle feet made of Doria stone and lead at Dumbarton Oaks, designed by Ruth Havey.

23. This cast-iron figure of George Washington, called a "heating stove figure," dates from 1843 and was originally used indoors as a source of radiant heat.

24. A cast-iron dog with a highly textured coat and a steady gaze.

25. This small-scale cast-iron squirrel was made in the late nineteenth century.

26. Pan, as sculpted by Janet Scudder for Brookgreen Gardens in South Carolina.

27. A vase of acquia sandstone and iron flowers as designed by Beatrix Farrand and carved by Frederick Coles in the early 1930s.

28. Lady Londonderry created the gardens at Mt. Stewart in Northern Ireland just after World War I. The salon she hosted there included many prominent politicians and thinkers of the day. Here, on the Dodo Terrace, some of her favorite guests are depicted as the animal she imagined them to be.

29. Oil jars displayed as a sculptural group.

30. A wellhead provides a large lawn with a sculptural focal point.

31. An abstract metal sculpture rises out of a ravine and lifts the eye.

32. Steps for mounting a horse remain in this garden as an ornamental note.

33. Pink hippos join the ranks of kitschy pink flamingos and elephants.

garden ornaments was readily available in cast iron, artificial stone, and zinc—not just for the wealthy, but for middle-class gardeners as well. Of course, there were those who saw the downside of mass production and the inevitable backlash ensued. The arts and crafts movement of the late 1800s eschewed mechanically made pieces in favor of the fruits of skilled artists and artisans. Handcraftsmanship, local materials and simplicity of design, in harmony with local architecture, characterized this aesthetic philosophy. Concurrently, but at the other end of the spectrum, a new class of extremely wealthy "Gilded Age" Americans set about erecting enormous mansions featuring expansive formal gardens. They looked to Europe for inspiration and hired agents to procure the finest classical sculptures—some antiques and some reproductions.

American sculptors, such as Frederick MacMonnies (1863–1937) and Janet Scudder (1869–1940), became known for their contemporary garden art inspired by classical themes.

As the Gilded Age gave way to the realities of a world at war, gardens became more intimate. Abstract and nonfigurative sculpture began to appear. Artists experimented with such materials as mesh, mirror, stainless steel, aluminum, concrete, and fiberglass. Found objects, including columns, weathervanes, well heads, and olive oil jars, took on purely ornamental functions. Natural items with pleasing forms, such as rocks and driftwood, were treated as sculpture. And finally (though not, thankfully, universally), "kitsch" ornaments such as gazing balls, pink flamingos, and garden gnomes could be spotted in suburban and exurban gardens.

DESIGN When selecting a sculptural ornament for the garden, consider the form, scale, material, intended placement, and desired effect. You'll find a bewildering array of both representational and abstract sculpture at garden centers, art galleries, flea markets, antique shows, salvage shops, and elsewhere. The Internet is another bountiful source and, if you are on the hunt for something truly unique, many artists welcome commissions.

Arguably, there is no right or wrong choice of form and style when it comes to garden ornamentation, as long as you strive for overall harmony. The scale of a sculptural element should suit its immediate surroundings—but size can be used to produce a desired effect. A small sculpture can get lost in a large expanse, but cleverly positioned, it might be viewed as a subtle surprise. A thoughtfully underscaled figure at the end of a path will make the path seem longer. Obversely, an over-scaled sculpture can be melodramatic and actually make the space feel larger.

34. A wood rooster with natural bark, carved with a chainsaw.
35. At the Griffis Sculpture Park outside of Buffalo, New York, surreal figures created by Larry Griffis, Jr., inhabit the fields.
36. Reclaimed columns add sculptural and architectural elements to this private garden in Washington.
37. A floating metal sphere, as created by contemporary artist Neil Dawson outside Christchurch, New Zealand.
38. Acrobats reach for the sky in a sculpture by California artist Aristoides Demetrios.
39. These wrought-iron figures were placed in barns in Pennsylvania during the nineteenth century in hopes of protecting livestock from disease.
40. A dapper gent made of lead peers into the garden.

Sculptures and statuary can be found in marble, stone, iron, steel, lead, zinc, bronze, aluminum, terra-cotta, clay, wood, glass, artificial stone, mirror, and resin. Your choice of material will help convey a sense of formality or informality, ostentation or understatement, antiquity or modernity.

In ancient Rome, the placement of a sculpture had symbolic as well as aesthetic value. For example, when a statue of Hercules was sited at the junction of two paths, it was meant to represent the choice between vice and virtue.

As you contemplate placement, you probably won't be grappling with such matters—but there are a number of factors to consider. Is your piece meant to be a focal point within the space or a delightful surprise to the viewer? Is it meant to be seen from a number of locations or just one? Should it stop the eye or encourage viewers to look beyond it? Do you want it to mask a view or engage with and enhance it? Addressing these questions should help you place sculptural elements perfectly within your landscape.

41

42

43

41. This howling wolf may have been carved from stone found in the mountains behind him.

42. A bronze Turtle Train created by W. Stanley Proctor in 1939 makes its way through the Children's Garden at Brookgreen Gardens, South Carolina.

43. A large terra cotta orb in the Swiss countryside.

44. An exquisitely carved and crafted wood finial at Bodnant in Wales.

45. These sapling bundles held together with vines can be found in a woodland garden in Tryon, North Carolina.

46. The dark tone of this graceful female figure continues the rhythm of the upright evergreens.

47. A sculptural surprise recessed into a stone wall.

48. This sculpture visually replaces the tree trunk of the Pyrus salicifolia, or Pendula, in the white garden at Sissinghurst.

49. Bathers play in and on the pond at Griffis Sculpture Park near Buffalo, NY.

44

45

46

47

48

49

Trompe l'oeil ("trick of the eye") panels are two-dimensional sculptural elements that create the illusion of depth. They are best employed in smaller gardens to provide a sense of expansiveness. More traditional two-dimensional sculptures can add interest to any garden wall.

Classical architecture and formal gardens are best complemented by traditional, representational forms rather than abstract creations. Informal gardens lend themselves to more rustic ornaments, whereas modern architecture can provide a pleasing backdrop for contemporary, abstract sculpture.

50. This trompe l'oeil panel at Dumbarton Oaks can be found at the terminus of a path that ends abruptly. The tunnel-shaped trellis culminating in a mother of pearl wall fountain creates the feeling of three-dimensional space.

51. A sheet-metal cow weathervane with the directionals removed, made in Pennsylvania around 1860.

52. This sculptural, espaliered pear tree helps incorporate the imposing brick wall behind it into the garden.

53. A long horizontal wall comes alive with the motion of waves in Marine Relief by Stanley Bleifeld, installed at Brookgreen Gardens in the mid 1990s.

54. An unexpected sleepyhead resides in a meadow at Chanticleer in Pennsylvania.

55. A stone leaf "floats" downstream at Chanticleer.

56. At the baroque gardens of Herrenhausen, a multitude of sculpture defines the various corners of the elaborate parterres.

57. A pair of lions at the entrance suggests a formal garden awaits within.

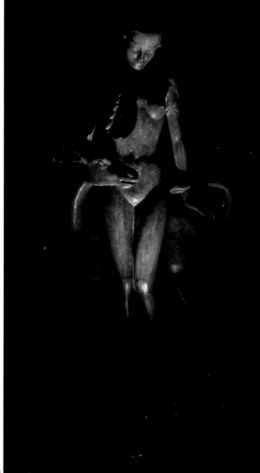

58. The circular shape of the sculpture is echoed by the shape of the sheared trees and the mounds of santolina.

59. "Diana and the Fawn" at Dumbarton Oaks.

60. Diana and the Fawn, here highlighted by thoughtfully designed night lighting.

61. A mask of large proportions, perhaps ten feet tall, made of Corten steel, at Griffis Sculpture Park.

When a piece of sculpture is meant to be a focal point, plantings should complement it rather than compete with it. An exception would be a formal parterre in which the sculpture is but one component of an intricate design scheme.

Consider lighting important pieces of sculpture so that they might be appreciated and lend drama to the nighttime garden.

CLIMATE AND WEATHERING The contemporary American sculptor Raymond Kaskey reminds us that, "Works sited outside must be created in anticipation of the weather. You cannot leave anything outside in the rain without regular maintenance, including your car."

Materials weather differently, and climate should be considered as you make your choice. Porous stone, whether natural or man-made, is particularly vulnerable to the effects of the freeze-thaw cycle, as is terra-cotta. Cast iron rusts. Bronze oxidizes to a green copper-sulfate patina that rain will wash onto its base or surrounding paving, causing stains. Lead is quite durable in cold climates, but if the internal armature is made of iron, it will rust as rain permeates the exterior. Eventually, the rusted form will expand and split the lead.

An alloy called Corten, or weathering steel, came into use in the 1960s. It does not need to be painted or sealed and will form a rustlike coating that in most cases is stable and resistant to corrosion. However, it is sensitive to salt air and may corrode in seaside environments. If the form of the piece allows rainwater to collect in crevices, this too can cause corrosion.

Some materials, in particular certain resins and fiberglass, are sensitive to UV rays. Wood will crack when exposed to shifts in humidity. Limestone, sandstone, marble, and granite deteriorate in the presence of acid rain.

INSTALLATION AND MAINTENANCE The larger the sculpture, the more complex its installation may become. In most cases, it is best to avoid direct contact between the sculpture and the earth, so some sort of base or stand is required. (Garden gnomes, on the other hand, are perfectly at home on the ground.)

When installing a substantial sculpture, take note of the slope and drainage of the site and avoid standing water. If necessary, devise some sort of drainage system so that the piece never comes into direct contact with water. If it is to be placed on a platform or base, the base should be well drained and properly waterproofed. Any fasteners used to anchor the sculpture to its base should be of a compatible material.

Sculptures should be sited out of range of sprinklers and protected from damage by lawn mowers, trimmers, and snow removal equipment. If the piece is made of a delicate material, it might be wise to shelter it under a roof. Cast-iron sculptures are sometimes protected by a coat of paint.

Keep sculptures well away from trees that have invasive roots, attract birds, or produce sap. Deep shade encourages algae growth on a variety of materials. Care should be taken

62

63

62. *Born Free*, by Serena Litofsky, features deer made of steel, polymer, and resin.
63. A limestone sculpture shows the effects of time and weather.
64. Gilded lead figures in dramatic poses decorate the outdoor theater at Herrenhausen.
65. "The Sweet Patootie" at the House of the Giants in Akaroa, New Zealand, is a mosaic applied to durably reinforced concrete.
66. Stacked pieces of wood form the body and well-chosen branches the feet and head of this rustic turtle in Germany, protected from contact with the soil.
67. A cast-iron dog doing what dogs love to do.
68. Painting cast iron is both protective and ornamental.

64

65

66

67

68

when using fertilizers or herbicides near sculptures since some may cause damage.

Sculptures should be routinely inspected for damage. Cracks and splits will allow water to permeate and should be repaired as soon as possible. Any crevices that hold water or leaves should be examined and cleaned regularly.

Most metal sculptures require maintenance at least once a year. Cleaning with mild soap and water, followed by an application of wax, will help preserve their beauty and durability for years to come. In temperate climates, porous objects should be stored before the first frost. If that isn't practical, they should be covered carefully.

Although introducing sculptural elements into your garden requires careful planning and adds a few items to the to-do list, it is a worthwhile touch, creating new focal points and adding texture, color, and style to outdoor spaces large and small.

69. A well-planned tulip bed leads the eye to a ghostly horse and rider.

STAIRS

A little step may be the beginning of a great journey.
ANONYMOUS

1. Stone slabs interplanted with colorful perennials are set into a slope to create a delightful transition between levels at Chanticleer in Pennsylvania.
2. Many cultures have considered the ziggurat a symbol of the "stairway to heaven." The island garden of Isola Bella in Italy is a striking example of a ziggurat design that carries the eye from the water's edge to the top of its soaring obelisks.

The first stairs were probably formed naturally, as primitive humans traveled up and down well-trodden slopes. Moving to higher ground with ease was critical to survival in the face of invaders or quickly rising floodwaters, so better and better stairs were engineered. As they evolved, they took on a symbolic significance as well as a practical one, elevating man to the spiritual plane—bringing him closer to the divine.

Ancient cultures all over the world placed their houses of worship at the highest elevations—as close to their gods as humanly possible and visible to their followers from great distances. The ancient Babylonians, Egyptians, Maya, and Aztecs built steplike edifices, such as ziggurats and pyramids of great heights, for use as tombs, temples, and public gathering places.

An early form of ascent was the inclined ramp formed from compacted soils or stone rubble. It retained the symbolism of the stairway but was more efficient for transporting building materials to higher ground. As one civilization succeeded another, new temple sites were rarely created. Rather, the ascendant ruler tended to embellish existing structures, adding to their height and size. Ramps made the process considerably easier.

In the Shandong province of China, north of the city of Tai'an, stairs stretching to the top of the sacred mountain Tai Shan have been in use for thousands of years. The area has been a cultural center since the Neolithic era (10,000–2000 BC). Some seven thousand steps carved into the granite mountain traverse about six miles in a symbolic link between earth and heaven. Generations of pilgrims, including Confucius, have made the journey.

A wood staircase dating to the Bronze Age (circa 1300 BC) was found at an ancient salt mine in Hallstatt, Austria, miraculously well preserved thanks to the salty environment. Made from the trunks of spruce and fir trees, its treads were about 3 feet wide and were fitted into slits in the trunks and supported by triangular wedges.

Greek temples were erected in places where sacred events were believed to have taken place. Purposely set apart from the earthly realm, they were built on pedestals with identical sets of ascending stairs on all sides. In this way, they could be seen from near and far and entered from any approach.

The Romans built their temples on rocky promontories, accessible via one set of wide, ceremonial, precut masonry stairs leading to a single entrance. In *De Architectura*, Vitruvius made note of both the spiritual and functional qualities of stairways, stating that stairs leading to temples should be odd in number so that visitors might begin and end their ascent on the propitious right foot. He further specified that the height of the risers should be between 9 and 10 inches to ease the difficulty of the climb.

In medieval times, castles featured spiral staircases that wound upward always in a clockwise direction. There was an ingenious reason for this: Presuming that any intruder would be right-handed, this forced him to keep his sword-bearing arm against the adjoining wall, limiting his striking range and providing an advantage to the defender. As further protection, sometimes these staircases included a trick or stumble step of a different dimension, meant to slow down interlopers.

In the Far East, palace stairways often included one squeaking tread to warn of trespassers. This early "security alarm" was created by placing nails so that they rubbed against clamps when stepped on, making a chirping sound. Floors made in this manner were called or *uguisubari* ("nightingale floors").

It was not until the Renaissance that garden steps were conceived and built on a grand scale. Thanks to the country's hilly terrain, staircases became an essential element of Italian garden design during the period. Linking multiple levels, the stairways were often monumental in scale and highly ornamented with balustrades, vases, statues, and fountains. In more rustic or informal areas, they might take the form of a ramplike *scala cordonata*, with long, sloping steps on shallow

3. A gently inclined ramp of bricks set on edge in a circular pattern eases the climb through the garden of Deeg Palace in Bharatpur, India, while bands of sandstone provide traction for the descent.
4. Symmetrical staircases scale the steep hillside and connect the terraces both visually and functionally at Villa Garzoni.
5. A series of urns alternating with troughs of water encloses a stairway at Villa Lante.
6. Random rectangular slabs of limestone set into turf form an informal ramp at Montjuïc in Barcelona.

7. Master designer André Le Nôtre tucked stairs into the edge of the parterre at Vaux-le-Vicomte.
8. The baroque stairway at Troja Palace, built in the late seventeenth century, incorporates sculptures depicting a battle between Olympic gods and Titans.
9. An elegant curved stairway leads from the castle terrace to the gardens at Veitschöchheim in Germany.

stone risers, topped by turf, gravel, or occasionally paving.

In France, where the terrain was not as hilly, stairs were used more subtly. André Le Nôtre placed them cleverly within his grand schemes to provide views or hide certain features so that they might emerge as a visitor grew nearer. In his book *Cours d'Architecture*, Jacques-François Blondel (1705–1774) dismissed the ornamental value of the staircases, instead focusing on how to design them ergonomically, based on the length of the human pace.

Baroque gardens throughout Europe incorporated highly ornamented stairways that combined utility with keen visual interest.

In his 1792 plans for the US Capitol, Benjamin Latrobe designed steps of whose dimensions differed according to their intended use. The central ceremonial steps, meant to be mounted in a leisurely way, have 5-inch risers and 17-inch treads, whereas the stairs leading to the House and Senate, designed for speedier ascent, have 6-inch risers and 14-inch treads.

Much governmental, religious, and monumental architecture around the world continues to reflect the classical Greek tradition, with buildings erected on raised bases accessible via grand staircases.

DESIGN Each year, accidents on stairs account for more than four thousand deaths and 1.4 million injuries in the United States alone—that's one accident every two minutes and one death every two hours! Even when building codes—which are far from stringent—have been followed to the letter, owners and architects may be held liable for accidents. Common hazards include risers and treads that are not uniform; treads that are too shallow, cracked, or otherwise damaged; improperly illuminated stair areas; and the absence of handrails.

The code requirements for stairs vary from place to place and according to the building's use and occupancy. Most codes do stipulate that stairs must be slip resistant, have handrails with 12-inch extensions at the top and bottom, be at least 44 inches wide with closed risers, and be maintained throughout all seasons. When you are installing stairs, it is essential to check local building codes.

Almost all codes dictate that there should never be more than 3/8-inch difference from one tread or riser to the next. Beyond that, it is not a good idea to group fewer than three steps together, as one or two steps in a path may become a tripping hazard. The nose of a tread should never project past the riser more than an inch as it may catch the foot and cause a fall.

To meet code guidelines, every door opening requires a landing that is at least 5 feet wide—but even this is too narrow to permit clearance for two people and the outward swing of the door. Landings must be placed at least every 12 feet in rise of the staircase, but an ideal design locates landings every four feet in rise.

All staircases exceeding 30 inches in height are required to have handrails 34 to 38 inches above the steps. The rails should fit comfortably in the hand with a diameter of between 1 and 2 inches, and be separated from the adjoining wall by at least an inch. On the open side of a stair, a railing must have pickets spaced no wider than 4 inches apart.

Outdoor stairs usually have a subbase of reinforced concrete with footings below the frost line. In unstable soils, landings and steps that adjoin structures should not be tied in, and

should have separate footings. Stairs can be finished with textured or broom-finished concrete, stone, oversize brick, or tile. It is most important that surfaces not reflect glare or become slippery when wet. Thermal-finished granite provides the most durable surface; marble, limestone, and sandstone are more fragile.

Although whimsical, the stairs at "The Giant's House" in New Zealand are built on a sturdy base. More about the construction of these and other creations of Josie Martin can be found in the design section of our "Walls" chapter.

Stair risers should match the material, color, and coursing of the stone or brick used for the adjoining façade or walls. Selecting one color for treads and another for risers will help

10. Stone steps lead to a wooden landing and are surrounded by a gracefully curved wrought-iron handrail in Williamsburg.

11. A wood front entrance stoop and railing at Williamsburg are painted to match the trim of the house. Although visually attractive, the landing is a bit small to accommodate two visitors.

12. A garden staircase rises to meet a mulched landing and then curves up to a paved one before reaching the next garden level at Pinewood in Florida.

13. At Pinewood, wrought-iron handrails are set into brick steps with tile risers.

14. These steps constructed by Josie Martin at the Giant's House in New Zealand feature mosaics of cobalt blue tiles, pottery shards, and pebbles resting on weathered timber risers.

15. This mosaic stairway scheme, also at the Giant's House, employs treads of varying depths, its colors complemented by plantings of lamb's ears and a low boxwood hedge.

16. Shimmering polka dots of varying sizes float in steps of dyed concrete lined with a low mosaic wall.

17. Mosaic treads and risers in a floral pattern connect two turf terraces.

18. Sophisticated semicircular stairs with stone treads and brick risers at Williamsburg.

19. The lower risers of this flared stairway at Hidcote in England are covered with greenery.

20. In contrast with the aged surrounding courtyard ruins in Antigua, Guatemala, a modern set of stairs with open risers leads to a circular stairway.

21. A handsomely detailed ramp of granite setts in Berlin, Germany.

22. This ingenious construction in Dresden, Germany, serves as both a stairway and a ramp for bicycles

23. This steep stone staircase in a garden in France includes a central ramp for wheelbarrows that also channels water during heavy rainfalls.

24. Convex and concave steps meet to form an elliptical landing.

25. A congregation of gilded sandstone sculptures sip tea on the scalloped steps of the Chinese House in Sanssouci.

those with poor sight navigate the stairs. Open risers can be very dramatic and will reduce the visual mass of the steps—but they are distracting and may cause people to trip on the way up. They should certainly be avoided if there are small children around who would be in danger of falling through one of the openings. In fact, open risers are prohibited in many locales. If you have your heart set on an open look, tempered glass risers offer the same effect without the hazard.

The code for most exterior ramps used commercially specifies a maximum slope of 1 inch of rise to every 20 inches of length. Residential ramps may be a bit steeper but, as always, check with your local authorities. Landings are required at the top and bottom of ramps and whenever they change directions.

Handrails are required for ramps just as they are for stairways.

Steps and ramps should be uniformly illuminated without glare or shadow lines and treads should always be nonreflective. It's best to light stairs from above, mounting the fixtures inside the handrail or on the sidewall. To save electricity, motion detectors may be used to activate the lamps.

If storage space is at a premium, you might want to use the area created beneath your stairs or ramp for that purpose. Curved stairs and railings are extremely elegant, but keep in mind that they can cost up to twice as much as straight steps.

Spiral staircases are space savers but they can be treacherous and should only be considered if you really don't have room for straight or double-back stairs.

26. Curved steps disappear into a slope at Ludwigsburg in Germany.

27. A cast-iron spiral stairway in Jodhpur, India.

28. Buttressed and cantilevered steps carved out of red sandstone in Jodhpur, India.

29. These stone steps set into turf seem to have been carved out of the earth.

30. Steps carved into existing rock.

31. Refined steps carved from single slabs of marble include boot scrapers set in granite at the sidewalk level. Note that the sweeping iron handrail is mounted separately.

32. Large, rough blocks of rock with minimal mortar joints create an informal and sturdy stairway.

Steps can be dramatically cantilevered out from a masonry wall, but it's important to protect people from bumping their heads. Situating well-defined planting beds under the overhanging steps is an attractive solution to the problem.

Rustic stairs may be carved directly into the stone of a hillside, or native stone may be collected on site and used to construct an informal stairway.

CLIMATE AND WEATHERING Special thought must be put into exterior stairs in temperate climates, where they will be subject to freeze-thaw cycles and deicing compounds. Concrete stairs and mortar joints are always the first to fail and should not be exposed on all four sides. They should be deiced with non-corrosive materials and the treads should include a non-skid metal nosing. Ideally a tread should be made from one full paving unit without joints, which means that most brick should be avoided.

In temperate climates, exterior stairs should be located so that they are exposed to the winter sun and will not trap wind-blown snow. Steps exposed on all four sides will be the first to ice over.

Use only safe, chloride-free substances or environmentally friendly (though somewhat less efficient) ones, such as sand or kitty litter to deice stairs. Avoid metal-edged shovels in favor of those edged in plastic or rubber, which will not scratch or dislodge paving on steps. If snow removal is excessively burdensome, consider installing heating cables under the treads.

Although you may not have a choice in this, stairs built on an east-west axis will be more difficult to navigate during the rising or setting of the sun, due to glare.

Brass, stainless-steel, aluminum and bronze handrails are the most resistant to corrosion. Cast-iron and steel handrails should be powder coated or painted with epoxy paint and then coated with a urethane finish to prevent UV degradation.

Metal handrails can become too hot to touch in bright sunlight, so consider a coat of light-colored paint to reduce the solar gain—or better yet, choose wooden handrails, which stay coolest of all.

In arid climates, rills with flowing water are often placed down the middle or to either side of stairs to cool the air.

In humid climates, wood steps are the first to deteriorate. They promote moss and algae growth and are slippery when wet. If wood is your choice in this situation, consider coating it with an abrasive paint.

INSTALLATION AND MAINTENANCE Stair design and construction must be precise, so it's best to engage only the most qualified and experienced masons or carpenters. Before pouring

33. These detached carved marble steps are well suited to the mild winters at the Taj Mahal.
34. A narrow rill of flowing water in the center of a stairway provides a sense of coolness, though its actual effect on the temperature is negligible.
35. Wood garden steps set directly in soil create a rustic feeling but require careful maintenance to keep them sturdy and slip-resistant.

the concrete subbase, review the formwork for overall design, dimensions, and elevations. All treads should have the same thickness of 1 to 2 inches. The front edge can be flamed, hammered, bull nosed, or covered with abrasive metal. Abrasive strips can be recessed into the front edge to prevent slipping. All treads should slope 1/4 inch per foot to shed water and all tread slopes should be uniform. The joints on treads should be staggered and never line up.

All risers should be of a material and color that will not crack or show scuffmarks from shoes. For this reason, it's best to avoid stucco or painted finishes.

Before installing handrails, measure all treads and risers and accept no variation in size greater than 3/8 inch. The posts for railings are usually core-drilled into the finished landings and treads. In the past, lead was the preferred filler, but this has been replaced by high-compression cement products that can be dyed to match the tread or landing material. The post's grout joints can also be concealed with foot caps, which should be made of cast aluminum and powder coated to prevent rust stains.

Turf steps with brick or stone risers require quick drainage and constant maintenance. Ideally, the treads should be the same width as a lawn mower and have a mowing edge meeting each riser.

Avoid placing plants that are thorny, shed bark, or produce messy flowers and fruit next to exterior steps. Wet leaves on stairs can be lethal.

Stairs located in the shade should periodically be power washed to eliminate all moss and algae.

Although stairs are a primarily functional element of garden design, when well thought out they can add much to the ambience. Narrow stairs add mystery, wide ones with generous treads are welcoming, landings provide rhythm and can even become inviting terraces. Consider the many ways a utilitarian set of stairs might add drama to your garden as well as a way to get from here to there.

36

37

38

39

36. These concrete steps have a slip-resistant nose for safety and handrails of simple but flowing S-scrolls mounted in only two places.

37. A curved brick stairway embraced by a flared wood railing.

38. These "French steps," designed by Beatrix Farrand at Dumbarton Oaks, have risers of brick set vertically and turf treads bordered with beautifully carved limestone scrolls.

39. A turf ramp in a private garden in Tryon, North Carolina, employs bands of bricks as risers.

41

40

40. Front steps in a pyramidal form allow access from all sides. Williamsburg.

41. A moveable, wood step that doubles as a bench provides direct access to a shop in Verre, Holland.

SUNDIALS

But what minutes!
Count them by sensation, and not by
calendars, and each moment is a day.
BENJAMIN DISRAELI

1. This square brass sundial was brought to Tudor Place in Washington, DC, from Crossbasket Castle, the Scotland home of the Peter family dating from the seventeenth century. Oddly enough, the hour lines on the plate are for the latitude of Augsburg, Germany—meaning that it has yet to tell the time accurately.

2. Jantar Mantar (literally "House of Instruments") was constructed by Maharaja Jai Singh II, a scholar of ancient astronomy, between 1727 and 1733. The Samrat Yantra ("Supreme Instrument"), with a ramp of 90 feet as gnomon, is in the background while a pair of black-and-white hemispheric bowls called Jai Prakash Yantra sits in the foreground.

The sundial was one of our earliest scientific instruments. Although used to determine time, it is not a clock but an astronomical device that charts the progress of the sun across the sky.

The relationship between time and celestial movement was recognized by the earliest humans, who devised a simple shadow stick—a twig stuck into the ground in full sunlight—to determine the time of day. At what we now call noon, when the sun was directly overhead, the stick cast no shadow.

As the day progressed, the shadow grew longer. The vertical part of a sundial, called the *gnomon* (from the Greek for "indicator") is really no different from that primitive shadow stick.

As early as 3500 BC, the Egyptians and Babylonians (inhabitants of present day Iraq) were erecting tall obelisks or pillars in public spaces to serve as indicators of the times for work and midday meals. Hieroglyphics from the Middle Empire (2033–1710 BC) reveal that measuring time continued to be central to Egyptian daily life.

In China, archeological finds from the Eighteenth Dynasty (1540–1307 BC) include an L-shaped object called a *merkhet* ("instrument of knowing"). The portable sundial was also developed during this era. During the eleventh century BC, it is believed that the Duke of Zhou (author of the *I Ching*) built a *ceyingtai* ("terrace for gnomon measurement") at Gaocheng.

The pre-Socratic Greek philosopher Anaximander (610–546 BC) is credited with introducing the sundial to his country and refining it to indicate solstices and equinoxes.

Roman architect and engineer Marcus Vitruvius described thirteen types of sundials, including some that were portable, in his best-known work, *De Architectura*. Obelisks plundered from the Egyptians were erected as gnomons in Rome, and although the Romans used sundials extensively, they did little to advance their design.

It was not until 100 AD in Greece that sundials were constructed with a slanted gnomon similar to ones we find today. When the slanted gnomon is placed parallel to the Earth's axis, it keeps pace with the seasonal changes in the sun's angles.

During the Middle Ages, vertical sundials were commonly placed over doorways to indicate the hour of the day. Medieval peasants in northern Europe carved sundials into the bottoms of their wooden clogs, then placed them upright in the ground so that the heels cast a shadow.

The Renaissance heralded the golden age of many things, including sundials. They were soon being crafted in a variety of forms, including the armillary, a sphere surrounded by calibrated rings. In addition to time, the exceedingly sophisticated sundials charted the season, the date, and the time of sunrise and sunset.

At the same time that sundials were evolving, the first mechanical clocks driven by counterweights were coming into being. These timepieces were thought to be more modern because they did not rely on the sun—but the truth is that until the late 1800s, mechanical clocks had to be adjusted periodically by consulting the unfailingly accurate sundial.

The cannon sundial—in which a magnifying glass caused the sun's rays to ignite a gunpowder charge and signal the hour with a boom—was a common feature in late-eighteenth-century gardens. Benjamin Franklin described this instrument as the "striking sundial" in *Poor Richard's Almanac* and noted the advantage of knowing the time without the having to look at the instrument (on sunny days, at least).

Thomas Jefferson designed a sundial for Monticello, made from a 10-inch wooden sphere. Although the original disappeared some time ago, a reproduction has been made according to the drawings and description Jefferson sent to the architect Benjamin Latrobe in a letter dated August 27, 1816. The spherical sundial was common in Europe but rarely found in American gardens.

3. A horizontal sundial made of cast iron with sparse decoration, inscribed with the year 1840.
4. An armillary sphere is the focus of a flower-filled garden room at Insel Mainau.
5. This faithful reproduction of a spherical sundial designed by Thomas Jefferson sits on a carved stone base set on a wooden pedestal at Monticello.

Once the mechanical clock had been perfected, the sundial became obsolete as a chronometer, but it has remained a popular ornament in gardens around the world, valued for its beauty and simple utility. Unlike clocks and watches, the sundial reminds us of our connection to the rhythms of our cyclical universe. The writer Hilaire Belloc was fascinated by sundials and wrote many short poems about them, including:

Save on the rare occasions when the Sun
Is shining, I am only here for fun.

DESIGN The most common types of garden sundials are horizontal, vertical, and armillary. To be accurate, a sundial must be designed and calibrated for the latitude and longitude of the proposed location. Most mass-manufactured sundials are set for a latitude of 45 degrees. If you'd like your sundial to be useful as well as attractive, your best bet is to commission one from a knowledgeable craftsman.

The horizontal sundial features a round dial plate and a vertical gnomon; the plate is often inscribed with a humorous or inspiring phrase about the passage of time. These instruments are usually mounted on a freestanding plinth.

The vertical sundial consists of a projecting gnomon that casts a shadow line on an inscribed vertical wall.

The armillary sundial is a sphere with encircling rings and a central shaft that functions as the gnomon, casting a shadow on the hour ring. It is the most advanced form of sundial and quite pleasingly decorative as well. Like its horizontal counterpart, the armillary sundial is freestanding.

Horizontal and armillary sundials make lovely focal points

6. In the gardens of Montpelier in Virginia, where President James Madison lived as a child, this sundial is set on an ornately carved stone plinth. Thought to be Italian, the dial is inscribed "Feare God and obey the King."

7. A brass dial plate from around 1730 sits on a limestone plinth in the Baroque gardens of Herrenhausen in Germany.

8. A stone plinth holds this horizontal sundial with upright hour markers.

9. A vertical sundial at the Bok Tower Gardens in Florida features a bronze gnomon supported by the figure of a snake—the symbol for time. The hours are marked by zodiac symbols inscribed in the marble.

10. This bronze armillary sphere some four feet in diameter, titled *The Cycle of Life*, was created by Paul Manship in 1924 for Brookgreen Gardens in South Carolina. Its complex array of imagery includes signs of the zodiac, the cycle of life and the four elements.

11. A cast-iron armillary of modest design set on a fluted stone column.

12. On this unusual bronze sundial at Brookgreen Gardens, created by Brenda Putnam in 1931, a semi-circle of hours is completed above by a sculpture of a boy teasing a young goat. It is mounted on a pink marble pedestal carved with rams' heads.

for formal gardens. As such, they should be placed so they may be viewed from all sides and approached closely enough that they may be read.

So as to function, vertical sundials should be placed on southern walls in the northern hemisphere and northern walls in the southern hemisphere. (There are examples of eastern and western vertical sundials, but these function only in the morning or afternoon.) Common sights in Europe and South America but all too rare in the United States, vertical, wall-mounted sundials nicely enhance any barren wall.

Sundials can be found in granite, marble, flagstone, lime-stone, slate, bronze, brass, copper, lead, iron, aluminum, and wood. Their pedestals are most often made of stone or metal.

CLIMATE AND WEATHERING If a sundial can't cast a shadow, it becomes purely ornamental—so clearly, it is best to place it in full, all-day sun.

Sundials weather in much the same way as any sculpture of the same material, so for specific information on weathering, consult the "Climate and Weathering" section in our "Sculpture and Statuary" chapter.

13. A horizontal sundial made completely of metal serves as an ornament in a parterre border.
14. This vertical sundial marks both the hour and half hour.
15. This bronze sundial was placed in Savannah's Johnson Square in 1933 in honor of Colonel William Bull, who helped lay out the city two hundred years earlier.
16. A sundial amusingly set on a bust mounted on the pier of a stone wall.

INSTALLATION AND MAINTENANCE All calibrated sundials should be accompanied by precise instructions on their proper mounting and orientation. Follow these carefully if you'd like your instrument to be useful as well as attractive.

The plinth for a freestanding sundial should be set on a concrete footing that extends below the frost line.

Stone sundials can be cleaned with a mild bleach solution and can be painted with a mixture of buttermilk and ground-up moss and lichen to convey a weathered look.

Bronze and brass sundials will age to a natural brown or verdigris finish, but may be kept brilliant with metal polish. If you prefer some shine, polished brass and bronze may be sealed with a clear polyurethane lacquer finish. Aluminum sundials should be powder coated and cleaned with a mild soap.

Cast-iron and iron sundials will rust and require the most maintenance. These should be galvanized and powder coated.

A wide variety of mottoes and quotations have graced the faces of sundials over the years. Here are a few of our favorites:

Come along and grow old with me; the best is yet to be.
Let others tell of storms and showers, I tell of sunny morning hours.
Be as true to each other as this dial is to the sun.
Hours fly, Flowers die. New days, New ways, Pass by. Love stays.

17. A horizontal sundial found at the Bruton Parish Church, established in 1674 in Williamsburg, Virginia.
18. This sundial seems right at home in an herb garden, set on pervious stone paving interplanted with creeping thyme.
19. A two-tiered base of weathered limestone holds a bronze sundial showing signs of patina.
20. This sundial is both sculptural and functional; detailed instructions for "How to Read the Analemma [Sundial]" are included on its plinth.

SWIMMING POOLS

In one drop of water are found all the secrets of the oceans.
KAHLIL GIBRAN

1. **The swimming pool at Dumbarton Oaks was designed by architect Frederick Brooke (1870–1960) in the early 1920s. Beatrix Farrand suggested that limestone paving would blend with the limestone "brim of the pool" and the Italianate character of the design.**

The earliest known example of a swimming pool, the "Great Bath," was built in the sophisticated city-state of Mohenjo-Daro in Pakistan during the third millennium BC. Upon discovering it in 1922, British archaeologist Sir John Hubert Marshall wrote, "Its plan is simple. . . . In the midst of the open quadrangle is a large swimming-bath, some 39 feet long by 23 feet broad and sunk about 8 feet below the paving of the court, with a flight of stairs at either end, and at the foot of each a low platform for the convenience of bathers who might otherwise have found the water too deep. The bath was filled from the well . . . and the waste carried off through a covered drain." Constructed of brick set on edge, the bath was covered with gypsum plaster and sealed with natural, waterproof tar.

Swimming in the Nile River was a popular activity among the ancient Egyptian population. Stone carvings depict swimmers performing identifiable strokes, such as the breaststroke and crawl. Private, man-made swimming pools were reserved for royal palaces.

Gaius Maecenas (circa 70 BC–8 BC) was a wealthy advisor to Emperor Caesar Augustus and a patron of the arts. He is credited with designing the first heated swimming pool in ancient Rome. Supported by a ring of pillars, the pool was set over a chamber in which a fire burned constantly, stoked by slave laborers.

Both the Greeks and Romans were known for their public

2. One of several pools at Hadrian's Villa (second century AD) outside Rome. During the Renaissance, many marble facings and ornaments were transplanted to nearby villas such as the Villa D'Este.

3. In the fourteenth-century Garden of the Partal at the Alhambra, stone lions feed water to the pool from a source miles away, in the mountains.

4. A baoli (step tank) or in Ranakpur, India, has been used in the same way for centuries.

baths and valued swimming as an important part of every boy's education and military training. Artificial pools were constructed for these purposes. At the Battle of Salamis (480 BC), the Persians greatly outnumbered the Greeks, yet the Greeks were victorious because of their ability to swim to safety from their sinking ships. The untrained Persians drowned before reaching shore.

In his book *De Architectura*, written around 25 BC, Vitruvius wrote in detail about the construction and design of swimming pools. Pliny the Younger (circa AD 61–112) boasted both warm and cold pools at his villa in Tuscany.

In Sri Lanka, pools dating back to the eighth century have been dubbed *kuttam pokuna* ("twin pools"). In fact, they are not identical: one is 132 feet by 51 feet by 18 feet deep, while the other is 91 by 51 feet by 14 feet deep. Made of granite, they are fed by water that passes through cleansing filters and into the first pool through a carved lion's mouth. It then flows into the second pool via an underground pipe and drains out through an opening in the bottom. The pools are intricately ornamented with scrolls and stone vases and were probably used for bathing rituals by monks at a nearby monastery.

Step wells large and small were common in India between the eleventh and sixteenth century, designed to safeguard much needed water during the dry season. Elaborately ornamented with columns, friezes, scrollwork, and carvings of deities, their scale depended on the size of the local population. In some cases, they were large enough and deep enough to accommodate stone diving platforms for swimmers. They served as cool and inviting spots to gather and socialize.

In Mexico, Nezahualcoyotl (AD 1402–1472) developed sophisticated hydraulics at Texcoco. Water was brought from more than 5 miles away to feed carved rock pools used for bathing, tiled pools used to irrigate orchards, and holding pools for fish. A series of canals connected the pools, and all were surrounded by lush gardens.

In his essay, "Of Gardens," Sir Francis Bacon (1561–1626) described the pools of his day: "As for the other kind of Fountain, which we may call a bathing-pool, it may admit much curiosity and beauty . . . that the bottom be finely paved, and with images; the sides likewise; and withal embellished with coloured glass, and such things of lustre; encompassed also with fine rails of low statues: but the main point is the same which we mentioned in the former kind of Fountain; which is, that the water be in perpetual motion, fed by a water higher than the pool, and delivered into it by fair spouts, and then discharged away underground, by some equality of bores, that it stay little."

Thermal baths fed by natural hot springs have been in existence since the Roman era, and spas with large pools could be found all over Europe and England throughout the centuries. But, during times of epidemics and plagues, bathing water became a scapegoat and public baths were shunned as a source of disease.

Swim clubs became popular in England in the nineteenth century, and by 1837, six indoor pools could be found in London. Swimming events were included in the Olympic Games for the first time in 1896.

The first municipal pools in the United States were built in an effort to limit the number of raucous and often naked young men swimming in local rivers and lakes. They caught on quickly, and by the 1890s, could be found in large and small communities around the country. A. J. Eilers Sr. built the first concrete pool in Texas in 1915, at the site of a local spring-fed swimming hole in Austin. It soon became known as Deep Eddy Pool. A bathhouse was added during the Depression by the Works Progress Administration and the pool can still be enjoyed today.

Among the first private pools in the United States were those constructed in such Gilded Age gardens as Villa Vizcaya in Coconut Grove, Florida, and Dumbarton Oaks in Washington, D.C. Soon, Hollywood celebrities were getting in on the act, building lavish private pools adjoining their mansions.

At Pickfair, Douglas Fairbanks and Mary Pickford built one that measured 55 by 100 feet, abutted by a sand beach.

5. The early twentieth-century swimming pool at Vizcaya in Florida flows under the house into a sheltered grotto. It was designed to be filled with either salt or fresh water.
6. The pool at Dumbarton Oaks features rocaille panels of cast stone surrounding a red marble fountain.
7. The Venetian Pool in Miami, Florida, built for public use in 1923 on the site of a coral rock quarry, includes waterfalls, grottoes, and stone terraces.
8. Another view of the 820,000-gallon Venetian Pool, which is spring fed and drained daily.

9. An oval pool, set in lawn and filled to the rim, blends into the landscape of this private garden in Peapack, New Jersey.

10. A rectangular pool surrounded by a flagstone terrace is enlivened by a jet of water from a wall fountain.

11. An irregularly shaped swimming pool is tucked into the surrounding plantings to give it a natural feeling.

Jack Benny was photographed canoeing across his swimming pool.

In the 1930s, public pools were open to all races but segregated by gender. When men and women began swimming together, nonwhites were relegated to their own public pools. Until well into the 1950s, public pools were seen as a manifestation of the good life, emphasizing the importance of leisure time activities and community camaraderie. But as the '50s wore on and construction techniques evolved, private pools became accessible to the middle class and they abandoned local swimming spots for their own backyards.

The development of a substance called gunite, a mixture of cement, sand, and water that could be applied through a pressure hose to produce a dense lining, made pool construction easier and less expensive. As more people moved to the suburbs there was a greater demand for private pools that could serve as hubs for wholesome family activity.

Since the 1950s, swimming pool design has continuously evolved, the basic rectangle giving way to rounded shapes, biomorphic designs, vanishing edges, lap pools, and more. Today, swimming pools may be formal or naturalistic, meant to stand out from or blend in with the surrounding landscape. The only limits are personal taste and budget.

DESIGN There are five types of pool construction: aboveground, vinyl lined, fiberglass, poured concrete, and gunite.

Above ground pools are the least expensive and easiest to install, but there are distinct limits on their size, shape and depth. They are not considered permanent structures so they won't affect property-tax rates, but permits are usually required before installation. These pools are functional—and can be fun for kids—but are less than aesthetically pleasing.

Vinyl-lined pools are the least expensive of the in-ground options and can be installed relatively quickly. The vinyl liner has a limited life span, however, fades with the use of chlorine, and can be punctured. Steps and benches usually do not match the liner.

Fiberglass pools are prefabricated one-piece structures, installed easily but available only in set sizes, shapes, and depths. They are more expensive than vinyl-lined pools but more durable and long lasting. Originally available only in white, they can now be found in other colors, including tan and many shades of blue. Fiberglass pools require less maintenance than do those of concrete or gunite because they are nonporous, made with fewer chemicals, and never need resurfacing. An added benefit: Their smoothness is kind to feet.

Gunite and poured-concrete pools can be fabricated in any size, shape, and depth. They are the most expensive choice, but when installed properly, are quite durable and long lasting. These pools are plastered and can then be finished with pebble aggregate, colored plaster, polished marble, or tile. Dark-colored pools appear deeper, more fountainlike and are the most reflective. As an added luxury, a hot tub or spa may be integrated into the design. (If you'd like to be able to use the spa elements year-round without the expense of heating and maintaining the larger body of water, consider a separate heater and filter system for the spa.)

Gunite and concrete swimming pools are sold and priced according to four standard sizes: 15 by 30 feet, 18 by 36 feet, 20 by 40 feet, and 25 by 50 feet. So, for example, if you design a pool that is 19 by 37 feet, you will be billed for a pool that is 20 by 40 feet. Standard pool depth is 3 feet in the shallow end up to 8 feet in the deep end, but the depth differential should be reduced in smaller pools so as to avoid a steep bottom that might be uncomfortable to walk on. Keep in mind that you'll probably spend a lot of time in the shallow end and be sure it is sufficiently spacious. A diving pool should have a minimum of 13 feet in the deep end, though this depends somewhat on the height of the board.

When designing a pool for people who do not actually swim much, consider wide, long steps and underwater pool benches, all of which should be curved or rounded to avoid injury.

Pools can be filled with either salt or fresh water. Saltwater is easier to sanitize, with the use of a chlorine generator that runs along with the pump and eliminates any need to handle toxic chemicals. A freshwater pool requires both a pump and a filtration system to circulate the water and remove contaminants, as well as a feeder that releases chlorine into the water. The amount of chlorine needed is based on the pH content of the water, which must be checked at least twice a month. Chloramines are created when chlorine disinfectants are added to water and combine with perspiration and other organic waste. "Chlorine smell," red eyes, dry skin, and respiratory discomfort are the result of chloramines rather than the chlorine itself.

A recent innovation that is gaining in popularity is the natural swimming pool (NSP), which filters water biologically. The NSP was developed in Austria and uses a combination of hydraulic design, a fine filter, and the introduction of plants that naturally keep down algae. The cost of an NSP is comparable to that of a traditional swimming pool, but NSPs tend to be larger because the natural filter zone (composed of vegetation and rocks) must be separate from the swimming area. Long-term maintenance costs are lower than those of traditional pools because natural pools don't require chemicals.

Automatic covers are available for rectangular pools in widths up to 25 feet. Irregular-shaped pools can be fitted with automatic covers, but the surrounding terrace must be cantilevered and this will increase the overall cost of installation. The box that houses the automatic pool cover is usually capped with aluminum that is both flimsy to walk on and unattractive. Painting the cover to match the pool's coping will make it less visible. An alternative is to install removable paving to conceal the cover and provide secure footing.

Swimming pools are usually tiled at the "scum line" because accumulated organic residue from perspiration, sunscreen, and so forth, is difficult to remove from plaster or concrete. Ideally, the tile should be of the same material or color as the coping. Glazed tiles are the easiest to clean. The water level in most pools is set at 6 inches below the top of the coping, but should be as close to the brim as possible.

12. The floor of this pool offers up a lively mosaic pattern of a school of fish.
13. Full-width entry steps make an ideal place for children to play and a relaxing place for all to cool off.
14. This pool is filled nearly to the rim and tucked into a stone wall with splashing jets.

Deck-level pools are designed so that the water level matches that of the surrounding deck. A continuous overflow channel around the circumference takes care of splash-over. Although more expensive, deck-level pools can be most effectively filtered and they offer a sense of greater surface area and enhanced reflectivity.

Infinity-edge pools that appear to vanish into the horizon represent the latest trend in pool design. Because they require extensive engineering, they are far more expensive than other options, while limiting the seating area to only three sides. Another trendy choice is the zero-entry pool, which replaces steps with a sloping, beachlike approach to the water.

If the construction of your pool will require an adjacent retaining wall, consider engineering the bond beam of the pool to support the proposed wall. This will reduce costs by eliminating the need to excavate and pour a second footing. The wall adjacent to the pool can be fitted with spouts or cascades, or even protruding rocks for climbing, evoking the feeling of swimming in a quarry.

If the pool is located some distance from the house, a pool house is a practical addition to the plan, providing bathrooms, changing rooms, and housing for unsightly pool equipment (filters, heaters, and the like). This machinery is usually set on a 4- by 6-foot concrete pad, never more than 50 feet away from the pool itself, and will last longer if it is protected from the elements.

If the primary purpose of the pool is exercise, consider a lap pool. These long, narrow, and relatively shallow pools take

15. In this private garden in Provence, a pool is surrounded by a large limestone terrace decorated by symmetrically placed topiaries.

16. An unsymmetrical swimming pool overlooks the Pacific Ocean in Maui, its angles designed to accommodate a palm tree in a stone planter on one side and a sculpture on the other.

17. This infinity edge pool in Antibes, France, appears to flow into the Mediterranean.

18. This swimming pool in Ranakpur, India, is edged with beach pebbles and filled to the maximum level.

19. A swimming pool in a private garden in Far Hills, New Jersey, is set in lawn and built into a hill with a wall that is often used for diving.

20. This pool is tucked into a side garden and concealed from the house's primary view of the garden.

21. A pavilion provides a shady retreat and a graceful entry to the pool.

22. A pool house at Chanticleer in Pennsylvania offers gracious, private changing areas as well as a gazebo open to the pool.

up far less room, are easier to maintain, and are less intrusive in the overall landscape.

A current pool, usually about 12 feet in length, simulates the resistance of a river current and eliminates the swimmer's need to turn around. In effect, one is swimming in place. These are quite inexpensive to install and maintain but are really more like a piece of exercise equipment than a body of swimmable water. They are often enclosed so they can be used year-round.

CLIMATE AND WEATHERING Pools in temperate climates should be located in full sunlight and should be dark in color to facilitate the absorption of solar heat. Because they tend to be covered for many months of the year—not a pretty sight— they should be camouflaged with screens or fencing or located away from primary house views.

Pools in temperate climates can be left filled and uncovered year round as long as the water is kept above 40°F. Be aware that this can be an expensive proposition and comes with a constant concern about burst pipes caused by power outages or malfunctions. What's more, a lot of water will be lost to evaporation. On large properties, geothermal heating and a generator can lower the cost of heating and reduce the likelihood of burst pipes, but the problem of evaporation remains. That said, pools in temperate climates should never be fully emptied during the winter, as hydrostatic pressure of the soil below could pop the pool out of the ground.

Most pool owners in temperate climates elect to install pool covers. Automatic or retractable covers are not surprisingly the most expensive kind, but can be used year-round to limit evaporation, conserve energy, reduce the need for maintenance, and keep young children safe. Manual winter covers can be put in place as part of the winterizing process, and come in a variety of materials, including solid vinyl (these require a pump on top to remove accumulated rain water); leaf-net covers, which allow rain through but trap debris and may

23

24

25

23. This lap pool, painted black to appear bottomless, can be entered through a loggia.
24. In a design by Michael Bartlett, this lap pool in Washington, DC, features stairs that lead directly from the house, providing easy access for daily exercise.
25. A fiberglass SwimEx current pool set in a flagstone terrace.
26. This light-colored paving was chosen specifically to counter the effects of hot summer sun on bare feet.

26

promote algae growth; and mesh covers, which allow water to penetrate but block light so that no algae will form.

Terraces adjoining swimming pools should be light in color to reflect solar heat. Gray flagstone in full sunlight can heat up to a foot-searing 140°F. Limestone and light-colored sandstone reflect solar heat but can be stained by suntan lotions and other spills and etched by high concentrations of chlorine. Pools with a 2-foot coping surrounded by lawn are the most attractive and the least expensive choice, but other options for surrounding surfaces include travertine marble and nonslip tile. Whatever material you choose, be sure it is suited to your climate—particularly if you live in a freeze-thaw climate.

In hot climates, the paving around a pool can be cooled with jets of mist, which also reduce the surrounding air temperature.

INSTALLATION AND MAINTENANCE Local regulations regarding swimming pools dictate setback and fencing requirements, and building permits are required almost universally. The addition of a swimming pool will probably make your homeowner's insurance premiums go up. In any case, you must notify your insurance company if you add a swimming pool to your property.

Pool companies are extremely competitive so seek out a number of estimates and carefully compare bids for price, completion time, and the type and quality of the equipment provided—and get personal recommendations from former clients if possible.

Pool costs increase significantly if the contractor encounters bedrock or disturbed soils. If this is a concern, it is a good idea to bore test the area before breaking ground. Your money will go further if the pool site is easily accessible and the soil from the excavation can be used rather than carted away. Most pool contractors do not include tree and stump removal in their estimates.

Pool manufacturers have worked hard to improve the quality and efficiency of filters, sanitizers, and automatic pool covers. Among the labor-saving devices now generally available are remote-control systems that activate heaters, filters and lights with the touch of a smartphone, and pool security systems that warn of unwanted guests, human or animal.

Shallow pools require less filtering. Pools featuring intricate shapes or compound curves are more difficult to construct and more time consuming to maintain because floating debris can get caught up in eddies.

Paved areas around pools should not be slippery when wet and should always be set to drain away from the pool. As for the surrounding plantings, consider your choices carefully.

Avoid plants that are deciduous, shed, or produce fruit that might litter the pool—and remember that chlorinated water is lethal to all plants.

In rural areas where there are no fire hydrants, the presence of a swimming pool may reduce the cost of fire insurance for the property.

27. Plants are set back from this pool to frame rather than overhang it, reducing the need for maintenance.
28. A pool of traditional design, subtly set into serene pastoral surroundings.
29. Sited away from the house and set in lawn, this pool becomes the focal point of a garden room.

TOPIARY & ARCHITECTURAL PLANTS

The best time to plant a tree was twenty years ago. The next best time is now.
CHINESE PROVERB

1. Parterres of clipped boxwood filled with seasonally changing annuals have obelisks of metal latticework at their center, in an entrance court in McLean, Virginia, designed by Michael Bartlett.
2. Small-leafed satsuki azaleas trained in *karikomi* (cloudlike forms) at the 320-year-old Rikugien Gardens, Tokyo.
3. Evergreen shrubs trained with the straight lines of *hako-zukuri* at the Geishan Bridge in Ritsurin Park in Takamatsu, Japan.
4. A sheet of moss represents the sea and the boxlike *hako-zukuri* the islands floating in it, at Tofuku-ji in Kyoto.
5. A venerable pine branch is supported by a technique called *hozue*, which is also the term for a person resting his head on the palm of his hand, at Kenrokuen Garden in Kanazawa, Japan.

In his book *Naturalis Historia* (circa AD 77–79), the Roman naturalist and philosopher known as Pliny the Elder wrote of gardens filled with cypresses clipped to represent "hunt scenes, fleets of ships, and all sorts of images." His nephew, Pliny the Younger (AD 61–112), described the gardens at his villa in Tuscany as including box hedges spelling out his name and the name of his *topiarius*, or topiary gardener (probably a Greek slave).

Without a doubt, the art of topiary was inspired by the fact that only a limited number of evergreen plant species (cypress, pine, juniper, box, and myrtle) could be found in Italy at the time. Training them into a variety of shapes added visual interest and detail to what could have been a monotonous landscape.

The early topiary gardeners of the Far East (also drawn from the servant class) pruned and trained plants in a variety of styles. In some cases, the goal was simply to reveal the beauty of a particular plant's unique form. Other topiary styles included *bonsai*, in which plants were painstakingly miniaturized; *karikomi*, the art of creating cloudlike forms; and *hako-zukuri*, the design of geometrical, boxlike shapes.

The popularity of topiary has waxed and waned. During

6. Topiary layered in the estrade form at El Retiro Park in Madrid, Spain.

7. A shaded passage between the Alhambra and the Generalife is planted with hedges trained in abstract shapes.

8. Architectural yew hedges shaped like ramparts enclose a *parterre de broderie* at Villa Garzoni in Collodi, Italy.

9. This 250-square-foot parterre made of indigenous boxwood dates from the late seventeenth century, and can be found in La Fronteira near Lisbon, Portugal. Behind it, a water tank decorated with Portuguese tiles called *azulejos* is topped with a balustraded promenade featuring twin corner gazebos.

10. Espaliered orange trees on the walls of a courtyard at Palacio de los Marqueses de Viana in Córdoba, Spain.

11. Pear trees espaliered to a wall form a four-tier horizontal cordon outside a kitchen garden.

medieval times, it languished, persisting mainly in monasteries in the form of simple, nonrepresentational shapes. Woody plants were trained to "standards" in which the lower branches were removed to create a single straight stem with a sheared ball of foliage on top. Another popular form was the *estrade*, in which a plant was trained and sheared into tiers.

Italian Renaissance gardeners, fascinated by the accomplishments of ancient Rome, revived the art of topiary in human, animal, and architectural forms. During the Baroque period, topiary artists created figures of fantastic intricacy.

Espalier, which today refers to fruit trees or shrubs trained to grow flat against walls, fences, or latticework, originated as an agricultural form of topiary. Egyptian tomb paintings dating to 1400 BC portray espaliered fig trees growing in the pharaoh's garden. The term originally referred to the framework used to train the plant but has come to encompass the plant as well and is currently used as a verb in horticultural discussions.

Throughout the Middle Ages, the espalier was a popular technique for growing fruit trees in monastery and courtyard gardens, where space was at a premium. In subsequent eras, the method took hold in climates less than favorable for fruit production, where a wall could provide protection and warmth for the plants. Freestanding espaliers allowed sunlight to reach more parts of the tree, resulting in more flowers and ultimately more fruit.

Eventually, ornamental plants were espaliered as well. Today, trees, vines, and shrubs are often trained to walls or two-dimensional forms. There are several reasons to consider an espalier. It can be a lovely way to cover an expanse of wall or a graceful way to conserve space and/or provide a warm microclimate for tender plants. And of course an espalier provides reliable support for a climber. Plants that take well to an espalier include *Camellia sasanqua*, *Magnolia grandiflora* or *stellata*, ficus, wisteria, *Malus* species (apple or crab apple), and *Parthenocissus species* (Boston ivy or Virginia creeper).

12. Conifers, infrequently used as espaliers, are informally trained flat against a brick wall in Charleston, South Carolina.

13. *Parthenocissus* spp. vines (a variety of Boston ivy), trained to a trellis in Prague, are planted in an extremely narrow bed next to the wall.

14. English ivy trained as swags may look simple but requires high maintenance due to the vine's rampant growth.

15. *Magnolia grandiflora* espaliered in a natural form to an iron trellis set in a niche in a brick wall.

16. Self-supporting cacti climb a wall in Oaxaca, Mexico.

17. Blossom-laden wisteria gracefully climbs a brick wall with the help of well-hidden but essential supports anchored into the brick in Boston, Massachusetts.

18. *Parthenocissus tricuspidata*, planted in containers, attaches itself to a wall using clinging rootlets called holdfasts, in Konstanz, Germany.

19. Young street trees being pleached, or trained, as an aerial hedge in the town of Schwetzingen, Germany.

20. The pleached Lime Walk at Arley Hall in England, sometimes referred to as a "hedge on stilts," dates back to the 1850s. The trees are clipped regularly to prevent flowering, thus creating a hedge that remains the trunk size and height of twenty-year-old plants.

21. A double row of American hornbeams have been trained as a pleached hedge since 1958, in the Ellipse Garden at Dumbarton Oaks.

Pleaching is an architectural form of topiary in which branches and twigs are woven together to create living walls, fences, roofs or latticework. (The word derives from the Latin word *plectere* ("to weave or plait"). Julius Caesar described formidable pleached hedges that served as defensive barriers in Flanders in his *Commentaries on the Gallic and Civil Wars*: "Having cut young trees and bent them, by means of their numerous branches on the sides, and the quick-briars and thorns springing up between them had made these hedges present a fortification like a wall, through which it was not only impossible to enter, but even to penetrate with the eye."

A more ornamental form of pleaching is a raised hedge, sometimes called a pole-hedge, formed by planting a row of trees, stripping the branches from the lowest 8 to 10 feet of their trunks and then weaving the upper branches together.

In pollarding, a tree's uppermost branches are removed to promote the growth of a dense head of foliage. It is speculated that this was first done in Medieval Europe, when all tree trunks were considered the property of the feudal lord. Peasants were allowed to cut the tops of the trees and use the branches and leaves for firewood and food for livestock. Over time, pollarding became primarily an ornamental practice with the practical advantage of controlling the size of large trees.

22. Pollarded trees at the Japanese Embassy show their "knuckles" or pollard heads, from which new shoots are beginning to grow.

23. Double rows of pollarded plane trees line the central promenade in Tremp, Spain.

24. In southern Spain, these young trees are being trained as pollards to control their size. They form an allée leading to a glorieta that houses a fountain.

25. The Theatre de Verdure ("Green Theater"), featuring impeccably clipped wings of yew, sits on an elevated stage of turf in the eighteenth-century gardens at Bodnant in Wales.

26. In 1764, Nicolas de Pigage designed Schwetzingen's Theatre de Verdure with the Temple of Apollo as its backdrop and a turfed viewing area below. The open-air theater was the site of intimate performances of drama and opera.

27. This parterre at Villandry is called the Garden of Love. The beds are filled with boxwood hand-clipped into shapes that symbolize the various kinds of romantic of love: hearts for tender love, broken hearts for passionate love, fans for fickle love, and daggers for tragic love.

28. Sweeping hedges of contrasting green and golden yew mimic the shape of the parapet wall at the Château de Hautefort in the Dordogne region of France.

29. A low boxwood hedge in a "Greek key" pattern at Château de Hautefort.

30. Dome-shaped yews line a path paved with stones set in a diamond pattern in the arts and crafts–style gardens at Tintinhull in England.

31. An ancient hedge of dense yew clipped to manifest a natural rippling form at Powis Castle in Wales.

32. The vegetable garden at Mount Vernon is edged with single-cordon apple tree espaliers. The enclosing brick walls are lined with fruit espaliers.

33. At Chanticleer in Pennsylvania, beds of vegetables are surrounded by low horizontal apple espaliers. In the distance, additional espaliers are trained in a U shape to a wood frame.

34. An American interpretation of the *glorieta* creates a room formed from clipped hemlock embellished with swags at Ladew Garden in Maryland.

35. Curved beds edged in clipped boxwood give this vegetable garden finished edges, creating a sense of formality.

36. A mixed planting of ilex, boxwood, and deciduous azaleas creates a tapestry hedge of fall colors in Nara, Japan.

All of these topiary techniques were used exuberantly—often simultaneously—in France and Germany during the sixteenth and seventeenth centuries. In France, sophisticated *parterres de broderie* were formed from border hedges of yew and boxwood laid out in elaborate, precise patterns. Hedges took on an architectural function in so-called *glorietas* ("green summerhouses") in Spain; as outdoor rooms in the expansive gardens of Germany; and in "green theaters" throughout Europe.

The trend eventually reached England, where enthusiastic gardeners created elaborate topiary, endless labyrinths and impeccably maintained hedges. Unfortunately, most of this work was obliterated by proponents of the naturalistic landscape movement of the mid-1800s, driven by the notion that "nature abhorred a straight line."

Early American gardeners undertook topiary gardening on a more modest, domestic scale by bordering their vegetable gardens with hedges. The earliest known garden maze in the United States was created at the Governor's Palace in Williamsburg and a reproduction can be visited today. George Washington is known to have trained fruit trees against walls and used espaliered hedges extensively at Mount Vernon.

As an element of the cottage garden style of the 1920s, simple garden rooms and whimsical shapes were created from topiary, along with herbaceous borders. Boxwood, yew, hornbeam, beech, and English holly were the preferred mediums. Tapestry hedges made from combinations of many species, often conifers, were popular as well.

Topiary and precise hedging demands constant, skilled maintenance and can be as stressful to gardeners as to the plants themselves. Today, vines growing on sculpted iron or wood frames are popular substitutes for sheared plants. The frames may be stuffed with a soil mixture held in place by sheets of moss, promoting rapid growth with a minimum of skilled labor.

DESIGN Never commit to the use of topiary and architectural plants lightly. A hallmark of this style is precision, and a poorly maintained topiary garden defeats the purpose entirely. Given the need for constant maintenance, be sure to provide adequate workspace around the plants. For example, adjacent to any hedge that will need more than a short ladder to reach its extremities, consider creating a path or lawn rather than a planting bed.

Keeping in mind that leaves require adequate sunlight to thrive, topiary plants should be tapered so that their lower

37. Dichondra grows over a wire form and becomes a unicorn at the Phipps Conservatory in Pittsburgh, Pennsylvania.

38. An upright frame sandwiching sphagnum moss is planted with sedums of contrasting colors arranged in a diagonal pattern.

39. An array of annuals trained to an armature is shaped and coordinated to create a colorful peacock at Insel Mainau in Germany.

40. The art of topiary clearly requires skill, thoughtfulness and balance.

41. A rhythmic allée of conical Thuja, or arborvitae, gives way to a progression of small-scale standardized trees with orb-shaped tops at Schwetzingen.

42. The *parterre de broderie* at Vaux-le-Vicomte is a composition of boxwood fastidiously clipped to maintain low hedges of intricate patterns. It is accented by rosy dustings of powdered brick.

portions receive as much light as their tops. Obelisks tend to thrive, whereas arched gateways often grow twiggy underneath. The healthiest topiary and hedges are sited in sunny, well-ventilated locations with good drainage.

Avoid large-leafed plants unless you are willing to hand prune them, as sheared leaves develop unsightly brown edges. In low-light situations, such as on the northern side of a house, consider introducing plants with light green, glossy leaves, such as *Hydrangea anomola petiolaris* or *Camellia sasanqua*. (Be sure to check for hardiness in your zone as, even under the best conditions, these plants require considerable effort to establish and train.)

Topiary and architectural plants provide year-round interest in the garden. They are best sited as a collection of "artworks" within their own garden, symmetrically placed or serving as accents among other flora. Elaborate architectural hedges can function as living fences, walls, tunnels, and roofs.

CLIMATE AND WEATHERING In temperate climates, evergreens planted on the exposed southern and western sides of buildings may "winter burn." To guard against this, wrap susceptible plants in open-weave burlap or spray them with an antidessicant during the coldest months.

Heavy, wet snow can be disastrous to topiary. In areas prone to severe winter weather, net and stake the plants or remove snow manually before too much of it can accumulate and turn to ice. Yew and juniper are far more tolerant of snow loads than boxwood or privet, and a sharply tapered form sheds snow the best. In windy areas, topiary should be reinforced with wood or metal poles.

43

44

45

46

47

48

43. At Ladew Gardens, a hemlock hedge provides both walls and a gate between garden rooms.

44. Conical shaped topiaries readily shed snow while shapes with flat tops allow potentially destructive accumulation.

45. Yew topiaries provide whimsy and architecture in the Arts and Crafts garden at Hidcote in England. It was created by an American, Lawrence Johnston, in the early 20th century.

46. An elephant and a giraffe hold court from their pedestals in the flower garden at Green Animals in Portsmouth, Rhode Island.

47. Crape myrtle with stems crossing in the Belgian fence pattern provide a backdrop for a flower bed at the Norfolk Botanical Garden in Virginia.

48. Boxwood clipped into bowl shapes that become plant containers at Helen Dillon's garden in Dublin.

In temperate climates, tender plants and fruit trees fare better when espaliered to a protective south-facing wall. The heat absorbed by the wall during the day protects the plants at night and may also extend the growing season. In hot locations, on the other hand, south- and west-facing walls may become too hot and "cook" the fruit. Plants trained to any wall of a heated home will be somewhat insulated.

Care must be taken when positioning hedges. When they are planted on the south side of a flower or vegetable bed, they will limit the amount of sun the bed receives. When planted across a slope, they will trap cold air and create frost pockets that may damage marginally hardy plants.

INSTALLATION AND MAINTENANCE Before making the long-term commitment to topiary, it is wise to have your soil tested for pH and nutrient composition so you can select hardy species well suited to the site. The location should have uniform solar exposure, soil and drainage throughout to ensure that the plants will grow uniformly. Good ventilation is most important for, with the constant shearing required, the foliage can become so dense that the interior leaves lack adequate light and air and become subject to lethal fungus disease.

The gardeners of the Far East have long been believers in root pruning to reduce growth. Exact techniques vary from species to species so it is prudent to check with an expert before pruning any roots.

Preparing your beds for planting is crucial. The soil should be well drained and not too rich in nitrogen, which promotes quick, leggy growth. Hedges bordering flower or vegetable beds should include a barrier to contain the roots. There are various types available, some made of plastic sheeting. Optimal depth varies based on the vigor of the specific plant's roots.

An evergreen topiary or hedge should never be pruned late in the season because the resulting new growth will brown and die after the first freeze. Antidessicants can minimize winter damage while protecting inner leaves from "sunburn" after a heavy pruning. Hornbeam and beech trees will retain their tawny leaves throughout the winter if pruned a month before the first freeze.

If there are deer in your area, consider installing an enclosure that is at least seven feet high or stick with plants they have little interest in. Yew is considered a delicacy by deer while boxwood is rarely nibbled. You can find out more about local deer-resistant species at your garden shop.

The rewards of training plants are many. Topiary shapes add sculptural drama that can be either informal and whimsical (even humorous) or formal and architectural. You might even create a garden "room" with dense topiary walls. Espaliers can turn a bare expanse of wall into a lush, verdant curtain with the side benefit of creating a microclimate for delicate fruit. A pleached hedge can become an impressive focal point, while simultaneously screening an objectionable view. With pollarding, you can introduce a favorite tree that might normally grow too large for the space. These techniques demand both patience and commitment, but the results are sure to provide endless satisfaction.

49

50

49. The hornbeam topiaries in the Allée des Charmes in the Manoir d'Eyrignac are hand pruned by five gardeners using a plumb-line for precision.
50. At Arley Hall in England, great cylinders of evergreen Quercus ilex, or Holm oak, were planted in the 1850s. They are clipped every August to maintain a height of about 26 feet and a diameter of slightly less than 10 feet.

51. Obelisks of clipped yew stand sentry around a fountain and echo the shape of the lichen-covered finials.

52. Newly planted trees at the earliest stage of pleaching must be securely supported to accommodate the added weight of the wooden framework.

53. Mature, freestanding trees are trained to maintain the flat plane necessary because of their proximity to a house in the Netherlands.

54. Trained to a height above the surrounding wall, these pleached trees will provide additional visual enclosure when in leaf without infringing on the ground-level space of a walled garden.

55. Pollarding controls the growth of these sycamore trees in the main square of Maastricht, Holland, so that they can be planted close together as a grove.

56. Pleached trees trained as one aerial hedge line several paths in Bruges, Belgium.

WALLS

When the deep purple falls over sleepy garden walls
And the stars begin to twinkle in the sky,
In the mist of a memory you wander back to me,
Breathing my name with a sigh.
MITCHELL PARISH

1. Bricks were made on site of Boone Hall Plantation, an antebellum mansion near Charleston, South Carolina, in the early nineteenth century. Some believe that salvaged brick from that time was used to build this serpentine wall in 1936.
2. A brick wall faced with plaster and capped with terra-cotta tiles on the grounds of Prague Castle. Although parts of the castle date back to the ninth century, this wall is of an undetermined later date.

Walls Made of Brick or Clay

The first brick walls that we know of, hand-made of sun-baked clay, date back to 7500 BC in the Tigris River valley. "Rammed clay" walls, made by packing a wet clay-and-sand mixture between two parallel wood forms, were used throughout Asia by early civilizations. They were often sealed with wax or plaster and capped with terra-cotta tile, wood, thatch, or bamboo.

Walls didn't change considerably over the ensuing centuries. Those of the early American farmers of the Great Plains, an area with a limited supply of wood and stone, were made of sod stripped from the earth's surface, its intact roots and rhizomes providing a weblike structure. Eventually, some blacksmiths designed a special plow called the "grasshopper" that could cut large, uniform blocks of sod. These were then subdivided into bricklike units sometimes called prairie marble.

With the construction of canals and railroads for easy shipping, brick surpassed stone as the building block of choice—and has remained so for the past 150 years. It's no wonder: It is less expensive than stone, more readily available and easier to install. What's more, brick offers endless options for coursing, color, finish, and size.

DESIGN Brick comes in many sizes, densities, shapes, colors, and finishes. When designing and installing bricks in a full spectrum of color, never set two bricks of the same hue next to each other.

Reclaimed bricks are valued for their patina and individuality and, if used in their original region, are likely to withstand the climate. Keep in mind, though, that particles of mortar, dirt, and airborne material may have accumulated in the pores, which can affect the bonding quality of the new joints. When using salvaged brick, purchase 3 percent more than is required to allow for flaws, cutting, and breakage.

Brick walls under 3 feet in height can be a single brick thick, but taller walls need to be at least two bricks thick and may be bonded in a variety of structural patterns. These include stretcher bond, ⅓ running bond, English bond, Flemish bond, Flemish double bond, sixth-course header bond, sixth-course Flemish header, Flemish double stretcher, English cross, Flemish diagonal, and Flemish cross.

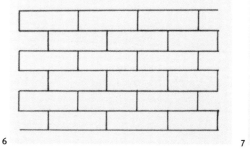

3

5

4

6

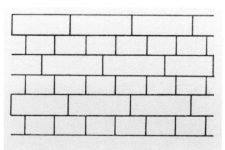

7

8

9

3. A brick wall with a pattern of openings is referred to as a "pierced" wall or a "screen wall" and defines the space while allowing air circulation and views. This one, at Brookgreen Gardens in South Carolina, deftly separates garden rooms and their sculptures. The bronze *Jaguar* was sculpted by the garden's owner, Anna Hyatt Huntington, in 1932 and is backed by a solid panel in the wall. Albert Wien's *Phryne Before the Judges* can be seen through and above the wall.

4. A brick wall in Charleston, South Carolina, in a running bond pattern with brick piers, is set on a stone base for sturdiness and privacy but has a pierced top for air flow.

5. A brick wall in the Flemish bond pattern, topped with a coping of crenellated brick caps in alternating heights, at Williamsburg, Virginia. Because of its profile, the wall's cap sheds water effectively, minimizing damage to its numerous mortar joints.

6. Line drawing running bond.

7. Line drawing English bond.

8. Line drawing Flemish bond.

9. Line drawing English cross bond.

10. A pierced wall sited in an elevated location makes the most of gentle breezes.

11. A circular *clairvoyee* in a brick wall allows the air to flow freely while serving as a window to the garden beyond.

12. Buttressed piers strengthen a screen wall at Middleton Place in South Carolina.

13. This wall is designed to protect the tree's root zone by spanning it with a segmental arch.

14. The height of a brick wall is adeptly modified to accommodate a tree branch.

15. Woody plants are tucked into the curves of a serpentine wall.

Long and tall brick walls should be punctuated with piers or buttresses at proportioned intervals and reinforced horizontally with gauged truss steel wire placed every six courses.

Rather than cutting tree roots that might be in the way of footings, consider the use of piers with spanning steel beams—a root-friendly solution that is also cost effective and extremely secure.

A serpentine brick wall is economical in that it can be built one brick thick at virtually any height. The math is simple: the radius of the curvature should be no less than twice the height of the wall. Serpentine walls have historically been used in Britain and other challenging environments to provide microclimates for tender plants.

Brick grout joints are important not only aesthetically, but because "striking" the joint properly ensures good bonding and sealing. Concave or V-shaped grout joints are the most effective in repelling water; grapevine, beaded, or weathered joints can work as well. Raked, flush, or struck joints are the most difficult to make watertight. Brick grout joints can be dyed for contrast or harmony. Frank Lloyd Wright emphasized horizontality in his famous Robie House in Chicago by specifying long, thin brick with white horizontal joints. The vertical joints were dyed to blend in with the brick.

Brick walls can be surfaced with plaster or stucco to cover all coursing, joints, and irregularities, but if the coating is not properly applied and maintained, it may crack and discolor. In most of southern Europe, Asia, and South America, brick walls are considered pedestrian and tend to be surfaced and painted. In the urban United States, on the other hand—par-ticularly in the East and South—well-crafted, exposed-brick walls are considered beautiful.

Walls should be made of a material that contrasts with the surrounding paving, though the elements can be linked by picking up the paving material in the capstone.

In fact, many of the principles of paving apply to walls as well, and a similar array of materials is available. For more information on these materials, consult our "Paving" chapter.

CLIMATE AND WEATHERING All brick walls in temperate climates must be S/W (severe weather) grade and capped with an overhanging coping to prevent moisture from seeping into the core. In tropical climates, coping also prevents plants from growing on top of the wall.

16

17

18

19

20

21

16. Light-colored mortar joints create strong horizontality while vertical joints of dark mortar disappear at Frank Lloyd Wright's Robie House in Chicago.

17. Applied ornamental plaster mutes the brick structure of this wall in Antigua, Guatemala.

18. Vanishing plaster is left unrepaired in order to retain the beauty of the weathered brick in the gardens at Herrenhausen in Germany.

19. The corbelling of its top throws rain away from this brick wall and guards against water running down its face and staining it.

20. The elegant, rounded corner of this wall in Charleston is a testament to its craftsmanship. Note the change in the color of the cap's mortar joints, which indicates that a portion of the wall has been repointed.

21. Vines soften this brick wall and are well managed to limit growth that might damage it.

23

22. The "Moat Walk" at Sissinghurst features a wall at its center that was uncovered by gardeners shortly after Vita Sackville-West bought the property in 1930. It is believed to be the foundation of a manor house dating back to the 16th century.
23. A brick wall with arched panels sits on stone to protect it from ground moisture.
24. Shade and humidity promote the growth of mildew on a brick wall surfaced with stucco.
25. Though visually pleasing, a brick wall with double caps encourages the growth of moss on the wall panel between the caps.
26. Bricks of unusual sizes are stacked to form elongated arches with keystone construction, then topped with a scored stone cap.
27. A combination of molded and angled bricks forms a capstone meant to direct water away from the wall—but because there is no overhang, rain runs down the wall's surface. Its path is obvious.
28. This wall is stepped down in segments to accommodate a steep grade change.
29. Brick set in a "dog tooth" pattern becomes a sculptural accent, adding texture and interest to the wall.
30. Tall brick walls have created walled gardens for centuries, protecting treasured plants, valued vegetables. and herbs from winds and critters.

For southern exposures, consider light-colored brick as darker brick will absorb heat. All south-facing brick walls create microclimates ideal for tender plants.

Brick walls that extend to the ground in poorly drained areas may wick moisture, resulting in efflorescence, moss growth, and possibly blistering of the brick face. In this situation, consider a granite or stone base course.

In areas that experience extreme freezing and thawing, stucco or plaster finishes will eventually crack and discolor. Patching and paint are the best repair solutions. In areas prone to strong winds, brick walls require vertical reinforcement, such as buttressing.

Do not encourage vines to climb brick walls that are soft and porous. Stucco and plaster walls can be damaged by climbing plants with aerial rootlets, such as English ivy. To encourage moss, pour a mixture of buttermilk and moss onto the brick surface.

INSTALLATION AND MAINTENANCE Brick walls are considered permanent structures, and usually require construction drawings and building permits. Check your local regulations—and make sure to locate underground utilities before beginning the job.

Quality construction is extremely important if your walls are to be secure and long lasting. Be sure the footings are of sufficient depth and size. (Some settling and cracking is inevitable, so examine and repair walls each season.)

Most brick retaining walls are actually brick veneer applied over concrete-filled cinder blocks with tie backs and waterproofing. The height of a standard cinder block is equivalent to three standard bricks plus their joints.

The pier-and-panel method of construction endorsed by the American Brick Industry is the least expensive option. The wall panel is one brick thick and is supported by galvanized mesh coursing connected to structural piers. Besides requiring half the number of bricks that a classically built wall does, the panel does not require a continuous footing.

For decorative purposes, many brick walls are capped with brick that is molded, set on edge or layered horizontally. In temperate climates, this practice should be avoided. Because of the small unit size, brick coping requires many mortared joints that will freeze, thaw and crack if not impeccably drained. Spot repair is always noticeable. Molded, oversized bricks or tile with a quick-draining profile make better choices for capping brick walls in mercurial climates. Flagstone or limestone capping is ideal in that large stones can be cut to uniform thickness, to minimize the number of grout joints. Beaded grout joints, which protrude beyond the face of the brick, are the most susceptible to freeze-thaw cracking. This technique should be used only in very stable climates.

Cracks larger than 0.014 inch will allow wind driven rain to penetrate the wall. Since water expands 9 percent when it freezes, it is essential to remain vigilant and repair cracks often, particularly in locations subject to freezing and thawing.

Position retaining wall weep holes close to the finished grade level and make sure there is adequate drainage. PVC pipe is often used for weep hole drainage; choose gray rather than white and recess it so that it recedes from view.

Again, consult our section on brick paving for more details.

25

26

27

28

29

30

1

◉ *Walls Made of Concrete* ◉

The terms *concrete* and *cement* tend to be used interchangeably, but this is inaccurate. In fact, cement is an ingredient of concrete, along with sand and gravel. When mixed with water, cement hydrates and hardens rapidly to bind the sand and gravel into solid concrete. (The word comes from the Latin *concretus*, meaning "compounded" or grown together.)

Throughout the millennia, concrete has been made from a number of materials including lime, burnt lime, gypsum, clay, volcanic ash, and finely ground bricks. The oldest surviving concrete we know of was discovered along the banks of the Danube River in Serbia and dates from 5600 BC. Egyptians used concrete as far back as 2500 BC and it has been theorized that some of the pyramids were made from poured rather than quarried stone.

The Romans discovered that adding *pozzolana* (volcanic ash) to the cement mixture resulted in stronger concrete that would set under water. This advanced form of concrete disappeared during the Middle Ages but was revived during the sixteenth century, when English builders began importing *pozzolana* and lime mixtures from Italy.

In 1824, a British stonemason named Joseph Aspdin created a strong form of cement by burning ground lime and clay together. He called the substance Portland cement because of its resemblance to Portland stone, a type of limestone. Portland remains the most commonly used cement in the production of concrete.

1. Retaining walls of tumbled concrete masonry blocks are dry stacked to support a series of terraces in Kauai, Hawaii.
2. The Neuer Börneplatz memorial is a concrete wall built in 1996, outside the Old Jewish Cemetery in Frankfurt, Germany. Some eleven thousand stones inscribed with the names of Frankfurt citizens killed during the Holocaust are set in the wall.
3. Perforated concrete units are staggered to create a "pierced" concrete wall that allows glimpses of the other side as well as air circulation.
4. Salvaged pieces of broken concrete are sometimes referred to as "urbanite." Here, they are used to build a retaining wall.

Beginning in the mid-nineteenth century, metal rods were embedded in concrete to increase its tensile strength. The result came to be known as reinforced concrete. Inexpensive, quick to form, and incredibly durable if properly installed and maintained, it has been used universally ever since. In fact, concrete is the most widely used man-made material in the world.

DESIGN Concrete can be surface textured to create patterns or given a rough finish without sharp edges. Despite its durability, it is neither indestructible nor without cosmetic flaws. It can be colored with a dye, but unless a sealant is applied every three to five years the color will fade. Even the best of paint jobs lasts only about two years.

Concrete walls should not extend more than 50 feet or come in contact with a separate structure without the addition of expansion and control joints (vertical separations between wall segments).

If your landscape budget is limited, cinder blocks, also known as concrete masonry units (CMUs), offer the best solution, as they do not require massive footings and are easy to install. Interlocking concrete blocks can be stained a dark green or black and covered in climbing plants—but avoid invasive vines, such as English ivy. They may also be coated with a surface-bonding cement that contains synthetic fibers for extra strength, or finished with stucco.

Dyed concrete wall bricks, which cost about 10 percent less than their clay counterparts and come in a better range of light colors, are also available. But if you are looking for bricks in rich reds or browns, concrete can't hold a candle to clay, which also tends to be more consistent in color, right through to the brick's core. If not properly cured, concrete brick may fade, effloresce, or shrink. Sealing will minimize these problems.

Stucco can be applied to concrete or cinder blocks in a variety of ways, to create finishes of various textures and colors. At the "Giant's House" in Akaroa, New Zealand, artist Josie Martin has painstakingly created extravagant mosaics on a base of reinforced concrete so strong that it has withstood three powerful earthquakes. Made from tiles she has collected as well as broken china and pottery contributed by others, her work continually evolves and grows atop the steadfast concrete that underpins it.

5. An application of stucco—there are endless color options—gives a concrete wall a refined look and highlights architectural detail.

6. Panels of wood pickets set into a concrete wall with a stucco finish provide visual interest, while allowing light and air to flow.

7. A *clairvoyee* featuring a nautical motif perforates a concrete-stucco wall in Naples, Florida.

8. A concrete wall, pierced at eye level with terra-cotta tiles arranged in a diamond pattern, allows views through the wall.

9. A heavily reinforced concrete wall, strong enough that it has withstood three earthquakes, has been turned into mosaic sculpture at the "Giant's House" in New Zealand.

10. Josie Martin applied pieces of porcelain to her base of engineered concrete to create a uniquely imaginative garden wall.

11. In contrast to its stark, motionless concrete core, the mosaic face of this wall moves to the tempo of the acrobats. Note how the neighboring orange trees and marigolds echo the color and shape of the balls being passed.

12. Gaudí, in conjunction with his associate Jujol, employed a Catalonian technique called *trencadís*, developed during the art nouveau period, to create mosaics such as those seen here. Salvaged materials that were easily fragmented were directly applied to wet mortar to create ever-varying patterns.

1. Slender pillars of granite overlay a bamboo fence to create an unusual open stone wall in Kyoto, Japan.
2. A dry wall of Otago schist blends with natural outcroppings of stone in the mining town of Arrowtown, New Zealand.
3. Thick mortared slabs of random ashlar stone form a substantial garden enclosure.

CLIMATE AND WEATHERING In temperate climates, concrete is prone to efflorescence, pitting, staining, bleaching, and corrosion. The surface of concrete walls may spall (flake) when exposed to freezing and thawing. Vertical surfaces may be damaged by high winds and are sensitive to acid rain. Sulfate-resistant cement should be used for any walls affected by saltwater spray.

Though you probably won't be doing the construction yourself, be aware of the type of concrete being used on your project, and make sure that the mix will be resistant to relevant environmental factors.

INSTALLATION AND MAINTENANCE Though it seems to be ubiquitous, concrete is not always economical, nor is it the lowest-maintenance or most aesthetically pleasing choice for walls. All concrete will effloresce and fade unless thoroughly cured and sealed every three to five years.

Efflorescence masks the color of dyed concrete. It is difficult to prevent but can be removed with a mild detergent.

Damaged concrete is difficult to repair seamlessly. One treatment for corroded, pitted or stained concrete is to bush hammer the first ⅛ inch off the surface—but this can be costly and could open cracks and expose the reinforcing metal bars. When exposed to air and moisture, the bars will rust and eventually disintegrate, compromising structural support.

❧ Walls Made of Stone ❧

Early walls were made from rocks that had heaved to the earth's surface and created obstacles. The rocks were gathered in order to clear fields for grazing or other purposes and then stacked to form enclosures for livestock, protect crops, or define boundaries. Building these "dry stone walls" required few tools and no mortar.

A hilltop sanctuary in Southeast Turkey, Göbekli Tepe, is distinguished by oval and circular dry stone walls featuring pillars weighing 15 to 20 tons. It was constructed between 9000 and 8000 BC.

During the Mycenean period (1600–1100 BC), the Greeks built walls of huge limestone boulders roughly fit together without mortar. Some boulders used in the lower courses were as heavy as 14 tons. Called "cyclopean walls," they were so monumental that some believed them to have been built by Cyclops, mythical one-eyed giants, as an impregnable defense for the settlement within.

Eventually, walls were set with mortar to increase their strength. In Europe, many cities, towns, and castles were surrounded by walls for defense—but as gunpowder became more widely available, fortifications lost their effectiveness as protection from invaders.

The Islamic tradition of shielding women from the public

eye has inspired the creation of elaborately carved filigree walls of marble or red or beige sandstone. They are awe-inspiring to look at, easy to look through, permit breezes to circulate and cast most interesting shadows.

Despite the inherent strength of mortared walls, dry construction can be longer lasting because of its flexibility and the fact that it doesn't trap damaging water. In Tokyo, the impressive four-hundred-year-old walls of the Imperial Palace are of dry stone construction called *ishigaki*, the preferred method in a land prone to earthquakes and torrential rains.

In 1650 Massachusetts, dry stone walls were mandated by law to control livestock. Walls were required to be 4 to 5 feet tall and "fence viewers" were appointed to enforce the law. Wandering livestock was placed in pounds, also made of stone, and owners paid a fine to retrieve their animals.

Stone walls continue to serve utilitarian purposes and their inherent beauty adds a natural yet elegant element to the landscape. Indigenous stone reflects the surrounding geology, becomes more beautiful with age and requires minimal attention. Of all the building materials, stone offers the widest array of color, texture, size, and installation method—and it is the most adaptable to the vagaries of climate. Stone

4. Meticulously carved marble panels create a wall of privacy but are open enough to allow the occupants to observe the goings on beyond the wall.
5. Carved red sandstone forms a sophisticated physical barrier that remains open to light, air and views.
6. A guard house on the grounds of the Imperial Palace in Tokyo is surrounded by traditional dry stone walls referred to as *ishigaki*.
7. A sunk fence, or ha-ha, at Newby Hall in England successfully keeps sheep out of the formal gardens.

masonry is an art that requires experience and patience, but a well designed and constructed stone wall will appear as if it has been in its spot forever.

DESIGN Selecting the proper stone and finish for your needs involves a variety of factors, all of which are outlined in our "Paving" chapter.

Reclaimed stone has great patina and is often mottled by moss and lichen. If you are reusing stone in its original climatic zone, you can be fairly certain it will hold up well—and unless it is considered antique, it will probably save you money, too.

Most stone walls are designed to work with gravity: the base stones are the largest and widest and the ascending stones get successively smaller. All stones should be oriented to emphasize their horizontal strata.

Stone walls can be constructed in a variety of patterns, including coursed random with roughly squared stone, uncoursed random with irregular-shaped stone, and coursed ashlar (a squared building stone cut more or less true on all faces adjacent to those of other stones to permit very thin mortar joints).

8. In Hokitika, New Zealand, a wall of local river stone bound with mortar of a similar color has no capstone.
9. A dry stack wall of flagstone capped with long slabs of the same stone in Potomac, Maryland.
10. A wall of large, natural-shaped fieldstone is mortared in place and capped with flagstone cut to follow its curves.
11. A dry stack stone wall capped with substantial pieces of the same stone features a rustic circular arch that provides a transition between garden rooms.
12. This gravity dry stack retaining wall consists of interlocking, irregular-shaped stones in an overall shape that tapers from bottom to top.
13. Walls of cleft-cut travertine imported from Italy frame views of the southern California landscape at the Getty Museum, designed by Richard Meier.

14

15

16

17

18

19

20

21

19. In a private garden in Connecticut, a stone wall that serves as an oversized plant trough has been designed to provide sharp drainage, optimal soil composition, and good light exposure for a carpet of Mediterranean plants.

20. The east wall of the walled garden called the "Pleasance" at Edzell Castle in Scotland was built between 1604 and 1610 by Sir David Lindsay to be used for leisure and entertaining. It features niches for plants or statues, narrative carved panels to spark intellectual curiosity and seven rayed stars with holes in their centers to welcome birds.

21. Walled terraces at Sanssouci (1744-1747) hold 168 niches with glazed glass doors enclosing fig trees. Grapes are espaliered on the alternating wall panels while fruit trees are trained as swag-shaped cordons and yews are clipped as obelisks.

14. Sizeable blocks of red sandstone are highly ornamented with carved columns and scalloped arches adorned with flowers.

15. Framing vistas of Jodhpur's Mehrangarh Fort in the distance, this low sandstone wall features panels carved into S-shaped scrolls that flow into leaves. Its piers are topped with a lotus motif. Note the drain channels carved into the beige sandstone base of the wall.

16. A railing of flowing sandstone vines has shed most of its gilding but still provides a shimmering foreground for the exquisitely carved façade beyond.

17. A recess in a stone wall becomes a bench in a flowery nook with the addition of an ergonomically contoured wood seat.

18. On the Planter's Viaduct at the Parque Güell, Gaudí used local stone to create a wall with a series of concave seats of jagged stones. The columns, resembling tree trunks of varying design, hold aloft planters containing agave plants.

Walls adjoining a formal house should be of ashlar quality, whereas informal architecture is more sympathetic to a rubble wall. Limestone, sandstone and marble panels may be intricately carved and incorporated into stone walls as a sculptural accent.

Stone retaining walls require adequate hydrostatic drainage. When designing your walls, consider how much taper is appropriate, as well as such extras as adjoining steps, pocket spaces for wall plants, a wall fountain, or a grotto and seating area.

All retaining walls except dry and semi-dry stacked walls should be waterproofed on the back side to prevent staining due to water and efflorescence from the mortar on the face side. Dry-set retaining walls should not exceed 6 feet in height. For heights greater than 6 feet, consider terracing.

Dry-set gravity walls require the least footing depth and exert the least impact on the root structure of adjacent trees.

22. In the 1670s, a rocky hillside was carved into four terraces to form the gardens at Powis Castle in Wales. Some of these clipped yews date to the eighteenth century.

23. The wave shaped Carob's Viaduct at Gaudi's Parque Güell is named for trees found on the site and is made from local stone.

24. A rammed earth wall in Japan is made of dried mud sandwiched in wooden frames and plastered to look like stone. It is set on a stone base, flanked by a channel drain to protect it from groundwater and topped by a coping with a generous overhang of wood finished with ornate tiles.

25. Sometimes referred to as the "grotesquery," this wall in Prague's Wallenstein Gardens, built between 1623 and 1630, is meant to represent a limestone grotto.

26. A zigzag pattern of brick, glowing with golden lichen, tops a wall of local stone at the Parque Güell in Barcelona.

27. A tall wall of thin, horizontal pieces of slate is dry stacked and meets its capstone with a mortar joint in Agra, India.

28. Dry stack stone walls and ramps at Opus 40 in Saugerties, New York, were all hand made by Harvey Fite (1903–1976), a professor of sculpture and theater at Bard College, to access and exhibit sculptures he created on site.

Piers with spanning steel beams are an economical and cautious alternative.

A stone wall should have a well-defined beginning and end; long and tall walls should be punctuated with piers or buttresses at proportioned intervals. Most places require a permanent 36-inch-tall barrier wall on top of any retaining wall over 3 feet in height. (In Europe, this regulation is not always enforced.)

CLIMATE AND WEATHERING Stone walls in temperate climates should be capped with overhanging coping to prevent moisture from entering the core. In tropical climates, coping prevents plants from growing on top of the wall. Coping mortar joints should be a uniform thickness of no more than ¾ inch and horizontal coping joints should be struck or pitched so they'll drain water quickly. Coping joints are the first to crack

29. The walled garden at the Biltmore Estate in Asheville, North Carolina, is surrounded by a tall stone wall capped with terra cotta tiles. It is sited to restrain the wind and capture the sun.

30. In Newport, Rhode Island, massive rocks capped with thick slabs of flagstone form a substantial dry wall mottled with gray, gold, and green lichens.

as freezing and thawing cause the wall to settle. It's important that they be re-pointed promptly to prevent water from seeping into the core of the wall.

Almost all stones with natural clefts will flake in the freeze-thaw belt. Stones with an absorption rating of less than 7 percent ASTM (American Society for Testing and Materials) make be the best choice. In temperate climates, soft sandstone, usually beige in color, will disintegrate over time. Although expensive, granite is one of the most durable stones.

When it comes to weathering, stone and brick behave in similar ways. For more information, consult our section on the weathering of brick.

INSTALLATION AND MAINTENANCE Walls generally require building permits, plans, elevations and, of course, knowledge of the location of underground utilities.

The height of a dry-stack gravity wall will determine the necessary width of the base and size of the stones. In temperate climates, the footings for mortared walls should go deeper than the frost line. It is best that stones be "wetted" before setting and pointing, so that the mortar doesn't dry out too quickly. Mortar joints can be tinted with a carbon-based dye to blend with the color of the stone.

Flagstone and limestone are ideal capping materials in temperate climates because they can be cut to uniform thickness in sizes that will minimize the number of grout joints needed. Stone walls in the Far East are often capped with terra-cotta tiles.

Try to find stones that fit together well, but when you experience the inevitable gaps, avoid using small stones to fill them. They are easily dislodged and just don't look very professional.

If more than one mason is working on your wall, insist that they rotate positions every hour to minimize the effect of any variation in their styles.

A straight vertical joint line should not exceed the length of the stone being set. Try to avoid crossing perpendicular joints where four corners line up.

Epoxy expansion joints should be located at the intersection of any wall with an adjoining structure. Caulking with epoxy is an art and should be done by a professional.

Never clean soft stones with muriatic acid. Instead, use a low-pressure power washer and moisten the stone with water before spraying with mild detergent. Avoid directing the power washer at mortar joints, and before cleaning, protect all nearby plants by covering or thoroughly soaking and spraying them.

Trees with extensive surface roots should not be planted near stone walls.

A well-designed wall fuses architecture with the garden, while adding a sense of timelessness, permanence, and durability. They can be as integral to a well-thought-out garden as the trees, flowers, and ornaments that dwell around and within them.

31. Stacked coral rock walls define garden spaces as a path passes through their arches.

32. A low stone wall with open panels employs chains to support its swags of wisteria and connect the stone pillars.

Appendix

We acknowledge the cooperation of all of the gardens and sites that appear on these pages with heartfelt appreciation. We've included the websites here of those that welcome visitors, to aid the garden explorer. Because many of them are off the beaten track or have irregular visiting hours, we suggest that you call prior to visiting and keep your GPS handy. Keep in mind, too, that all gardens change with the seasons and evolve in response to the forces of nature and human intervention. What you find may be different from what we've depicted in these pages. As we discovered over many years of travel, garden exploring can be a bit of an adventure–but supremely rewarding!

BELGIUM
Historic Center of Bruges http://whc.unesco.org/en/list/996
Parc de Bruxelles http://www.montdesarts.com/en/parks/Parc-de-Bruxelles
St Michael's Bridge Ghent http://www.visitgent.be/en/st-michaels-bridge

CANADA
Dr, Sun Yat-Sen Garden http://vancouverchinesegarden.com/
Le Quatre Vents http://www.ccpas.qc.ca/jardins-quatre-vents.php/

CZECH REPUBLIC
Troja Chateau http://www.czechtourism.com/c/prague-troja-chateau/
Vrtba Garden http://www.vrtbovska.cz/en/   http://www.prague.net/vrtba-garden
Wallenstein Palace Gardens http://www.prague.net/wallenstein-garden

FRANCE
Chateau de Chantilly http://www.domainedechantilly.com/en
Chateau de Villandry http://www.chateauvillandry.fr/en/
Courances http://www.courances.net
Villa Ephrussi de Rothschild http://www.villa-ephrussi.com/en/
Giverny http://fondation-monet.com/fr/
Le Bagatelle http://equipement.paris.fr/parc-de-bagatelle-1808
Manoir d'Eyrignac http://www.eyrignac.com/en/
Vaux-le-Vicomte http://www.vaux-le-vicomte.com/en/
Versailles http://www.chateauversailles.fr

GERMANY
Englischer Garten Munich http://www.muenchen.de/int/en/sights/parks/english-garden.html
Herrenhausen http://www.hannover.de/en/Welcome-to-Hannover/Gardens-Recreation/Herrenhausen-Gardens
Insel Mainau http://www.mainau.de
Linderhof http://www.schlosslinderhof.de/index.htm
Ludwigsburg http://www.schloss-ludwigsburg.de/
Neuer Bornplatz, Frankfurt http://juedischesmuseum.de/154.html?&L=1
Sanssouci http://www.potsdam-park-sanssouci.de/
Schloss Schwetzingen www.schloss-schwetzingen.de
Schloss Veitschochheim www.schloesserbayern.de
Wilhelmshohe www.museum-kassel.de
Worlitz Park, The Garden Kingdom of Dessau-Worlitz
    www.woerlitz-information.de/woerlitz
Zwinger Museum http://www.skd.museum/en/museums-institutions/zwinger-with-semperbau/

GUATEMALA
Casa Popenoe www.casapopenoe.ufm.edu/

INDIA
Deeg Palace www.rajasthan-tourism-guide.com/deeg-palace.html
Fatehpur Sikri http://whc.unesco.org/en/list/255
Gandhi Memorial Gardens, "Raj Ghat" http://www.viator.com/New-Delhi-attractions/Raj-Ghat/d804-a2407
Humayun's Tomb http://whc.unesco.org/en/list/232
Lake Palace Udaipur http://www.udaipur.org.uk/tourist-attractions/jagniwas.html
Lodhi Gardens http://www.gardenvisit.com/garden/lodi_garden-lodhi_gardens
Mehrangarh fort http://mehrangarh.org/
Ranakpur http://www.udaipur.org.uk/temples/ranakpur-temple.html
Rashtrapati bhavan http://presidentofindia.nic.in/rashtrapati_bhavan.html
Saheliyon-ki-bari http://www.udaipur.org.uk/gardens/saheliyon-ki-bari.html
Taj Mahal http://www.tajmahal.gov.in/

IRELAND
Dunloe Castle http://www.thedunloe.com/gardens
Mount Usher http://www.mountushergardens.ie/
Powerscourt http://www.powerscourt.ie/gardens

ITALY
Bomarzo http://www.bomarzo.net/index_en.html
Hadrian's Villa http://whc.unesco.org/en/list/907
Isola Bella http://www.stresa.com/borromeanislands
La Mortola (Hanbury Botanic Garden) http://www.giardinihanbury.com/hanbury4/
Villa di Maser http://www.villadimaser.it/
Villa Carlotta http://www.villacarlotta.it/
Villa d'Este http://www.villadestetivoli.info
Villa Garzoni http://www.provincia.pistoia.it/museievaldinievole/ing/m_garzoni.htm
Villa Lante http://www.gardenvisit.com/garden/villa_lante
Villa Marlia (Villa Reale) http://www.parcovillareale.it
Villa Melzi www.giardinidivillamelzi.it

JAPAN
Heian Jingu http://www.heianjingu.or.jp
Isuien http://www.gojapango.com/travel/nara_isuien_garden.htm
Kenroku-en http://www.pref.ishikawa.jp/siro-niwa/kenrokuen/e/
Korakuen http://www.okayama-korakuen.jp/
Kyoto Gosho http://sankan.kunaicho.go.jp/english/guide/kyoto.html
Nijo-jo http://www.city.kyoto.jp/bunshi/nijojo/english/
Rikugien http://teien.tokyo-park.or.jp/en/rikugien/
Ritsurin Garden http://www.prcf.kagawa.lg.jp/ritsurin/index_e.html
Saiho-ji (Kokedera, Moss Garden) http://www.japan-guide.com/e/e3937.html
Shisen-do http://www.kyoto.travel/2009/11/shisen-do-temple.html
Shugaku-in http://sankan.kunaicho.go.jp/english/guide/shugakuin.html
Tofuku-ji http://www.tofukuji.jp/english/index.html

NETHERLANDS
Floriade http://www.holland.com/us/tourism/article/floriade-2012-26.htm
Keukenhof http://www.keukenhof.nl/
Abbey Abdij http://www.eupedia.com/netherlands/middelburg.shtml
Vrjithof Square, Maastricht http://www.orangesmile.com/travelguide/maastricht/#
Historic town of Veere http://www.eupedia.com/netherlands/veere.shtml

NEW ZEALAND
Avon River Park http://www.avonotakaronetwork.co.nz/
ChristchurchBotanicGarden http://www.ccc.govt.nz/CITYLEISURE/parkswalkways/christchurchbotanicgardens/index.aspx
Oamaru Public Gardens http://www.gardens.org.nz/waitaki-gardens/oamaru-public-gardens/
Ohinetahi http://chsgardens.co.nz/about/open-gardens/ohinetahi/
Ora Garden of Wellbeing http://www.gardens.org.nz/lake-taupo-gardens/ora-garden-of-wellbeing/
The Giants House, Akaroa http://www.thegiantshouse.co.nz/

PORTUGAL
Palacio de Fronteira http://www.gardenvisit.com/garden/palacio_de_fronteira
Sintra http://www.sintraportugal.net/attractions/palacio-monserrate-palace-sintra

SPAIN
Alcazar Seville http://www.alcazarsevilla.org/?p=129
Alhambra http://www.alhambradegranada.org/en/
Catedral de Sevilla, Patio de los Naranjos
http://www.andalucia.com/cities/seville/cathedral.htm
El Retiro Park http://www.esmadrid.com/en/retiro-park
Empuries Ruins http://www.historvius.com/empuries-1713/
Generalife http://www.alhambradegranada.org/en/info/placesandspots/thegeneralife.asp
Merida http://www.travelinginspain.com/Merida.htm
Montjuic http://www.viator.com/Barcelona-attractions/Mountain-of-the-Jews-Montjuiec/d562-a836
Palacio de los Marqueses de Viana http://www.palaciodeviana.com/es/home.asp

SWITZERLAND
Bad Ragaz, Tamina Gorge http://www.myswitzerland.com/en-us/tamina-gorge-circular-tour-bad-ragaz.html

UNITED KINGDOM
Arley Hall http://www.arleyhallandgardens.com/
Athelhampton http://www.athelhampton.co.uk/
Bodnant http://www.nationaltrust.org.uk/bodnant-garden/
Castle Drogo https://www.nationaltrust.org.uk/castle-drogo/
Cawdor Castle http://www.cawdorcastle.com/
Chiswick http://www.chgt.org.uk/
Crathes Castle http://www.nts.org.uk/Property/Crathes-Castle-Garden-and-Estate/
Dunham Massey https://www.nationaltrust.org.uk/dunham-massey/
Edzell Castle http://www.historic-scotland.gov.uk/
Hestercombe http://www.hestercombe.com/
Hidcote Manor https://www.nationaltrust.org.uk/hidcote/
Kew Gardens http://www.kew.org/
Kiftsgate http://www.kiftsgate.co.uk/
Mount Stewart https://www.nationaltrust.org.uk/mount-stewart/
Newby Hall http://newbyhallandgardens.com/site/
Powis Castle http://www.nationaltrust.org.uk/powis-castle/
Rousham http://www.rousham.org/
Scotney Castle http://www.nationaltrust.org.uk/scotney-castle/
Sezincote http://www.sezincote.co.uk/
Stourhead http://www.nationaltrust.org.uk/stourhead/
Sutton Place www.parksandgardens.org/places-and-people/site/4340
Tintinhull Garden https://www.nationaltrust.org.uk/tintinhull-garden/
West Dean http://www.westdean.org.uk/WestDeanHomepage.aspx
Westbury Court http://www.nationaltrust.org.uk/westbury-court-garden/

UNITED STATES
Allerton National Tropical Botanic Garden http://ntbg.org/gardens/allerton.php
Aristides Demetrios Sculpture http://www.demetriossculpture.com/
Arlington National Cemetery http://www.arlingtoncemetery.mil/
Beaufort House Inn http://www.beauforthouse.com/
Biltmore Estate https://www.biltmore.com/
Bok Tower http://boktowergardens.org/
Boone Hall http://boonehallplantation.com/
Brookgreen Gardens http://www.brookgreen.org/
Ca' d'Zan https://www.ringling.org/ca-dzan
Chanticleer http://www.chanticleergarden.org/
Chicago Botanic Garden http://www.chicagobotanic.org/
The Cloisters http://www.metmuseum.org/visit/visit-the-cloisters/
Colonial Williamsburg http://www.history.org/
Drayton Hall http://www.draytonhall.org/
Dumbarton Oaks http://www.doaks.org/
Getty Center http://www.getty.edu/
Greystone http://www.greystonemansion.org/
Griffis Sculpture Park http://www.griffispark.org/
Green Animals Topiary Garden http://www.newportmansions.org/explore/green-animals-topiary-garden
Harkness Park http://www.harkness.org/
Ladew Topiary Garden http://www.ladewgardens.com/
Leonard J. Buck Garden http://www.somersetcountyparks.org/parksfacilities/buck/LJBuck.html
Magnolia Plantation and Gardens http://www.magnoliaplantation.com/
Middleton Place https://www.middletonplace.org/
Mohonk Mountain House http://www.mohonk.com/
Montpelier http://www.montpelier.org/
Mount Vernon http://www.mountvernon.org/
Naumkeag http://www.thetrustees.org/places-to-visit/berkshires/naumkeag.html
NC Arboretum http://www.ncarboretum.org/
Norfolk Botanical Garden http://norfolkbotanicalgarden.org/
Oak Alley http://www.oakalleyplantation.com/
Opus 40 Sculpture Park http://www.opus40.org/
Owens Thomas House http://www.telfair.org/owens-thomas/
Paca House and Garden http://www.annapolis.org/
Phipps Conservatory http://phipps.conservatory.org/
Pinewood Estate http://boktowergardens.org/news/pinewood-estate/
Blessed John Paul II Shrine http://www.jp2shrine.org/en/index.html
Reynolds Mansion http://www.thereynoldsmansion.com/
Robie House http://www.flwright.org/visit/robiehouse
Shaker Village of Pleasant Hill, Kentucky http://www.shakervillageky.org/
Venetian Pool, Coral Gables http://www.coralgables.com/index.aspx?page=167
Vizcaya http://www.vizcaya.org/

Selected Bibliography

Baker, Martha. *Garden Ornaments: A Stylish Guide to Decorating Your Garden.* New York: Clarkson N. Potter, Inc., 1999.

Balston, Michael. *The Well-Furnished Garden.* New York: Simon and Schuster, 1986.

Bazin, Germain. *Paradeisos: The Art of the Garden.* Boston: Little, Brown and Company, 1990.

Bearsley and Brauner. *Entryways and Front Gardens.* Menlo Park, CA: Lane Books, 1961.

Bennett, Paul. *The Garden Lover's Guide to the Midwest.* New York: Princeton Architectural Press, 2000.

Beveridge, Charles E., and Paul Rocheleau. *Frederick Law Olmstead: Designing the American Landscape.* New York: Rizzoli International Publications, Inc., 1995.

Blomgren, Paige Gilchrist. *Making Paths & Walkways: Creative Ideas and Simple Techniques.* Asheville, NC: Lark Books, 1999.

Byne, Arthur, and Mildred Stapley. *Spanish Gardens and Patios.* Philadelphia: J.B. Lippincott Co., 1924.

Cabot, Francis H. *The Greater Perfection: The Story of the Gardens at Les Quatre Vents.* New York: W.W. Norton & Company, Inc., 2001

Cane, Percy S. *Garden Design of To-day.* New York: Charles Scribner's Sons, 1936.

Cautley, Marjorie S. *Garden Design: The Principles of Abstract Design as Applied to Landscape Composition.* New York: Dodd, Mead & Company, 1935.

Coats, Peter. *Great Gardens.* London: Weidenfeld and Nicolson, 1963.

Coats, Peter. *Great Gardens of Britain.* New York: G.P. Putnam's Sons, 1967.

Crisp, James, and Sandra Mahoney. *On the Porch: Creating Your Place to Watch the World Go By.* Connecticut: The Taunton Press, 2006.

Davis, John. *Antique Garden Ornament: 300 Years of Creativity: Artists, Manufacturers & Materials.* Suffolk: Antique Collector's Club, 1991.

Dunn, Teri. *For Your Garden: Garden Gates and Arches.* New York: Michael Friedman Publishing Group, Inc., 2000.

Farrand, Beatrix. *Beatrix Farrand's Plant Book for Dumbarton Oaks.* Washington, D.C.: Dumbarton Oaks Trustees for Harvard Univ., 1980.

Fell, Derek. *Garden Accents: The Complete Guide to Special Features for Creative Landscaping.* New York: Henry Holt and Company, 1987.

Fox, Helen Morgenthau. *Patio Gardens.* New York: The Macmillan Company, 1929.

Griswold, Mac, and Eleanor Weller. *The Golden Age of American Gardens: Proud Owners: Private Estates: 1890-1940.* [LR1] New York: Harry N. Abrams, Inc., 1991.

Harper, James, and Margie Roe. *Fence Style: Surround Yourself with Charm and Elegance.* New York: Sterling Publishing Co., Inc., 2000.

Harpur, Jerry. *The Gardener's Garden.* Boston: David R. Godine, Publisher, Inc., 1985.

Hawkins, Reginald, and Charles H. Abbe. *Walks and Paths, Driveways, Steps, Curbs, and Edgings.* New York: D. Van Nostrand Company, Inc., 1951.

Hern, Mary Ellen W. *Art of the Olmstead Landscape.* New York: The Arts Publisher, Inc., 1981.

Hicks, David. *My Kind of Garden.* Suffolk: Antique Collector's Club, 1999.

Holmes, Caroline. *Icons of Garden Design.* Munich: Prestel Publishing Ltd., 2001.

Hyams, Edward. *Capability Brown and Humphry Repton.* London: J.M. Dent & Sons LTD, 1971.

Israel, Barbara. *Antique Garden Ornament: Two Centuries of American Taste.* New York: Harry N. Abrams, Inc., 1999.

Kipps, Kennedy. *Brookgreen Gardens.* Charleston, SC: Wyrick and Company, 1999.

Lane, Mills. *Architecture of the Old South.* New York: Abbeville Press, 1993.

Main, Alison, and Newell Platten. *The Lure of the Japanese Garden.* New York: W.W. Norton & Company, 2002.

Masson, Georgina. *Italian Gardens.* Suffolk: Antique Collector's Club, 1987.

Miller, Marcianne, and Olivier Rollin. *Making Arbors and Trellises: 25 Practical and Decorative Projects for Your Garden.* New York: Lark Books, 2002.

Moyer, Janet Lennox. *The Landscape Lighting Book.* New York: John Wiley and Sons, Inc., 1992.

Moynihan, Elizabeth B. *Paradise as a Garden: In Persia and Mughal India.* New York: George Braziller, Inc., 1979.

Newsom, Samuel. *A Thousand Years of Japanese Gardens.* Tokyo: Tokyo News Service, Ltd., 1955.

Offner, Elliot, and Charles Slate. *The Archer and Anna Hyatt Huntington Sculpture Garden.* Charleston, SC: Wyrick & Company, 2003.

Outwater, Myra Yellin and Eric B. *Garden Ornaments and Antiques.* Pennsylvania: Schiffer Publishing Ltd., 2000.

Paul, Anthony, and Yvonne Rees. *The Garden Design Book.* Topsfield, MA: Salem House Publishers, 1988.

Pereire, Anita, and Gabrielle Van Zuylen. *Gardens of France.* New York: Harmony Books, 1983.

Plumptre, George. *Garden Ornament: Five Hundred Years of History and Practice.* New York: Thames and Hudson Inc., 1998.

Proske, Beatrice Gilman. *Brookgreen Gardens Sculpture.* Murrells Inlet, SC: Brookgreen Gardens, 1968.

Salmon, Robin R. *Brookgreen Gardens Sculpture Vol. II.* Murrells Inlet, SC: Brookgreen Gardens, 1993.

Saudan, Michel, and Sylvia Saudan-Skira. *Orangeries: Palaces of Glass—Their History and Development.* Koln: Evergreen, 1998.

Schinz, Marina. *Visions of Paradise: Themes and Variations on the Garden.* New York: Stewart, Tabori & Chang, 1985.

Schuler, Stanley. *The Complete Terrace Book: How to Design, Build, Furnish, Plant and Enjoy Your Terrace, Patio, Lanai, Deck, Porch, Atrium or Engawa.* New York: Collier Books, 1974.

Singh, Rahoul B. *Gardens of Delight: Indian Gardens Through the Ages.* New Delhi: Roli Books, 2008.

Sinha, Amita. *Landscapes in India: Forms and Meanings.* Boulder, CO: The University Press of Colorado, 2006.

Skinner, Tina. *Hardscaping with Decorative Concrete.* Pennsylvania: Schiffer Publishing Ltd., 2007.

Slawson, David A. *Secret Teachings in the Art of Japanese Gardens: Design Principles and Aesthetic Values.* Tokyo: Kondansha International, 1991.

Southworth, Susan and Michael. *Ornamental Ironwork.* New York: McGraw-Hill, Inc., 1992.

Strong, Roy. *Ornament in the Small Garden.* Buffalo: Firefly Books, 2002.

Symmes, Marilyn. *Fountains: Splash and Spectacle: Water and Design from the Renaissance to the Present.* New York: Rizzoli International Publications, 1998.

Takei, Jiro, and Marc P. Keane. *Sakuteiki: Visions of the Japanese Garden: A Modern Translation of Japan's Gardening Classic.* Boston: Tuttle Publishing, 2001.

Turner, Roger. *Capability Brown and the Eighteenth-Century English Landscape.* London: Weidenfeld and Nicolson, 1985.

Van Sweden, James. *Architecture in the Garden.* London: Frances Lincoln Ltd, 2002.

Vercelloni, Virgilio. *European Gardens: An Historical Atlas.* New York, Rizzoli International Publications, Inc., 1990.

Waugh, Frank A. *Formal Design in Landscape Architecture.* New York: Orange Judd Publishing Company, Inc., 1927

Wharton, Edith. *Italian Villas and Their Gardens.* New York: The Century Co., 1920.

Whitner, Jan Kowalczewski. *Gardening With Stone: Using Stone Features to Add Mystery, Magic, and Meaning to Your Garden.* New York: Macmillan, 1999.

Wilson, William H. W. *How to Design and Install Outdoor Lighting.* San Francisco: Ortho Books, 1984.

Winterbottom, Daniel M. *Wood in the Landscape: A Practical Guide to Specification and Design.* New York: John Wiley and Sons, Inc., 2000.

Glossary

ABLUTION: Cleansing the body with water or other liquids, as in a ritual or ceremony.

ACCORDION GATE: Used mainly in urban settings to accommodate vehicles, this large gate folds to the side like an accordion, minimizing the swing area required.

ALLÉE: A walkway lined with trees used in gardens throughout the ages to connect and feature outbuildings, create focal points, frame garden vistas, and provide shade and shelter.

ANTI-DESSICANT: A compound applied to plants during transplantation to prevent dehydration.

ARBOR: A leafy, shady niche formed by tree branches or shrubs, or a latticework bower intertwined with climbing vines and flowers.

ARCADIA: An idyllic paradise, named for a peaceful, pastoral area once under Roman rule.

ARCH BRIDGE: A bridge that incorporates arches into its structure, thus allowing a large volume of floodwater to pass under it and providing ample headroom for boats.

ARMILLARY: A spherical sundial with encircling rings and a central shaft (gnomon) that casts a shadow on the hour ring. In addition to its decorative quality, it is the most sophisticated kind of sundial.

ARTS AND CRAFTS MOVEMENT: An international design movement that began in England as a reaction to mass production and flourished between 1880 and 1910. Its focus was on traditional craftsmanship and simplicity of form.

ART NOUVEAU MOVEMENT: An international movement and style of art that peaked between 1890 and 1905 in Europe, featuring highly stylized, organic, and flowing curvilinear forms. It is considered a bridge to the modernism of the 20th century.

ASHLAR: A squared stone cut more or less true on all faces adjacent to other stones, so as to permit very thin mortar joints.

AQUACULTURE: The cultivation of aquatic plants and animals in either a natural or controlled environment.

BAFFLE: A protective flange set below a birdhouse or birdfeeder to keep out small mammals such as squirrels.

BALLOON FRAME: A building frame constructed of small units nailed together rather than large, heavy units joined by mortise-and-tenon construction.

BALUSTRADE: A row of balusters (upright supports), often vase-shaped, topped by a railing to create an open wall.

BEE SKEP: A traditional straw beehive, conical in shape. Harvesting the honey often means killing the colony, so they are primarily used decoratively today.

BELVEDERE: Literally *fair view* in Italian, a structure designed specifically to take advantage of a pleasing aspect.

BENTONITE: An absorptive and colloidal clay formed from volcanic ash.

BONDO: The trademarked name for body filler intended for use in automobiles but sometimes used to mask imperfections in ornamental ironwork.

BORE TEST: A process of soil-testing that involves digging a small, deep hole, most often with the intention of locating bedrock.

BOLLARD: A small post, usually of metal or wood, used in gardens and other urban environments to direct traffic flow, both vehicular and pedestrian, and provide decoration.

BONSAI: A Japanese art form in which miniature trees are grown in small containers. Pruning of both the crown and roots limits growth and produces plants that mimic mature trees.

BRICK GOTHIC STYLE: A style of architecture found in Northern Europe, most abundantly in Germany, that relies solely upon bricks.

BRONZE AGE: The period of history (3300-1200 BC) that came between the Stone Age and Iron Ages, during which most metalwork involved the smelting of copper and tin to make bronze.

BUTT JOINT: The simplest and weakest kind of joint, in which two members are simply butted together.

BUTTRESS: An architectural structure built against or protruding from a wall to provide support and structural reinforcement.

CANTILEVER: A beam supported on one end only.

CANNON SUNDIAL: A sundial common in 18th-century gardens in which the sun's rays, directed through a magnifying glass, would ignite a cannon's gun powder charge and signal the hour with a "boom."

CARBON ARC LAMP: A lamp in which an arc of light is created between two carbon rods—first demonstrated in the early 19th century by the British chemist and inventor Sir Humphry Davy.

CAST IRON: A brittle form of iron first used in China during the 4th century BC, made by pouring molten metal into molds.

CAST STONE: A material manufactured from cement, sand, gravel and other materials, meant to simulate the look of natural stone. Some speculate that the pyramids of Egypt were constructed with it.

CATCH BASIN: A device usually located just beneath the grating on a drain, used to prevent debris and silt from entering the drain.

CEMENT: A gray powder made from ground limestone and clay that, when mixed with water, hardens rapidly to bind sand and gravel into solid concrete. The technique for making it dates back to the early Romans.

CHAMFERED: Grooved, as in a column.

CHANNEL DRAIN: Also known as a *trench drain*, a long, narrow channel used to remove water from a site.

CHIPPENDALE STYLE: Inspired by the work of cabinet maker Thomas Chippendale, this style, popular in the United States during the 18th and 19th centuries, is characterized by a series of interlocking diagonals or rectangles.

CHINOISERIE: A french term, meaning "Chinese-esque," referring to a European style dating back to the 17th century characterized by the use of fanciful Chinese imagery.

CHOZUBACHI: An ornamental water basin carved into stone.

CLOSE-BOARD FENCE: A fence with very little room between the boards, providing privacy, security, and protection from the elements.

COADE STONE: Artificial stone made of a ceramic material invented by Eleanor Coade in the late 18th century.

COLUMBARIA: Latin for *dovecote*.

CONCRETE: Building material made from a mixture of sand, gravel and cement, first used in ancient times and still widely used today.

COPING: The top course of a wall, usually placed at an angle to facilitate drainage.

COR-TEN STEEL: A brand of steel meant to take on a rust-like appearance over time, alleviating the need for painting.

COTTAGE GARDEN STYLE: An informal gardening style developed in England in opposition to the grandeur of formal gardens.

CUPOLA: A small, decorative structure that sits atop the roof of a building and sometimes mimics the larger structures around it.

CURRENT POOL: A small pool with a resistant current for stationary swimming.

CYCLOPEAN WALL: Built by the Greeks during the Mycenaean Period (1600–1100 BC), a wall in which boulders weighing up to fourteen tons were fit together without the use of mortar. (The term cyclopean refers to the mythological creature Cyclops, who was strong enough to move such stones.)

DOVECOTE: A small house placed high on a building or on stilts as a habitat for pigeons. First used by the early Romans, these are often circular in design with a smaller box on top.

DOUBLE-SWING GATE: Two movable gates on independent hinges, never less than four feet wide, total.

DRAWBRIDGE: A bridge that can be raised or lowered for security purposes, often found on moated castles.

DRESSED FACE: Stone that has been "dressed" or sculpted to possess a smooth face and squared edges.

DRIP LINE: The area described by the outermost circumference of a projecting roof, where run-off from rain occurs.

DRY STONE WALL: A stone wall, often quite strong, built without mortar. Some of the earliest walls in history were built using this method.

EFFLORESCENCE: A chemical process of evaporation or crystallization of water and other chemicals on stone, brick or masonry, causing discoloration.

ELIZABETHAN PERIOD: The peaceful period in English history covering the reign of Queen Elizabeth (1558–1603), considered a Golden Age for the arts.

ENGLISH LANDSCAPE TRADITION: A gardening style favored in the 18th century, featuring naturalistic settings rather than the extravagant design and sculpture that had been popular previously.

ESPALIER: An ancient agricultural practice of training plants by pruning and tying their branches along horizontal planes. It is used both decoratively and functionally to make efficient use of limited space and enliven plain walls.

EXEDRA: From the Greek for *outdoor seating area*, a semi-circular bench or set of seats tucked within the walls or colonnades of a building or forming a garden room.

EXPANSION JOINT: A joint that allows for the expansion and contraction of the materials due to settling and temperature change.

FALSE GATE: A nonfunctional gate that conveys the illusion that the garden continues beyond its walls.

FILIGREE: Ornamental metalwork of intricate and delicate design, usually made of thin wires of gold, silver or copper.

FILLER COMPOUND: Putty, caulk, or the like, used to fill cracks or form a seal between building materials.

FINIAL: A crowning ornament or detail, often found atop the vertical posts of iron fences or gates.

FOLLY: A garden ornament that replicates its own surroundings, such as the ruins of a castle or a miniature gazebo.

FOOTING: The base or foundation of a wall, column, or pier that bears and evenly distributes the weight of the structure.

FROST LINE: The depth at which groundwater within the soil will freeze.

FREEZE-THAW CYCLE: The reaction of natural matter to seasonal changes in temperature.

FRENCH DRAIN: A drain for directing run-off, in which a trench is filled with gravel or a similar material and covered by turf.

GALVANIZING: A process in which iron or steel is coated or fully immersed in zinc.

GAZEBO: A roofed, freestanding structure (sometimes referred to as a belvedere, pagoda, or pavilion) open on all sides but providing shelter, ornament, and a quiet place to enjoy a view.

GEOTEXTILE: A permeable fabric that can filter, reinforce, protect, or drain the soil.

GILDED AGE: The post-Civil War period in America characterized by an ostentatious display of wealth among the privileged class.

GILDED IRON: Iron decorated with a coating of gold or silver.

GLORIETA: Spanish for *green summer house*, a form of ornamental topiary in which plants are trained into architectural shapes resembling windowed rooms.

GNOMON: The shadow stick or pin of a sundial whose shadow indicates the time of day.

GRAVITY WALL: Often made of dry-stone construction, a wall that depends on the mass of its components to exert the pressure necessary to maintain it.

GREEN ROOF: Also known as a *living roof*, a roof that is completely or partially covered in vegetation, either in small pots or planted evenly over a waterproof membrane. Among other advantages, it absorbs rainwater and lowers surrounding air temperatures by limiting reflective heat.

GROTTO: Any natural or artificially made cave, such as those traditionally found in Italy, where they were designed to mimic the caves found along the rocky coast.

GUNITE: A type of dry concrete invented in the early 1900s, well suited to lining swimming pools.

HA-HA: A sunken ditch faced on one side by a vertical that allows uninterrupted views from a garden to a field or park but prevents livestock from crossing over.

HAKO-ZUKURI: Japanese topiary fashioned into box-like shapes.

HAMMERED: A rough, pockmarked surface finish applied to natural stone to create the appearance of weathering and age.

HELLENISTIC ERA: The period just before the Common Era, following the conquests of Alexander the Great, marked by the spread of Greek cities and culture throughout Asia and Africa.

HONED: A smooth, non-reflective surface finish applied to natural stone.

HORIZONTAL SUNDIAL: The most common sundial, in which the gnomon is set perpendicular to the ground and casts its shadow onto a round, calibrated plate.

HORTICULTURE: The science and industry of plant cultivation.

HOT-DIPPED GALVANIZING: The process of immersing iron, steel or aluminum into zinc at temperatures of up to 860 degrees Fahrenheit.

HYDROSTATIC PRESSURE: Pressure exerted by a fluid at equilibrium due to the force of gravity.

IN SITU: Latin for *in position*.

ISHIGAKI: A Japanese style of dry-stone wall construction.

JUNCTION BOX: A container for electrical connections, usually concealed from view.

KARIKOMI: Japanese topiary resembling abstract, cloud-like forms.

LANGSTROTH HIVE: A prototype of today's standard beehive, invented by Lorenzo Lorraine Langstroth in 1851, that can be harvested without causing damage to the hive or its inhabitants.

LAP POOL: A swimming pool of long and narrow dimensions ideally suited for swimming laps while not taking up much space.

LATTICE: A visually pleasing framework of lightweight, criss-crossed materials open to light and cooling air.

LEACHING: The dissolution of substances due to the percolation of liquid around and through them.

LED: Short for Light Emitting Diode, a semiconductor light source that produced bright, long-lasting light.

LIVING ROCK: Rock sculpted by the elements, left in its natural setting— e.g., the Great Sphinx of Egypt.

LOUVERED FENCE: A fence whose vertical or horizontal boards are set at an angle to allow for some light and air flow while maintaining privacy.

MEDIEVAL AGE: The period following the fall of the Roman Empire (5th-15th century) that was a bridge between ancient and modern times.

MERCURY VAPOR LAMP: Invented in the late 19th century but not used widely until the 1930s, a gas discharge lamp that produces light when mercury reaches an "excited" state.

MERKHET: Egyptian for *instrument of knowing*, a timekeeping device used to track the alignment of major stars that, unlike a sundial, can be used at night.

MICROCLIMATE: An area ranging in size from a few square feet to many square miles whose climate is markedly different from those surrounding it. South- and north-facing walls create microclimates by blocking or trapping sunlight.

MORTISE-AND-TENON JOINT: A joint in which the male piece or *tenon* is set tightly into the female piece or *mortise* and then sealed.

MYCENAEAN PERIOD: The era in Greece at the end of the Bronze Age (1600-1100 BC) when much Greek mythology and literature are set, including the epic stories of Homer.

Natural Swimming Pool: First built in Austria in the early 1980s, a pool in which no chemicals are used. Cleanliness is maintained using a system of biological filters and plants.

Neolithic Era: Known as the final period of the Stone Age (beginning around 9500 BC), the time when agrarian societies developed, stone tools came into use, and pottery was first made.

Obelisk: An upright, four-sided tapering pillar or monument that terminates with a pyramid. In ancient Egypt, obelisks symbolized the sun god Ra.

Parterre: A French term referring to a formal garden on a level surface, composed of planting beds edged in stone or tightly trimmed hedges traversed by paths in symmetrical patterns. The *parterre* originated during the French Renaissance of the 15th century, as exemplifed by the gardens at Versailles.

Pagoda: A tiered building with multiple eaves, found throughout Asia.

Pale: A single unit or stake within a palisade. Palisade: A fence made of small tree trunks with their tops sharpened to points to provide protection.

Palladian Style: Neo-classical architecture inspired by the designs of the 16th-century architect Andrea Palladio—who himself was following the principles of the ancient Greeks and Romans.

Paradise Garden: An Islamic garden of Persian origin, enclosed and geometric, usually including canals to symbolize the four rivers of the Garden of Eden and divide the garden into quarters.

Patina: A green film or tarnish that forms naturally on bronze and copper as a result of oxidation or other chemical processes due to age and exposure.

Pavilion: A free-standing structure, often highly decorated, used for pleasure and relaxation.

Pergola: A garden feature consisting of balustrades and an open roofing surface of spaced girders or beams upon which vines or climbing plants may grow, providing relief from the sun. *(These are more substantial and permanent than arbors.)*

Pervious Paving: A paved surface through which water may pass.

Picturesque Garden Movement: A style that emerged in England in the 18th century as part of the larger Romantic Movement. Designers of this period often emulated the allegorical landscape paintings of the time, resulting in highly manicured gardens.

Pitting: A technique for dressing stone that results in an irregular surface marked with cavities and depressions.

Pleaching: A topiary technique in which trees are trained to form a raised hedge or "living fence" commonly used to shade a path.

Pointing: The process of renewing mortar joints in masonry construction.

Powder coating: Applying dry powder to metal electrostatically and then curing it under high temperatures to make the material stronger and more resilient than when simply painted.

Pollarding: A pruning technique in which the upper branches of a tree are regularly cut back to create dense foliage at a desired height. The practice developed as a way to maximize the cultivation of firewood.

Pozzolana: A Latin term for the volcanic ash added to cement mixtures to strengthen them so they could set under water.

Qanat: An ancient system that used underground tunnels, often several kilometers long, to channel water from its source to civilized areas requiring it for irrigation and drinking.

Rain Garden: A depression, ideally planted with native vegetation, created to collect run-off from impervious surfaces such as pavement and roofs for the purpose of minimizing erosion, flooding and pollution of groundwater.

Raised Hedge: A topiary technique in which rows of plants, commonly deciduous trees, are trained into a tight hedge which is then trimmed a few feet off of the ground to create an open wall.

Rammed Clay Wall: Also known as a *rammed earth wall,* a structure made of natural clay, lime or gravel tamped into shape by hand or simple tools. The ancient technique has recently come back into fashion for its sustainability and durability.

Reinforced Concrete: Concrete that has been made stronger by the introduction of other materials—most often rebar, though a variety of organic and inorganic materials have proved effective.

Rejas: A Spanish term referring to the iron gates and grilles found in churches and cathedrals for the protection of relics or to separate the choir from the congregation.

Rejeria: The art of ornamental ironwork dating back to 9th-century Spain.

Renaissance: The cultural movement in Europe that spanned the 14th – 17th centuries, noted for a flowering of art, literature, music, education, religion and politics. It is considered the cultural bridge between the Middle Ages and the Modern Era and generally believed to have begun in Florence, Italy.

Repoussé: A French method of metal decoration in which parts of the design are raised in relief from the back by means of a hammer or other tool.

Restraining Edge: A border that holds pavers together.

Rill: Any sort of channel or canal, natural or manmade, intended to carry water through the garden. Most are narrow, designed to flow along a walkway, staircase or out of a fountain, and are sometimes used to cool warmer areas of the garden.

Risers: The vertical elements in a set of stairs.

Rocaille: An elaborate, 18th-century style of decoration using pebbles and shells, typically applied to grottos and fountains.

Rococo Period: The era at the end of the Baroque period in 18th-century France marked by a move toward very ornate and fluid designs.

ROMANTIC MOVEMENT: A movement in Europe during the second half of the 18th century during which emotion was valued as the inspiration for art, literature and thought. It arose primarily as a reaction to the Industrial Revolution, Age of Enlightenment, and emphasis upon scientific explanations of nature.

SCALA CORDONATA: A ramp featuring broad, slightly inclined steps topped with turf or gravel and occasionally paved with risers.

SERPENTINE WALL: A wall built in an undulating wave pattern for the sake of aesthetics. Functionally, the nooks and crannies created can form individual microclimates ideal for plantings as well as outdoor rooms for seating.

SETT: A small rectangular paving block made of stone such as granite.

SHAKKEI: Japanese for borrowed scenery, a gardening principle based on the incorporation of a background landscape, scene or setting into the composition of a garden.

SINGLE-SWING GATE: Perhaps the most common type, a single gate that operates on hinges within a wall or fence.

SLIDING GATE: A type in which the gate itself slides behind the connecting member of the wall or fence. Its advantage over a hinged gate is that it takes less room to maneuver.

SMELTING: The process of melting or fusing metals, usually at temperatures high enough to trigger a chemical process.

SOD WALL: A wall built with "bricks" of sod stripped from the ground mainly used when other materials are unavailable.

STRAIGHT-BEAM BRIDGE: Perhaps the most simple type, it usually consists of one or two beams placed over a span and covered with another material.

SUMMERHOUSE: An garden building meant to provide shelter from the sun and foul weather.

SUNDIAL: A device for measuring time by the position of the sun. These range in design from the simple to the complex, but all must be calibrated specifically to their location and time of year.

SUSPENSION BRIDGE: A bridge in which the deck is suspended by cables attached to vertical pillars that support its weight. These range from simple rope bridges with small wooden planks, to the monumental Golden Gate bridge in California.

SWALE: a low-lying depression in a piece of land, often filled with water.

TAPER ENTASIS: An intentional distortion, first used by the Greeks, that incorporates a slight bulge in the center of a column to corrects the illusion of concave tapering created by parallel straight lines.

TESSERAE: An individual tile in a mosaic.

TOPIARUS: Literally, a *well-trained gardener*, and the root word of topiary.

TOPIARY: The art of training perennial plants, trees or shrubs into defined shapes, from geometrical forms to fanciful creatures.

TREAD: The horizontal element in a set of stairs.

TREILLAGE: Lattice work for vines or climbing plants.

TSUKUBAI: The Japanese term for a small basin, often carved of stone and used primarily for the purpose of ablution.

VERSAILLES BOX: A wooden planter built with one hinged wall to allow for easier removal of the plant at the end of its season. The gardens of Versailles include thousands of these.

VENEER: A protective facing.

VERTICAL SUNDIAL: A sundial designed to hang on a wall.

VICTORIAN ERA: The period of British history comprising the reign of Queen Victoria (1837-1901). It was a time of great prosperity, noted for the clash between Gothic and Classical ideals.

WALL CAP: A stone or metal covering atop a wall, meant to seal and protect its interior from water.

WATERCOURSE: A large rill in a garden, more akin to a small stream or river.

WATTLE FENCE: An ancient type of barrier in which small sticks and twigs are woven together between wooden posts.

WEEP HOLE: A small opening in a wall meant to allow proper drainage and evaporation of water.

WELL LIGHTS: Lights placed in a protective can or box and set within the ground so as to keep them hidden from view.

WROUGHT IRON: Superior to cast iron, this durable material is made using a smelting process that dates back to the 2nd century BC in Asia Minor.

ZIGGURAT: A pyramidal structure most often used for religious purposes and found throughout the major cities of Mesopotamia dating from 2200 to 500 BC.

ZILLIJ: A major feature of Moroccan architecture, ornamental terra cotta tile work covered with enamel and set in geometric patterns. It is used to decorate.

Acknowledgments

A book that has been over thirty years in the making requires the acknowledgment of so many who have helped along the way.

First and foremost, I must thank Michael Bartlett, my co-author and late husband, who was the driving force behind its conception and organization. His imagination was its inspiration, his energy got the project going and his determination ensured its completion. The striking images in this book reflect his eye for detail, and it was his generous spirit that drove him to share his decades of hands-on gardening and design knowledge with the world.

Michael's parents, Martha and Charles Bartlett have been a source of inspiration to both of us. Their love of gardening and design influenced Michael from a very young age. After I was warmly welcomed to their family, I realized the depth of their passion and it was contagious. Over the years, they reveled in our garden explorations and couldn't wait to see the latest set of photographs. They were the ones who first suggested we share our photos with others via the talks we gave as a duo. Those talks were the foundation for this book.

Helen Bartlett worked tirelessly to get this book into the hands of those who might consider publishing it. She collaborated with Scot Ribera to create a beautiful mock-up of several chapters that would showcase the project's potential. Her enthusiasm, encouragement and relentless resolve to see the book in print have remained constant over the years.

The first time I met David Godine he had already read the prototype of the book. He responded with wonderful enthusiasm that warmed my heart and provided the incentive I needed to complete the book without my co-author. It has been a long process, his enthusiasm has remained steadfast and I can't thank him enough. Sue Berger Ramin of Godine provided an objective eye and constructive insights, matched by her patience, commitment and kindness.

I will be eternally grateful to Jon Winokur for introducing me to an editor of extraordinary talent, Laura Ross. Laura worked relentlessly to transform a mountain of facts and technical information into a flowing text that is both enjoyable and enlightening. She did this without altering the vision or voice of the book ... now that's magic! I thank her from the bottom of my heart and I know Michael would feel the same way.

Family and friends have cheered us on over the years, attending our garden talks and reading through outlines and drafts. Their support and encouragement were so important, particularly when the project seemed extraordinarily complex.

Several assistants have been crucial to the realization of the book. John Nixon worked with me for a year and a half and has been an indispensable help in editing, evaluating photographs and creating a working layout. Early on, Susan Hollingsworth and Adam Elliott provided momentum in getting the project going. Julie Porterfield assisted with organizing photo files for the more than 1,200 photos.

Mark Oxley of Outdoor Illuminations provided much appreciated technical advice on the lighting chapter. He also arranged for the inclusion of three photos of night lighting by Robert Foley.

The proprietors of all the gardens included here enthusiastically gave permission for their images to be included; without them, there would not be a book.

ROSE BARTLETT

Colophon

The text of this book is set in ITC Galliard, a wonderfully robust and
celebratory serif typeface designed by Matthew Carter in 1978,
and based loosely on 16th century typeface Granjon. Galliard reads
well in small sizes, but also flourishes in large format documents.
The captions are set in Meta designed by Erik Spiekermann in 1990.
Meta is a humanist sans serif typeface well known for being
highly legible in small sizes. Meta is typographically appealing
because of the automatic non-aligning figures.
This book was designed by Sara Eisenman,
with assistance from Michael Babcock.

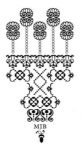